The Theory and Practice of
Cultural-Historical Psychology

The Theory and Practice of Cultural-Historical Psychology

Edited by Seth Chaiklin

Acta Jutlandica LXXIV:2
Social Science Series 22

AARHUS UNIVERSITY PRESS

ISBN 87 7288 838 5
ISSN 0065 1354 (ACTA JUTLANDICA)
ISSN 0106 0937 (SOCIAL SCIENCE SERIES)

Published with financial support from the
Danish Research Council for the Humanities

AARHUS UNIVERSITY PRESS
Langelandsgade 177
DK-8200 Aarhus N
Fax (+ 45) 8942 5380

73 Lime Walk
Headington, Oxford OX3 7AD
United Kingdom
Fax (+ 44) 1865 750 079

Box 511
Oakville, CT 06779
USA
Fax (+ 1) 860 945 9468

www.unipress.dk

Cover illustration: Wassily Kandinsky, "Fröhlicher Aufbau
(Structure joyeuse, July 1924)", 35 x 23 cm, private collection

Foreword

The cover of this volume was painted by Kandinsky in the same year often indicated as the start of Vygotsky's 'career' as a research psychologist. In this painting, one sees communication between two individuals who are free-floating, yet grounded against blocks of historical tradition. This image reflects a central problem within cultural-historical psychology, both as an object of its research and as a characteristic of its research community's present-day state.

The title, *The Theory and Practice of Cultural-Historical Psychology*, has a ring of definitiveness and finality that is no doubt premature, at least if read with meanings given traditionally to 'theory' and 'practice'. There is no coherent community of researchers practising this theory. At the same time, this judgement may reflect an ideal about theory and practice that is tied to an epistemological tradition that is rejected in cultural-historical theory. This raises a challenge for the practice of cultural-historical psychology. By negating traditional theory/practice relations, one must understand practice as a necessary moment in the development of theory. In many ways, we have not achieved a full reflective understanding and practice of the implications and demands that lie in this negation.

It is my hope that this volume will contribute to the development and dissemination of knowledge about cultural-historical psychology, and to the development of an institutionalised research community that will contribute to developing practices worth theorising about.

It has been a pleasure to work with the chapter authors in preparing this volume, and to experience the multinational diversity in cultural-historical psychology so directly. Special thanks to Mariane Hedegaard, Joachim Lompscher, and Falk Seeger for their help with diverse substantive questions, and to Falk Seeger for finding the cover art.

Finally, I would like to thank the multinational team of editors at Aarhus University Press, Pernille Pennington and Mary Waters Lund, for their patience and dedicated hard work, which is reflected in the final product.

Seth Chaiklin
Aarhus, Denmark
August 2000

Contents

Contents

List of Figures and Tables

Contributors

Angela Uchoa Branco is Professor at the University of Brasilia and Head of the Laboratory of Microgenesis of Social Interactions. From a sociocultural constructivist perspective, her team has been developing research projects, particularly oriented to investigate moral and gender development, as well as metacommunication processes in child-child and teacher-student interactions. Among her recent publications are 'Changing Methodologies: A Co-constructivist Study of Social Interactions' (with J. Valsiner) and 'Metacommunication as a Source of Indeterminism in Relationship Development' (with A. Fogel). Email: abranco@tba.com.br

Seth Chaiklin is Associate Professor in Pedagogical Psychology at the Department of Psychology, University of Aarhus. His research interests include subject-matter teaching, education for cultural minorities, and development in societal perspective. He has edited *Understanding Practice* (1993, with J. Lave, Cambridge University Press), and *Activity Theory and Social Practice* (1999, with M. Hedegaard and U.J. Jensen, Aarhus University Press). Email: seth@psy.au.dk

Mercedes Cubero is Associate Professor in the Department of Experimental Psychology, Seville University. Her recent publications are about heterogeneity of verbal thinking and cultural psychology and more specifically about investigations of the relationship between activity settings, ways of thinking and modes of discourse. Her publications in English include 'A Sociocultural Perspective on Adult Education Activities: Literacy as the Dialogical Construction of Text' (with A. Santamaría and M. Marco) and 'Modes of Discourse and Ways of Thinking: Actual Debates in Sociocultural Studies' (with J.D. Ramírez). Email: cubero@psicoexp.us.es

Mariëtte de Haan is researcher at the Faculty of Social Sciences, Utrecht University from 1988 until the present, working at different times for the Departments of Psychonomics, Educational Sciences and the Netherlands' School for Social and Economic Policy Research. Her research has focused mainly on education/socialisation and cultural diversity, but also on literacy and curriculum development. She received her Ph.D. from Utrecht University in 1999 for her book titled *Learning as Cultural Practice: How Children Learn in a Mexican Mazahua Community*. Her current research focuses on communication practices in multiethnic classrooms (Turkish, Moroccan and Dutch students) in the Netherlands and how these practices relate to other socialisation practices outside the classroom. Email: M.deHaan@fss.uu.nl

Manuel L. de la Mata is Professor at the Department of Experimental Psychology and member of the group Laboratorio de Actividad Humana at the University of Seville. His research and publications are oriented to the study of the relationship between cultural practices as formal education and human mental actions. In particular he is studying teacher-student interaction and text memory. Email: mluis@cica.es

Mohamed Elhammoumi is researcher and Adjunct Professor at Edgecombe Community College, North Carolina, USA. He received his Ph.D. from Sorbonne University in 1984. He is editor of the forthcoming journals: *Arab Culture and Psychology*, and *Studies in Socio-Historicocultural Psychology*. His research focuses on the interrelations between the social-historical-cultural environment and children's cognitive development. Recent publications include articles and monographs on contemporary cultural psychology, developmental psychology, and cognitive development of children in the Arab societies, paying special attention to the cognitive growth of children living under nomadic, transitional, and non-nomadic life.
Email: elham@rockymountnc.com

Gloria Fariñas León is Professor in the Department of Applied Psychology at the Faculty of Psychology, University of Havana. She received her Ph.D. from Lomonosov University, Moscow, in 1983. She is the vice-president of the cathedra 'L.S. Vygotsky' at the University of Havana, where she also heads the graduate studies in educational psychology. Her recent publications include two books on learning strategies and articles on theoretical problems in educational psychology. Email: glofaleon@yahoo.com

Peter E. Jones is Senior Lecturer in Communication Studies at Sheffield Hallam University. His recent publications are in the areas of Marxist philosophy of language, discourse analysis, and problems in general linguistic theory. Email: p.e.jones@shu.ac.uk

Zilma de Moraes Ramos de Oliveira is Professor of Developmental Psychology at the University of São Paulo — Ribeirão Preto Campus, and advisor at the State of São Paulo Secretary of Education. Since she received her Ph.D. at the University of São Paulo in 1988, she has been doing research and publishing articles on early peer interactions and early education.
Email: dpe@fde.sp.gov.br

Roxane Helena Rodrigues Rojo is Professor in the Department of Applied Linguistics at the Catholic Pontifical University of São Paulo, Brazil, where she is currently Head of the Postgraduate Studies Program in Applied Linguistics. Her main research interests are oral and written language construction, language teaching and learning, literacy, schooling and curriculum and classroom discourse and interaction. Her recent publications include several papers and the following books: *Literacy: Linguistic Perspectives* (1998, Mercado de Letras) and *National Curricula Parameters: Classroom Practices* (forthcoming). Email: rrojo@globo.com

Andrés Santamaría is Associate Professor in the Department of Experimental Psychology at Seville University. He is currently working on the role of semiotic mediation in text comprehension and remembering in teacher-student interaction. He usually works and gives classes on the relationship between thinking and speech. His recent publications include book chapters and articles on the semiotic nature of consciousness, semiotic mediation and interiorisation in instructional situations, and text comprehension and remembering. Email: santamar@psicoexp.us.es

Falk Seeger is Senior Lecturer in Psychology and Mathematics Education at the Institute of Mathematics Education, the University of Bielefeld, Germany. His current research interest focuses on external representations and on computer-mediated communication. His recent publications include articles on the relation of cultural-historical psychology and semiotics, an edited volume on selected writings of Arne Raeithel, and another edited volume on the *Culture of the Mathematics Classroom* (1998, Cambridge University Press). Email: falk.seeger@uni-bielefeld.de

Charles Tolman is Professor Emeritus of Psychology and Emeritus Fellow in the Centre for Studies in Religion and Society at the University of Victoria. He is book review editor for the journal *Canadian Psychology/Psychologie cana-*

dienne and former co-editor (with G. Rückriem) of *Multidisciplinary Newsletter on Activity Theory*. He is editor of *Positivism in Psychology* (1992, Springer Verlag) and *Theoretical Problems of Psychology* (1996, Captus), and author of *Psychology, Society, and Subjectivity* (1994, Routledge).
Email: tolman@uvic.ca

René van der Veer is Associate Professor in the Department of Education at Leiden University. He is interested in the history of education and developmental psychology. His publications include *The Social Mind* (2000, with J. Valsiner, Cambridge University Press), *The Vygotsky Reader* (1994, with J. Valsiner), *Reconstructing the Mind* (1994, with M.H. van IJzendoorn and J. Valsiner, Ablex), and *Understanding Vygotsky* (1991, with J. Valsiner, Blackwell). Email: veer@fsw.leidenuniv.nl

Vladimir P. Zinchenko is Head of the Laboratory on Man's Development at the Institute of General High Education, the Russian Academy of Education. He is a full member of the Russian Academy of Education, Professor (Head of Cathedra) of Psychology at the International University 'Dubna', and honorary member of The American Academy of Arts and Sciences. Recent publications include *Living Knowledge* (1998, Samara State University Press) and *Thought and Word of Gustav Shpet* (2000, Russian Academy of Education Press). Email: v.zinchenko@neuro.ps.msu.su

1 The Institutionalisation of Cultural-Historical Psychology as a Multinational Practice

Seth Chaiklin

Q: What is over 75 years old, but still a baby?
A: Cultural-historical psychology.

The preceding riddle offers an impression about the current state of cultural-historical psychology. If judged by the calendar and the historical span of empirical psychology, then cultural-historical psychology — as reflected in the research traditions that have developed from Vygotsky, Leontiev, Luria, and their colleagues — is relatively old. But when one examines the concrete manifestations of this research tradition, then it is harder to find the qualities typically found in well-established psychological and social scientific traditions. Cultural-historical psychology does not have the coherent institutional structures normally associated with a research tradition, thereby making it more difficult to define and locate the tradition in a singular manner.[1] As will be argued, the present-day institutional state of the tradition reflects consequences of its historical development, rather than fundamental conceptual flaws that prevent its growth. In other words, the chronological age of the tradition may not be a reliable indicator of its mental age. It can be salutary, therefore, to assess the status and health of cultural-historical psychology, a kind of self-reflection, that aims to clarify and develop the practice further. This chapter aims to contribute toward this end, while also providing a perspective from which to view the other chapters in this volume.

   In particular, I reflect upon the practice of cultural-historical psychology by considering the relation between its institutionalisation and current characteristics of its practice. Attention is paid to the consequences of the lack of

* Thanks to Mariane Hedegaard for her comments on the manuscript.
1. This is not to say that cultural-historical psychology must replicate existing traditions, but only to note that a productive scientific tradition has some characteristic material conditions that serve to support the practice and development of that tradition.

institutionalisation, both as part of understanding current practice and as a way to identify substantive questions in relation to ongoing institutionalisation of this practice. Among other points, I will characterise cultural-historical psychology as a multinational practice, and suggest that it would be valuable to maintain this aspect in its institutionalised practices.

The Institutional Practice of Cultural-Historical Psychology

As a practice, science is organised in institutional structures. Institutional resources serve a valuable function in facilitating and supporting the necessary dialogue and communication for developing and elaborating a scientific tradition of practice. In considering the theory and practice of cultural-historical psychology, it is necessary to examine the institutional processes by and through which it has developed. Cultural-historical psychology is young as an institutional practice, even if it is old as an intellectual practice. Just as individuals develop through the demands and constraints of institutional practices, so can we understand that cultural-historical psychology also develops through the institutional practices within the tradition.

At the same time, elements of institutionalised practice are not automatically valuable and productive in and of themselves. There are plenty of examples of how institutional practices become conservative, exclusionary, and distorted to serve narrow interests within a scientific community. Therefore, it seems appropriate to initiate more reflection and discussion about the ways in which cultural-historical psychology will organise itself in creating the (institutional) tools that enable further communication and development within the tradition.[2] Because we are in the relatively early stages of this institutionalisation process, we have the rare opportunity to attempt to form and develop these practices in ways that might be conducive to the epistemological assumptions that motivate cultural-historical psychology. Such assumptions are discussed here in more detail in chapters by Tolman, van der Veer,

---

2. My own view about the future is, unfortunately, pessimistic and cynical. I expect that institutional practices found in other psychological traditions will be recreated more or less in the cultural-historical tradition (partly because many researchers are socialised originally in these traditions). My optimism lies in the hope that attention to and awareness of the issue of institutional practices as a general research problem within cultural-historical psychology will help to make participants more conscious about and willing to influence the formation of the concrete artifacts (journals, societies, congresses, and so forth) that will be appropriate to the research being undertaken (or should be undertaken) in the cultural-historical tradition.

Elhammoumi, and Jones. In lieu of detailed, concrete analysis, I will only note the hypothesis that existing institutional forms reflect, in part, assumptions about the nature of knowledge and its communication. If cultural-historical psychology is developing from epistemological assumptions that differ from those in existing forms, then other kinds of institutional forms may be necessary in some cases.

As part of a self-reflective understanding of its practice, it is necessary to analyse the historical development of the material manifestation of cultural-historical psychology. This analysis, motivated by a dialectical theory of knowledge, can help to understand current forms of practice, as well as identify undeveloped potentials. Therefore, I want to review briefly the history of cultural-historical psychology from an institutional perspective, as a way to provide a background for understanding some characteristics of the present set of chapters.

When considering cultural-historical psychology, one can see traces of its institutionalisation in diverse academic departments around the world. However, most signs of contemporary institutionalised scientific practice (e.g., textbooks, formalised academic degrees, journals, and professional societies) are few and far between or non-existent when considering the cultural-historical tradition. For example, journals devoted primarily to this tradition have only appeared in the latter part of the 1990s (though some newsletters have been produced over the past two decades). None of them can claim to be a 'flagship' or leading journal, defining the main focus of the tradition, though there are definite movements in this direction[3] and it would seem that communications (e.g., informal, cross-national networks, facilitated by email and WWW) will continue to move in the direction of more integration and coordination. There have been no legally-registered international membership organisations that have organised around the cultural-historical tradition (though one can identify examples of loosely-organised groups in several countries or special-interest groups within professional organisations), and while international organisations are currently in formation, they are still not supporting regular (e.g., monthly or quarterly) communication. There are no annual international congresses in cultural-historical psychology, though some regular national meetings are or have been organised.

3.   See ISCRAT's homepage (http://www.iscrat.org), as well as journals oriented more to cultural-historical psychology such as *Human Development; Mind, Culture and Activity; Culture & Psychology;* and *Outlines.*

There are still no textbooks[4] written primarily from this perspective (I. Arievitch, personal communication, July 1999; A. Asmolov, personal communication, July 1999). Until quite recently, no academic departments have organised their education to present cultural-historical psychology in a systematic way. However, there are now at least two academic departments in Russia (the psychology institute of the Russian State University for the Humanities and the Moscow Institute of Education and Psychology) which started to offer, in the mid-1990s, systematic education organised around cultural-historical psychology. But in these departments the students have not yet started to work actively as researchers, and many of them will eventually work in professional jobs. There is one graduate departments at the University of Helsinki, Finland, that works primarily within the cultural-historical tradition.

How can it be that cultural-historical psychology has been so slow in establishing an institutionalised practice? A quick review of the tradition's history gives some explanations for this state, which in turn explains why it is so young. The suppression of the Vygotskian tradition in the Soviet Union, starting officially from 1936 with the Pedological Decree and continuing until the mid-1950s (for an English translation of this decree, see Wortis 1950, 242-45), was a major hindrance in its development.[5] And when it became possible to work openly in this tradition again in the Soviet Union, the tradition was not dominant (either in terms of the number of persons working in it or in

4. Textbooks are often an important way to identify the 'normal' science that is generally accepted within a theoretical tradition or scientific discipline, and an important dissemination mechanism for identifying central themes. The lack of a textbook is striking, despite the relatively long existence of cultural-historical psychology, and a clear sign of the weakly institutionalised nature of the tradition. This state of affairs is consistent with my claim that the tradition has not been established and passed through formal educational practices.

5. One historical account is available in Joravsky (1989). As a striking illustration of this point, look at the volume entitled *Psychology in the Soviet Union* (Simon 1957), a collection of translated papers published from 1953-1955 by Soviet researchers. Vygotsky's name does not appear, even though the topics include child psychology, development of speech and thought, and formation of psychic functions, and several of the contributors were Vygotsky's students or colleagues (e.g., Elkonin, Zaporozhets, Zankov, Slavina, Leontiev). There is, however, one exception. A paper about psychopathological research, written especially for this volume by Luria (1957), appears as an Appendix (because it arrived late). This paper, which was probably written sometime between January and April 1956, includes a detailed discussion of Vygotsky's central ideas. Note that 1956 was also the year that Vygotsky's *Selected Psychological Works* were published in the Soviet Union.

its institutional position). In the late 1960s and early 1970s, some researchers in other countries in Europe, Japan, and the Americas became interested, somewhat independently from each other, in the cultural-historical tradition, several of them studying for one or more years in Moscow. Also, some Cuban psychologists, starting in the 1970s, received their doctoral education in the Soviet Union. By the end of the 1970s and 1980s, the majority of Cuban research psychologists studied in the Soviet Union, where they learned about the cultural-historical tradition (though other traditions are also found in Cuba, see González Rey 1995)

At the same time, during the 1970s, translations of works by Vygotsky, Leontiev, Luria, started to appear in English, Spanish, Danish, German, and probably several other languages. Works by Vygotsky and Rubinshtein were being translated in Cuba in the 1960s (see González Rey 1995).

This impressionistic historical review (see Asmolov 1998, chap. 2, for a similar review) is meant to illuminate that there is not (yet) a canonical knowledge within the cultural-historical tradition, and there is not a well-established, coherent, international working community within which cultural-historical psychology is being practised and developed.[6] The lack of institutional infrastructure — which is now slowly starting to be developed — means that there has not been any formal educational training in the cultural-historical tradition in a systematic or common way. Furthermore, it has been difficult for researchers within the tradition to know about each other's work, even for well-established, long-time practitioners in the tradition. This international disjointedness among researchers in cultural-historical psychology, both in terms of their education in cultural-historical psychology and in their awareness of each other's work, has contributed to a heterogeneity in the development of particular themes or research issues. In short, a considerable diversity marks the knowledge and research questions within the practice of cultural-historical psychology.

6. For example, one cannot assume that the typical researcher in cultural-historical psychology has read certain texts from Leontiev, or Bakhtin, or Elkonin — much less Hegel, Marx, Ilyenkov — in same way that other theoretical traditions can assume certain basic or common knowledge (e.g., Piagetian psychology can assume knowledge of texts about concrete operations, or cognitive psychology can assume basic knowledge about the capacity and decay rate of short-term memory).

Unity in the Diversity? A Brief Survey of the Chapters

The diversity found in the historical origins of cultural-historical psychology raises the question of whether it is possible to speak about cultural-historical psychology as a singular or monolithic tradition. One way to approach this issue is to consider the chapters in this volume, all of which, except for this introduction, originated as papers presented at the Fourth International Congress for Cultural Research and Activity Theory, held in Aarhus, Denmark in 1998.[7] Even if cultural-historical psychology is not particularly well-established from an institutional perspective, it is geographically widespread (participants at the ISCRAT Congress came from 37 countries spread over 6 continents).

In assembling the chapters for this volume, no restrictions were imposed on maintaining a common theoretical view or methodological format. This liberal editorial policy entailed a risk that the volume could end as an incoherent set of chapters. On the other hand, if we are working within a tradition that is still in formation, where many ideas and directions have not been debated and evaluated sufficiently across the variations being developed within the tradition, then it can be a disadvantage to fossilise too quickly around the topics and arguments presented by some few individuals.

In this respect, it is refreshing to be able to read contributions from a wider range of researchers than 'the usual suspects'. The researchers in this volume are not novices or marginal by any means. All of them have been actively working and publishing in the cultural-historical tradition for many years now. From this point of view, it is interesting to look at the present volume as a kind of 'semi-random sample' of some topics and themes that concern persons who are working within the cultural-historical tradition. There is no reason to project from this set of chapters to a general picture of the work being done today, given there was no recruiting of specific chapters for this volume. But none of the chapters should appear extreme or alien in relation to cultural-historical psychology, and in this sense they are representative of current themes and interests being investigated within the tradition, though some may be considered somewhat provocative in relation to the cultural-historical tradition, offering challenges and criticisms.

---

7. The Congress was the event that enabled the assembly of these chapters, but each chapter in this volume has been substantially revised and reworked, and often extended or elaborated beyond that presented at the Congress.

At the same time, the diversity of research interests may reflect the heterogeneous origins of cultural-historical psychology's development across different nations. In particular, it is important to remember the likelihood of an interaction between local societal problems and research interests. However, it is still possible to see some common themes that emerge from this set of cultural-historical researchers who are working in different countries, with different theoretical perspectives. That is, shared views or issues appear across chapters, where the authors did not know in advance about each other's work. These similarities are interesting because they offer the possibility of indicating likely tendencies or trends in what captures attention and interest in cultural-historical psychology today, and I hope some of these themes will be continued and developed within this tradition.

For the sake of discussion, let me suggest a one-line definition of cultural-historical psychology as 'the study of the development of psychological functions through social participation in societally-organised practices.' This definition is quite useful for understanding a common core to the diverse contributions in this volume. All the empirical studies in this volume are grounded in the study of ongoing cultural practices, even if experimental methods are used as part of this investigation. Many authors in this volume (see in particular the chapters by Cubero & de la Mata; Tolman; Santamaría; Elhammoumi; and van der Veer) are concerned about the relation between societal practices and the development of psychological processes. Elhammoumi in particular expresses his concern about the insufficient attention to societal practices as the primary source for the development of mental processes, and argues for the need to use a more explicit materialist history in cultural-historical psychology. Consistent with my suggestion about the international disjointedness among cultural-historical researchers, it is understandable that he could not know, for example, that some researchers in Brazil are directly concerned about and struggling with the problems of finding a methodology to investigate this problem. In particular, Rojo is attempting to study language acquisition as a societal process in which social practices between parents and children serve to recreate societal practices. In this view, acquiring a language is seen as acquiring a way of being in society. Similarly, Oliveira discusses her approach to studying peer interaction, with a focus on the concept of 'role' as a way to understand a child's development as occurring within and through social and societal practices.

Several of the chapters were concerned about the need for developing a more systemic approach within the cultural-historical tradition. Branco presents a general overview, along with an empirical example, to describe an approach to the study of the cooperation and competition in social interaction in which one looks at co-construction of meanings at individual and collective levels. Van der Veer locates Vygotsky's holistic approach to psychology (a focus on genetic, explanatory analysis on the development of psychological processes) within a more general tradition found in continental psychology at the beginning of the 20th century, which he suggests has disappeared from much present-day psychology.

The concern about appropriate units of analysis is also found in chapters by Santamaría; van der Veer; Rojo; Cubero and de la Mata; and Oliveira. Santamaría's chapter concentrates on the details of the internalisation process, especially the use of semiotic mechanisms, in particular, referential perspective, as a way to understand the dynamics of the process by which joint understanding is developed. Differences in the use of semiotic mechanisms can be related to particular practices of the teachers. De Haan addresses this same issue directly in her chapter about differences between a 'teacher' style and a 'traditional parent' style of teaching. She interprets these style differences as reflecting different assumptions about intersubjectivity, which in turn result in different patterns of interaction between adults who are teaching children. This result, when considered in relation to Santamaría's chapter, suggests that internalisation is not only a matter of using particular referential mechanisms, but must also consider a person's capability to act in relation to the use of a particular mechanism.

The use of particular semiotic mechanisms, in this case, the acquisition and use of discourse genres in handling a common element of daily life (ways of categorising food items) was investigated empirically by Cubero and de la Mata. They show an interaction between a societal practice (literacy) and the thinking shown in a categorisation task. However, heterogeneity of thinking is not only to be found across groups of persons, but also for the same persons, where there is an interaction between the practices in which one engages and the forms of thinking that are used.

Zinchenko raises serious and important questions about the value of the internal/external pair for understanding mental phenomena, offering an alternative idea — own and not-own — from Mikhailov. The idea of ownership, which can be understood as a relation, rather than a location, may be a more useful way to understand the idea of the development of capabilities for action. From this point of view, both Santamaría's and de Haan's chapters can be understood as an analysis of how instructional intervention helps persons to make certain actions their own. Jones, in his extended presentation of the concept of 'ideal' emphasises the importance, in a materialist theory, of understanding the ideal (or the symbolic) as always connected to specific societal practices. From one point of view, Jones' discussion can be said to represent a theoretical background for some of the concrete studies presented here. Or it can be viewed as a horizon of the kind of explicit analysis of the relation between societal practices and psychological development such as Cubero and de la Mata are starting to develop. The further integration of this theory and practice is a clear concern to all the chapters in this volume.

To this point, it may appear that cultural-historical psychology is only concerned with the communicative and semiotic processes involved in the development of psychological processes. However, the idea of 'own' and 'not-own' implies that emotional relations and subjective meanings are also important in the development of psychological functions. Several chapters also mention or discuss the issue of emotional experience (see Fariñas León, van der Veer, Branco, and Zinchenko). Fariñas León discusses extensions to Galperin's theory of learning that would make it more comprehensive if it would also incorporate subjective aspects (such as emotional experience) of learning. She presents some examples of teaching experiments in which she illustrates the value of integrating subjective aspects in relation to learning specific content. She interprets these theoretical ideas as suggesting the importance of considering a personality level in relation to content learning. Her chapter provides an example of what Chaiklin is seeking in his historical review of the use of the concept of personality in cultural-historical psychology, namely some concrete elaboration in empirical work.

This brief survey of some common themes found in the chapters in this volume provides an indication that cultural-historical researchers are already addressing some of the problems to which others are trying to call attention. Despite the variations in specific theoretical concepts and sources that can be found across the chapters, there is still a consistent focus on trying to understand the development of psychological functions through participation in societally-organised social practices. This focus on unities among the chapters has not expressed adequately the detailed analysis of the relation between specific practices and the psychological functions that can be found in these chapters, nor discussed the relation between specific societal problems and research interests. In other words, cultural-historical psychologists are actively pursuing the concretisation of general theoretical principles found within the tradition.

Developing the Tradition

As a background for understanding how to further develop cultural-historical psychology, I consider three consequences of the under-institutionalisation of cultural-historical psychology that are reflected in these chapters. These are (a) the multiplicity of names or labels that are used to refer to the tradition, (b) the tendency to define the tradition as a negation of better institutionalised traditions, and (c) questions about the relation between the universal and the particular.

What's in a Name?

In this volume, we find chapters that are self-described as 'sociocultural psychology' (Santamaría; Cubero & de la Mata), 'sociocultural studies' (de Haan), 'sociogenetic psychology' (Oliveira), 'socio-historicocultural' (Elhammoumi), 'sociohistorical co-constructivist' (Branco), 'cultural-historical' (Chaiklin; Fariñas León) or refer to 'cultural-historical activity theory' (Seeger; Jones). One could say that we are in danger of having as many labels as we have authors. And this multiplicity is even more striking when one considers the semi-random process by which the chapters for this volume were assembled. That is, no attempt was made or conditions imposed to intentionally produce such a spread of labels, and there may be more than those listed here.

Given a tendency for academic traditions to totalise (i.e., to define themselves partly by excluding others and expanding their own scope), then it would seem that there is a danger for divergence in cultural-historical psychology, because these theoretical variations have started somewhat independently, even though they use some of the same theoretical sources. One way to confront the multiplicity of labels has been to create amalgamations such as CHAT or socio-historicocultural, or some other variation using combinations of socio, cultural, and historical. Another response is to appeal to Shakespeare's advice that a rose by any other name would smell as sweet. That is, despite the different labels, one could argue that to some extent the chapters all have the same basic orientation.

But there is one potential and serious problem with these eclectic approaches to resolving the multiplicity of labels. Even if the research traditions identified by the different labels trace their roots back to Vygotsky — either using his ideas directly, or ideas developed in relation to Vygotsky's ideas by researchers who were his students or assistants — these ideas are subsequently developed and refined among more local communities of researchers. The labels are a way of referring to and identifying oneself with a particular research tradition that reflects a structured approach for investigating the general problem of the role of social processes in the development of psychological functions. The label often serves to identify a particular tradition of problems and key persons. In other words, the variation in labels is not just a matter of linguistic taste, but rooted in a set of historical practices (e.g., visits between certain researchers and/or their students; reference to each other's work). It may be better to allow individuals to retain their preferred label, and find out in practice how they are to be concretised.[8]

For the sake of exposition, I will continue to use the expression *cultural-historical psychology*. I prefer this term primarily because it is the term Vygotsky used to describe his tradition.[9] Despite the occasional disputes about the relation between activity theory and cultural-historical psychology, it seems easier to me to keep the original term, and let it expand to encompass new theoretical developments that are inspired by the problems which emerge in that tradition. Ultimately, the concrete scientific practices and accomplishments that are encompassed by a label seem more important than the label itself.

In this spirit, we could ignore the problem of multiple labels used to refer to cultural-historical psychology, arguing that what matters is the content of the scientific work and not its label, while taking inspiration from Vygotsky's practice to read, evaluate, and integrate research from many different research traditions as part of his own theory development.

The goals and means determine whether a theory is scientific and no other factors. That is why to say 'scientific psychology' is equal to saying nothing or, more correctly, to saying simply 'psychology'.

8. In this connection, I think it better for researchers to use their preferred label in communicating face-to-face with other researchers, even if it means that one is saying 'cultural-historical psychology', while the other is saying 'sociocultural psychology'.
9. This choice is not free from complications either. The term 'cultural-historical' refers to a tradition that was developed by Wilhelm von Humboldt, which, among other things, promoted the idea of a hierarchical development of humans such that Western Europeans were more advanced. It is possible that Vygotsky got the term 'cultural-historical' from his teacher Shpet, but it is also likely that Vygotsky did not accept von Humboldt's theory about human development (V. Zinchenko, personal communication, November 1999).

It remains for us to accept this name. It perfectly well stresses what we want — the size and the content of our task. And it does not reside in the creation of a school next to other schools; it does not cover some part or aspect, or problem, or method of interpretation of psychology alongside analogous parts, schools, etc. We are talking about *all* of psychology, *in its full capacity*; about the only psychology which does not admit of another one. We are talking about the realization of psychology as a science.

That is why we will simply say: psychology. We will do better to explain other currents and schools with epithets and to distinguish what is scientific from what is nonscientific in them. (Vygotsky 1927/1997, 342)

Tulviste (1999, 77) argued in a similar spirit when he suggested that one day the name *cultural* will be dropped, such that only *psychology* will remain. There are, of course, many conceptual, theoretical, and practical problems that could be discussed here, including Vygotsky's definition of 'scientific', the institutional politics of academic-based science, whether 'scientific' should be the sole defining criterion, and so forth. Given Vygotsky's definition of 'scientific', one can conveniently define one's own goals and means as scientific and be finished with the other historical traditions (or let them all remain as separate sciences). If we ignore these conceptual puzzles for now, and continue naively forward, then two important principles or implications in Vygotsky's formulation (and practice) can be brought forward: (a) an openness to and interest in all problems that could potentially fall into the discipline of psychology, and (b) the avoidance of forming a special school.

In other words, in the long run, one should seek for cultural-historical psychology to become psychology, by virtue of its contribution to understanding psychological phenomena and not because it came from a particular school or tradition. If there are any modifying adjectives, then let them refer to substantive areas such as developmental psychology, clinical psychology, the psychology of learning, and so forth, or possibly we will retain diverse labels, but still find communication in this heteroglossia.

One can already see positive signs that researchers in this volume are moving in this direction. They are not interested in preserving Vygotsky's work as a museum piece, but use his writings as an inspiration source that needs to be clarified, concretised, elaborated, and revised and reconfigured when necessary. One sees a shift from explaining and interpreting the main authors, such as Vygotsky and Leontiev, to focus more on specific problems, drawing attention to, and trying to pull in other intellectual traditions. Just to name a few examples from this volume: Tolman uses the philosopher Macmurray; Oliveira draws on the concept of role as developed in a socio-genetic tradition; Rojo is trying to incorporate ideas from Wittgenstein and Bakhtin in her study of language acquistion; Cubero and de la Mata take inspiration from Lévy-Bruhl; Elhammoumi notes Wallon and Politzer; Zin-chenko points to Shpet, Ukhtomskii, among others; Jones focuses on the philosopher Ilyenkov. In short, one can see that contemporary practices of cultural-historical psychology are moving beyond the traditional sources (e.g., Vygotsky, Leontiev) in the development of ideas within a cultural-historical tradition. From this perspective, it would also seem that it is more important to continue to integrate diverse ideas into a unified cultural-historical psychology, than to invest too much effort into naming the 'baby'.

Negating the Mainstream

In the present volume, most attempts to criticise so-called 'traditional', 'mainstream', or 'positivist' psychology were edited out. This editorial policy reflected several considerations. First, these kinds of critiques have been widely available for at least 30 years. Second, people who are read-ing this volume are already likely to know, and have possibly made, similar critiques. Third, if the cultural-historical tradition has anything to offer to an international tradition of psychological thought and practice, then it should be able to formulate its contributions in positive terms, and not only as a negation of an existing (and established!) tradition of practice.

But why do authors who are working in a cultural-historical tradition still feel the need to make these critiques of the mainstream in their writing? My guess is that many persons working within the cultural-historical tradition still find themselves in a local and/or national intellectual community that sees cultural-historical psychology as questionable, inadequate, dubious. So it is understandable (to me at least) that some authors still want to establish their position as a negation of the dominating theoretical tradition of their proximal colleagues. If, however, authors start to recognise that it is possible to write to an audience that is educated within, understands, appreciates, values the cultural-historical tradition, then I expect that we will start to see more texts that push the edges and boundaries of our understanding of these concepts. Examples can be seen in the chapters in this volume that have grown out of doctoral dissertation projects (Cubero & de la Mata, de Haan, and Santamaría).

It is understandable that theoretical branches, when they are new, weak, underdeveloped in relation to institutionally well-established traditions, have some need for isolation in order to formulate and clarify their ideas. But at some point, it is also important to try to have dialogue and interaction across these variations. This is precisely what this volume is able to offer. Without trying to select the chapters in relation to a preconceived model of the current state of the field, it has been possible to obtain an interesting picture of the range of interests. The individual chapters do not attempt this dialogue, but perhaps the availability of this volume will make it easier for people to identify literature across the boundaries of their own branch of the river of ideas that has flowed from the early days of cultural-historical psychology.

The Universal and the Particular in Cultural-Historical Psychology

A second editorial problem concerns what information should be included in a scientific report in cultural-historical psychology. What is particular and what is universal? Normally in most psychological traditions it is considered boring or irrelevant to provide too much local detail when presenting a research report. The search for general principles of psychological operations inclines one to downplay specific or concrete characteristics. But this tradition can be problematic in relation to the cultural-historical tradition, which tends to place great importance on concrete details, as an essential part of understanding the origins and organisation of psychological functions. These concrete relations may reflect a universal that will be of wider interest to the research community. As editor, I sometimes found myself requesting more concrete details (which I meant were necessary to understand a phenomenon in a cultural-historical perspective), while other times requesting the removal of some practical aspects that seemed too local to the interests of the author. This was done to make the chapters have a more universal focus and appeal, but was it at the price of directing attention in a less useful direction? The problem of how to work with general principles, applicable across regional or national traditions of practice, while still remaining grounded in those practices has not been explored sufficiently within the cultural-historical tradition. It is clear that other psychological traditions will not be so useful in approaching this particular question, and this issue needs much more exploration in the ongoing development of communication among cultural-historical psychologists.

Problems for the Future

Having considered some characteristics of the present chapters as indications of the current state of cultural-historical psychology, and interpreted them in relation to the under-institutionalised state of cultural-historical psychology, I want to close by mentioning three issues that concern its further development: (a) the role of ideology, (b) the role of cross-national investigations, and (c) better integration of the implications of philosophical analyses for practice. Each of these issues are points in which institutional processes could have an important role in contributing to better conditions for further development.

Ideology

There is clearly a strong ideological component in the conceptual background for the cultural-historical tradition (see Elhammoumi, this volume), and there are clear examples of the distortion that can be introduced into scientific work when an ideological dimension becomes absolutely dominant (e.g., Soifer 1994). In the dominating epistemological traditions, ideology is often seen as opposed to science, or only to be treated as an object of study. However, if cultural-historical psychology is going to study societal practices, then it unavoidably meets ideological issues in research. Therefore, it will be necessary to see ideological issues as part of the content of scientific analysis that one is making (even if it is just to consider the norms that are used for evaluating and forming goals for development of psychological functions). But when we consider, as Seeger raised, that the research intervention can also be understood in relation to the societal practice, then there are also ideological issues connected to how we frame and interpret the questions in our research tradition. In other words, from a cultural-historical perspective, there is some (necessary) ambiguity about the relation between ideology and research. This reflexivity is not unique to the cultural-historical tradition, but one attraction of the tradition is that it has theoretical tools for considering the role of ideology in mental development (see Seeger, this volume, and Jones, this volume).

The topic of ideology is difficult to work with, because of the strong emotional aspects involved and because there is so little experience with how to handle these issues as part of the scientific analysis of psychological functions. One theme that cultural-historical psychology should confront is how to work with normative issues in its analysis, and the ways in which research practices are developed in relation to and maybe sometimes in opposition to existing practices about the relation between academically-based research and other societal practices (see Turner 1999). This is a point where developing new communication institutions within cultural-historical psychology may create conditions that enable development in this direction.

Cross-National Practices

In recent years, the concept or idea of *globalisation*, especially in the context of economic (such as in consumer marketing) and cultural processes (such as maintenance and transformation of practices), has been a source of attention, reflection, and often despair (because of the creation of questionable living conditions and values that seem to exceed existing processes of social control). However, it is also interesting to consider the phenomenon of globalisation in relation to the cultural-historical tradition of psychology. One implication of globalisation is a kind of homogenisation, at least in political-economic practices. This raises many questions about the kinds of explanatory models that should be developed for the psychological processes studied in this volume, and for the theoretical arguments about the relationships between societal practices and individual development.

At the same time, one could say that cultural-historical psychology is entering into a kind of globalisation through its developing institutional structures, and a growing dialogue across national boundaries. If its current state is marked by diversity and divergences (as suggested here), then what is gained or lost, especially with respect to the problem of the relation of the universal and the particular in the development of psychological functions? For example, the Brazilian authors in this volume (Branco, Oliveira, Rojo) are motivated by and concerned with the problems of developing adequate and appropriate conditions for child development in Brazil. However, it is difficult to see this interest in their work (partly as a consequence of my editorial requests that focused primarily on bringing forward issues likely to be of more general interest). This is the problem of the universal and the particular mentioned previously. Given the cultural-historical focus on historically-located practices, then how are we going to resolve problems of language, differences in educational traditions, and problems growing out of different practices in a way that supports an international dialogue without amputating an essential part of the research analysis.

These issues emphasise the need for cross-cultural and cross-national research. From the lens of institutional needs, several problems appear. If funding for research is justified in terms of its local relevance, then cross-national research is likely to seem less relevant to funding agencies and to one's local institution (especially because of the additional travel costs). Cross-national projects require personal contacts and communication across national borders, and this is not usually within the experience of many researchers (for such reasons as language, attendance of international meetings, specific research topics). Is it possible that institutionally-organised interventions from within the research tradition itself can help to overcome what has traditionally been organised at national or local levels? One challenge in developing cultural-historical psychology further is to develop ideas about how to sustain communication about the tradition that can preserve the differences in practices (which are often tied to local societal needs). For example, it may be necessary for researchers in a particular national context (e.g., Brazil) to produce a common text that provides an introductory overview of the cultural-historical conditions within which their work is being conducted, to which they could refer readers who do not have this background knowledge.

Theory/Practice and Knowledge Production

The title of this volume, *The Theory and Practice of Cultural-Historical Psychology*, indicates the interdependent relations between theory and social practice. These relations are central for cultural-historical psychology, and the epistemological tradition in which it is located. A key problem in cultural-historical psychology is understanding the relation between knowledge production and social practice. In principle, all psychological research traditions are concerned with such questions, but most of them do not have theoretical concepts *within* their theoretical tradition that allow them to reflect upon their practice. In this volume, Seeger discusses the simultaneity of theory and practice in a cultural-historical perspective. It is important to recognise that 'theory' here refers to scientific research focused on a practice, and that there is a possibility for that research to both articulate the practice as well as identify new ways to develop the practice. This interaction between theory and practice also makes it easier to see the reflexive possibilities in a cultural-historical psychology (and the ambiguity that arises in ideological questions), because the theory can be used to analyse the research practice itself.

The classical split between theory and practice reflects another epistemo-logical tradition. As Tolman elucidates in his chapter about the history of the concept of 'activity', there was a significant shift in philosophical thought from a focus on theoretical activity to collectively organised practical activity as the source for psychological interests and concepts. As Tolman suggests, the practical implications of this shift are still being investigated, and it is an intriguing and challenging idea to conceptualise cultural-historical psychology as part of societal practice.

One implication or consequence of this shift is that it is difficult to speak consistently about cultural-historical *psychology*, and several times in this chapter the expression 'cultural-historical tradition', appears. This difficulty arises because researchers and practitioners in other disciplines and professions are interested to use cultural-historical psychology in their own work, while the practices they study are important arenas for the development of cultural-historical knowledge. For example, there are a number of information technology researchers who are actively interested in and developing cultural-historical psychology (e.g., Berthelsen & Bødker, 2000). In Scandinavia, there are several occupational therapists (e.g., Fortmeier & Thanning 1994) who are working on trying to integrate cultural-historical psychology with their practice. Given the conceptual concerns about the relations between theory and practice in cultural-historical psychology, there should be an interest in having research dialogues with other disciplines and professions. But there is little tradition for dialogue between academic researchers and practitioners, even within the same discipline, as exemplified by the ongoing difficulties in the American Psychological Association in meeting the needs of researchers and practitioners. Is this a 'natural law' of professional organisations? A matter of differences in interest, either substantively or theoretically? Or is it also a challenge to see if we can find ways to support communication through our institutionalised practices that acknowledge the importance of practice in relation to theory.

Just as there are problems in communicating across nations, so are there also problems in communicating across practices. (This is another version of the universal/particular problem.) While most psychologists will not be specifically interested in the problems of occupational therapists (such as the rehabilitation of persons with spinal injuries), these are also rich situations which can be used to develop our understanding of cultural-historical psychology (e.g., personality development). As part of a growing self-conception about the practical ground for knowledge development, the cultural-historical tradition should attempt a more articulated dialogue and practice in relation to practice.

Instead of a Conclusion

This chapter has reflected upon some characteristics of cultural-historical psychology and presented some themes and problems that should be considered in the future development of cultural-historical psychology. Rather than offering any conclusions, this chapter is meant as a moment in the further development of the practice of cultural-historical psychology.

A main theme was that the practice of cultural-historical psychology is theoretically and internationally diverse, but because of under-institutionalisation, there have been insufficient opportunities for dialogue and communication. From that perspective, I would venture a hypothesis that the current practice that goes under the name of *cultural-historical psychology* is too diverse, both theoretically and practically. That is, the breadth of ideas and the complexity of the issues involved make it difficult at present to reach some clarity and agreement about important assumptions and research topics. Perhaps cultural-historical psychology will always remain theoretically and practically diverse, but then this creates new demands about what counts as progress within the tradition. This should not be a problem, so long as we, as a tradition, recognise that we may need to develop new practices (and their related institutions) that will sustain such a tradition.

References

Asmolov, A.G. (1998). *Vygotsky today: On the verge of non-classical psychology* (J.V. Wertsch, ed.). New York: Nova Science.

Berthelsen, O.W., & Bødker, S. (eds.) (2000). Information technology in human activity [Special Issue]. *Scandinavian Journal of Information Systems*, 12(1).

Fortmeier, S., & Thanning, G. (1994). *Set med patientens øjne: Ergoterapi og rehabilitering som patientens egen virksomhed*. København: FADL's Forlag.

González Rey, F. (1995). La psicología en Cuba: Apuntes para su historia. *Temas*, no. 1, 69-76.

Joravsky, D. (1989). *Russian psychology: A critical history*. Oxford: Blackwell.

Luria, A.R. (1957). Psychopathological research in the U.S.S.R. (H. Milne, trans.). In B. Simon (ed.), *Psychology in the Soviet Union*. London: Routledge & Kegan Paul, 279-87.

Simon, B. (ed.) (1957). *Psychology in the Soviet Union*. London: Routledge & Kegan Paul.

Soifer, V.N. (1994). *Lysenko and the tragedy of Soviet science* (L. Gruliow and R. Gruliow, trans.). New Brunswick, N.J.: Rutgers University Press.

Tulviste, P. (1999). Activity as explanatory principle in cultural psychology. In S. Chaiklin, M. Hedegaard, & U.J. Jensen (eds.), *Activity theory and social practice*. Aarhus, Denmark: Aarhus University Press, 66-78.

Turner, T. (1999). Activism, activity and the new cultural politics: An anthropological perspective. In S. Chaiklin, M. Hedegaard, & U.J. Jensen (eds.), *Activity theory and social practice*. Aarhus, Denmark: Aarhus University Press, 114-35.

Vygotsky, L.S. (1956). *Izbrannye psikhologicheskie issledovaniia* [Selected psychological works]. Moscow: Izdatel'stvo Akademii pedagogicheskikh nauk RSFSR.

Vygotsky, L.S. (1997). The historical meaning of the crisis in psychology: A methodological investigation (R. van der Veer, trans.). In R.W. Rieber & J. Wollock (eds.), *The collected works of L.S. Vygotsky: Vol. 3. Problems of the theory and history of psychology*. New York: Plenum Press, 233-343. (Original work written 1927)

Wortis, J. (1950). *Soviet psychiatry*. Baltimore: Williams & Wilkins.

2 The Complementarity of Theory and Praxis in the Cultural-Historical Approach: From Self-Application to Self-Regulation

Falk Seeger

When I started preparing this chapter, I first thought of starting with a brief historical account of the theory-praxis dichotomy in Western philosophy. I thought of beginning with Plato and Aristotle — having in mind the beautiful fresco of Raffaello, *La scuola di Atene*, with Plato and Aristotle in the middle, Plato pointing upwards and Aristotle, as if in a gesture of appeasement, stretching out his hand with his palm down in front of him.[1] I thought of discussing the eight or so different concepts of praxis that Aristotle had introduced, follow their fate in the Middle Ages when the Latin translation of the *Greek Commentaries on Aristotle's Nicomachean Ethics* done by Robert Grosseteste identified praxis as *operatio*,[2] when Duns Scotus and William Occam and their respective followers were fighting about the question whether praxis has to do primarily with human will or with human intellect (see Lobkowicz 1967). Finally, I would have arrived at Kant's separation of epistemology and ethics, discussed Hegel's idea that the practical consequences of philosophy must remain open and are not philosophy's business, while the young Hegelians in contrast proclaimed the practical nature of philosophy. Then I would have discussed Marx and his critique of philosophy, coming to the conclusion that praxis is the most revolutionary concept. After Marx I would have thought it necessary to mention Lukács' (1954) approach and

* I would like to thank Seth Chaiklin for critically reading and painstakingly commenting on previous versions of the chapter. These comments have helped me a lot in motivating myself to work previous versions over, but I am not sure if I have been successful in putting his clear ideas into equally clear sentences.

1. For an interesting approach to 'reading' this painting, see Most (1999).
2. *'Praxis autem … est secundum electionem hominis energeia, id est operatio'* (Mercken 1973, 12).

Horkheimer and Adorno's critical theory, briefly touching upon Marcuse's (1964) *One Dimensional Man*. Then, of course, it would have been necessary to present Habermas's (1968) separation of labour and interaction with eman-cipation as the mediating concept. To discuss Foucault's approach to praxis as discourse would have been a must, and I found Lacan's (e.g., 1964/1994) discussion of the relation of theory and praxis in psychoanalysis most inter-esting. Finally, I hit upon a couple of theory-praxis discussions inspired by the late Wittgenstein (see, e.g., Schatzki 1996). Here, at last, I began to doubt whether the whole idea would be feasible within a twenty-page chapter.

Searching for something like the core of the theory-praxis relation in the cultural-historical approach, I began to think about a story that would con-centrate on one central issue of the theory-praxis relation. I was looking for concepts that would mediate theory and praxis, very much in the spirit of 'bridging the gap' or 'transcending the theory-praxis dichotomy'. Things came to my mind like 'ascending from the abstract to the concrete' as one such mediating concept, or the 'thinking in action' theme that Sylvia Scrib-ner (1984, 1992) has written about, or the 'reflective practitioner' by Donald Schön (1983), or the 'teacher as researcher' theme in the theory-praxis discus-sion in educational research (see, e.g., Cochran-Smith & Lytle 1990; Goswa-mi & Stillmann 1987).

In the background of my thinking were a couple of ideas from the past, discussions about the 'crisis of psychology', issues of 'relevance' and the 'social responsibility' of researchers from the late 1960s and early 1970s (e.g., Caplan & Nelson 1973; Smith 1973; Walker 1969; and Tobach 1999 for a dis-cussion on the current crisis) where the problem of theory and praxis was discussed in themes like: 'if you are not part of the solution, you are part of the problem' (e.g., Nelson 1969) or the theme of 'giving psychology away' (Miller 1969), and so on.

Finally, I realised that Vygotsky had also written on the crisis of psychol-ogy (1927/1997b) saying that the problem of theory and praxis was lying at the centre of this crisis. Now, I decided to go back to his discussion and to some basic assumptions within the cultural-historical tradition.

Praxis as Situation

Two more or less implicit assumptions from the cultural-historical tradition were guiding my thoughts on the theory-praxis issue. One was that we have to acknowledge a fundamental complementarity of theory and

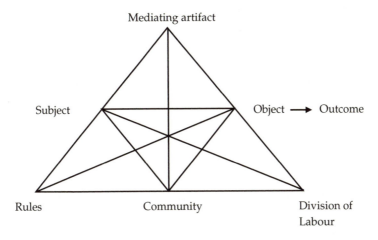

Figure 2.1. Engström's (1987) model of an activity system.

praxis in the sense that an activity can be seen as a system that is simultaneously theoretical as well as practical. It is important to recognise that this
complementarity is found both in activity as an object of reflection for an
observing scientist and also in the activity of an acting person. Therefore, a
satisfactory analysis of any theory-praxis problem has to apply equally well
both to the social scientist's work and to the practices that she or he is studying.

The second implicit assumption follows, in a sense, from the first. If each
activity realises a certain complementarity of theory and praxis, it can only
be grasped as a whole, in its totality — as a situation (cf. Jensen 1999). Therefore, a satisfactory analysis of any theory-praxis problem has to have a comprehensive model that can serve as a theoretical model of praxis, as well as
a model of scientific activity itself.

The need for representing theory-praxis as a totality is reflected in the
well-known triangle that Yrjö Engeström (1987) used in the development of
his model of a cultural-historical approach to changing societal praxis. This
diagram (see Figure 2.1) contains all elements and dimensions necessary for
the analysis of a given activity in any setting: subject, object, community, artifacts, rules, division of labour and object/outcome of that activity. It can be

applied to activity in the sphere of theory as well as in the sphere of praxis which is exactly what Engeström has done, beginning with *Learning by Expanding* (1987). The difference between theoretical and practical applications shows up only at the level of the concrete content of the categories, like subject, object, artifacts, community and so on, and at the level of primary, secondary, and tertiary contradictions.[3] There is no difference in principle between theoretical and practical activity: it only shows at the level of the concrete analysis. I consider this to be an essential element in a cultural-historical approach to dealing with the issue of theory and praxis. At the beginning there is no separation of activity and knowledge into two spheres, and consequently there is no need for an idea to be found as to how to reconcile these two spheres — which is the classical way to discuss the issue, as we will see later.

The preceding paragraph has emphasised the perspective of the unity of theory and praxis, a perspective that finds only differences in the concrete expression. In a certain sense, 'theory' and 'praxis' are two sides of a pair of contradictory concepts, a pair that is, like in Hegel's famous picture of master and servant, forming a unity in its contradictory relation. It remains, therefore, to find a qualitative difference between theory and praxis which expresses the fundamental contradiction between theory and praxis.

In psychology, the contradictory difference between theory and praxis should have something to do with the basic feature of reflexivity — or, as it is sometimes called — self-application (Groeben & Scheele 1977). For scientific activity, this means that the knowledge gained in psychological inquiry must also apply to the inquiring person (see also Raeithel 1998). This reflexive characteristic of psychological knowledge is like a categorical imperative expressing what should be done and what should not be done. Reflexivity also expresses a fundamental epistemological characteristic of psychological knowledge, namely, that it is relational. The hallmark of modern science, as analysed by Cassirer (1910/1980), has been that knowledge is no longer thought of as a 'substance' but as a relation, as a functional relationship between any process-structure and any other process-structure, and between any process-structure and an observer. Psychological knowledge, as it were,

3. Engeström (1987, 89) identifies the following levels of contradictions: primary contradictions arise *within* constituent components of the 'old' activity; secondary contradictions *between* the constituents of the old activity, tertiary contradictions between the motive/object of the old and a 'given new' activity, quaternary contradictions between the new activity and its neighbor activities.

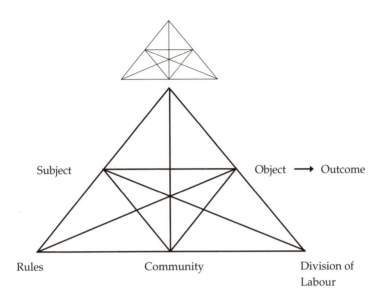

Figure 2.2. An activity system with a representation of an activity system as a mediating artifact.

receives its specific feature of relationality through self-application or, to express it another way, through reflexivity.

Figure 2.2 shows the addition of this feature of self-application into Engeström's diagram shown in Figure 2.1. This new diagram allows me to formulate the main themes for the remainder of the chapter. The diagram represents the basic situation of self-application through representations/artifacts given as psychological knowledge, concepts, and procedures. These artifacts mediate like other means or tools between subject and object. The process of self-application of psychological knowledge can be viewed as a mediational process leading to self-control in the sense that the mediational artifacts in Vygotsky's understanding are internally oriented, in contrast to artifacts like tools which are externally oriented. Thus, the problem of theory-praxis issues can be understood in terms of the role of mediational artifacts and self-control through mediational artifacts.

In the present case, psychological artifacts more or less reflect the totality of the situation.[4] The idea of reflecting a totality as a process of self-application is very much in the spirit of the rhetorical figure that Seth Chaiklin (1993) uses in a chapter on the theory-praxis issue. The 'totality of the situation' underlines the leading role of the perspective of societal praxis for a scientific analysis of the issue, or shows, in a slight variation of a quote from Vygotsky, how praxis informs the whole methodology of psychology.[5]

Artifacts Mediating Theory and Praxis

Given the importance of the mediating artifact in my argument, it would be useful to review the concept briefly before analysing how psychological knowledge can function as a mediating artifact. The main point here is that artifacts mediate different forms of activity and are used in gaining self-control of activity. Self-control, or self-regulation as one would prefer to say, is of fundamental importance for the theory-praxis issue (i.e., how is it possible to go beyond a situation through cognitive activity mediated by certain artifacts, especially secondary and tertiary artifacts such as language, diagrams, formulas, and number systems). An exemplary description of the central role of mediating artifacts and their function in self-regulation has been given by Vygotsky (1931/1997a) in his example of tying knots in a handkerchief as a way of remembering something (pp. 50-52).

In cultural-historical studies it is often found that Marx Wartofsky's (1979) distinction of primary, secondary, and tertiary artifacts is used.

Primary artifacts are those used in the process of producing something, which already gives a fairly broad range of things like hammers and axes, telephones and fax machines, words and computers.

Secondary artifacts are 'representations of primary artifacts and modes of action using primary artifacts' (Cole 1996, 121). Michael Cole gives as typical examples: recipes, traditional beliefs, norms, constitutions.

4. 'Totality of the situation' is meant here very much in the sense of Lewin's (1935) emphasis on the situation in 'The Conflict between Aristotelian and Galileian Modes of Thought in Contemporary Psychology' and 'The Psychological Situation of Reward and Punishment'. Lewin considered his treatise on the Aristotelian and Galileian mode of thought as an analysis of the reasons of the 'crisis of psychology', and he devoted much of his later career, in American exile, to find a practical solution to this crisis.
5. The original quote from Vygotsky (1927/1997b) is that 'practice reforms the whole methodology of science' (p. 306), where 'methodology', in Vygotsky's understanding, is not restricted to 'research methods', but embraces all methods used by scientific activity such as concept building or norms of discourse.

Tertiary artifacts in Wartofsky's understanding do not directly relate to practical activity. They constitute a 'relatively autonomous world' (p. 208). Knowledge gained in this world is not directly applicable, but through some form of transfer it can be applied to praxis — and this is so precisely because of its remoteness from actual praxis. The paradigm case of a tertiary artifact for Wartofsky are works of art, while Michael Cole extends the meaning of the concept to contain entities like schemas and scripts, and those most general concepts of the cultural-historical approach, like context, mediation, and activity. Cole's extension, as you can see, is a nice illustration of the idea of self-application: concepts like activity, mediation, and context function simultaneously as objects of inquiry and as mediating artifacts of the activity system.[6]

Psychological knowledge is a mediating artifact. To talk about psychological knowledge in theory and praxis means to talk about a mediating artifact that holds the identical position in theoretical and practical activity settings, with some differences. The theoretical way of talking refers traditionally to psychological discourse about practical tasks in the spheres of production or reproduction, in working and learning, in thinking and development. Applying psychological knowledge is thus seen as a problem of how to transport knowledge, rules, schemas that have been produced in the sphere of science to the sphere of praxis, so that participants can receive this knowledge, incorporate it, and make it part of their activity system. A typical barrier that complicates this vision is that the existing mediating artifact, often called 'folk psychology', resists the attempt of being replaced by artifacts elaborated in the sphere of science. The psychology 'given away' in the classical spirit is often not well received. If folk psychology is only seen as an obstacle to the implementation of artifacts produced in the sphere of science, the whole business of applying psychology is to outsmart the recipients.

The practical way of talking refers to discourse about the locus of the mediating artifact within the framework of a scientific psychology (e.g., in the sense of how scientific and theoretical study of mediating artifacts can

---

6. Here, we meet a difficulty. The separation of primary, secondary, and tertiary artifacts, as helpful as it may be, does not address how these artifacts are related to each other. Secondary artifacts seem to be abstractions from primary artifacts; are tertiary artifacts abstractions from secondary ones? What is the generative principle? Is it some form of Piagetian *abstraction réfléchissante* or something like Bateson's levels of learning where the higher level is defined as having the lower level as its object of change, thus including what is possible on the lower level (cf. Bateson 1972)?

lead to their application in practical situations). In practical settings the artifact is mediating between the subject and the production of some object disappearing within that process (very much in analogy to the use of the greatest artifact of them all: language), and only coming up when breakdowns occur.

In vivid contrast to these views on the relationship of folk and scientific psychology, Sylvia Scribner (cf. Tobach, Falmagné, Parlee, Martin, & Kapelman 1997) has shown in her work that the artifacts produced in everyday practical activity have the character of genuine knowledge. In her studies of dairy workers, she showed that an activity in a work setting that looked dull and routine (i.e., filling orders for milk products by collecting them in a warehouse, and loading them onto delivery trucks), did not mean that the workers lacked 'theoretical perspectives' about their work and their activity setting. Actually, they were extremely inventive in constructing artifacts, like algorithms, arithmetical procedures and graphical notations, which could help them organise their work. It was remarkable that these inventions mostly did not refer to any form of mathematics or knowledge taught in schools. They possessed, however, all the features of secondary artifacts.

It is noteworthy that the introduction of the concept of the mediating artifact is accompanied by a flattening of a common hierarchy that sees theory as being superior to praxis. I take it as a basic starting assumption that no knowledge form is *as such* superior to another knowledge form. If one cannot use superiority as a point of comparison or differentiation between theory and praxis, then on what basis can one talk about the relation between theory and praxis and their difference? In my view, this is possible only if one means that the difference between these two types of knowledge is defined through their respective theoretical and practical contexts — the principal difference being, as Bourdieu (1972/1977) puts it, the relation to time. The most obvious difference here relates to the non-reversibility of the structure of action in practical settings, whereas the structure of theoretical argumentation is reversible in the sense that it does not have to follow a strict temporal order. Also, in practical settings, there is often a strict time-boundedness of action, where something has to be done now and cannot be done later, or has to be done in a certain order. Theoretical thinking, in contrast, is distanced from this necessity of practical reason; it can arrange and rearrange elements of what then emerges as a whole by theoretical necessity, and not by temporal order. This does not mean that time (e.g., in the form of a time limit) can play an important and often decisive role in scientific activity as,

Theory	Praxis
Episteme:	*Phronesis*:
Scientific knowledge	Practical wisdom
universal	particular
conceptual	perceptual
abstract	concrete

Figure 2.3. Theory and praxis as *episteme* and *phronesis* (after Kessels & Korthagen 1996).

for example, Kedrov (1966/67) has shown in his analysis of D.I. Mendeleev's discovery of the periodic law of elements (see also Engeström 1987, 257-67). The decentering or distancing from praxis is a hallmark and an advantage of theory. This advantage turns into a disadvantage if theory does not succeed in re-centering on praxis, if what theory has to say about praxis is 'only theoretical'. This leads to a deepening of the split between theory and praxis, which in turn makes it difficult to see what is common and what is different in theory and praxis.

I will try to show that the split between the theoretical and the practical is kept alive by a conception of knowledge that is basically contemplative.

Contemplating or Acting?

Before discussing the question of secondary and tertiary artifacts and their role in self-control, I would like to discuss some examples of how the problem of theory and praxis has been dealt with in social scientific thinking. The problem is often seen as a purely epistemological problem: How can knowledge capture reality and then come back to reality in order to be applied in praxis?

Kessels and Korthagen (1996) present an interesting attempt to explain that the problems of today's educational praxis, in particular the praxis of teaching and teacher education, reflect a controversy that is about 2500 years old: the controversy about knowledge as *episteme* or as *phronesis*. Basically,

Plato is said to view knowledge as *episteme*, while Aristotle holds the knowledge as *phronesis* position. Figure 2.3 summarises the juxtaposition of the two types of knowledge discussed.

In Kessels and Korthagen's view the fundamental problems of teaching practice could be resolved if one would turn back to Aristotle's conception of practical wisdom (*phronesis*). For them the key to practically effective action is perceptual knowledge, because 'to be able to choose a form appropriate for the situation, one must above all be able to perceive and discriminate the relevant details' (p. 19). 'Practical wisdom' understood as something that is primarily grounded in perceptual knowledge still has to travel a long way from the distance receptors to practical activity. Because this knowledge remains fundamentally 'contemplative', its introduction reproduces the same difficulty that it was meant to overcome.

My point of departure for extending this figure was an idea of relating the concepts of self-regulation and praxis on the background of a critique of what G.E.M. Anscombe (1957) called the 'incorrigibly contemplative conception of knowledge':

Can it be that there is something that modern philosophy has blankly misunderstood: namely what ancient and medieval philosophers meant by practical knowledge? Certainly in modern philosophy we have an incorrigibly contemplative conception of knowledge. (p. 57)

Anscombe's view echoes nicely what Marx (1845/1983) identified in the *Theses on Feuerbach*, as the 'chief defect of all previous materialism', namely,

that the object, reality, what we apprehend through our senses, is understood only in the form of *object* or *contemplation*; but not as *sensuous human activity*, as *practice*; not subjectively. (p. 155)

It is well known that in the *Theses on Feuerbach* Marx advocates a view on human nature that emphasises the key role of practical activity (see also Jensen 1999; Tolman, this volume). Human sensuousness is conceived of as not only reflecting but also creating the world, as the product as well as the producer of history. Engagement in the world, activity within the world is not only the basis for a rational understanding, it is also the basis for a 'scientific morality', an ethical imperative: 'Philosophers have only interpreted the world in various ways; the point is to change it' (Marx 1845/1983, 158).

Vygotsky, very much in the spirit of Marx, also viewed social praxis as the 'cornerstone' of a scientific psychology. He did not, however, take Marx's advice, of using the history of industry as a necessary source for this science,[7] too literally. Vygotsky cared more about art, language, learning, ontogenesis and pedagogical and clinical problems of human development; he did not have much to do with the study of industrial work. However, in his manuscript about the 'crisis of psychology', Vygotsky took pains to analyse the 'psychotechnic' approach to psychology, where Hugo Münsterberg was the leading figure, and concluded that the neglect of the fundamental role of praxis was responsible for the crisis.

The principle and philosophy of practice is–once again–the stone which the builders rejected and which became the head stone of the corner. Here we have the whole meaning of the crisis. (Vygotsky 1927/1997b, 306)[8]

Another often-quoted point in the *Theses on Feuerbach* seems to have been still more important for Vygotsky's foundation of a cultural-historical psychology. It is the third thesis that talks about that changing the world requires that humans change themselves:

The materialistic doctrine concerning the changing of [men's] circumstances and education forgets that circumstances must be changed by men and that the educator himself must be educated. This doctrine therefore has to divide society into two parts, one of which is superior to society.
    The coincidence of the changing of circumstances and human activity or self-change can be comprehended and rationally understood only as revolutionary practice. (Marx 1845/1983, 156)

This basic metaphor of 'self-change' can be interpreted as the metaphor of the basic reflexivity of human activity that Marx is advocating in the 'psy-

7. As expressed in the oft-cited quote, that 'the history of *industry* … is the *open* book of the *essential powers of man*, the observably present human *psychology* …
    A *psychology* for which this book, that is, the most observably present and accessible part of history, remains closed cannot become an actual, substantial and *real* science' (Marx 1844/1967, 310-11).
8. The picture Vygotsky uses here is taken from Psalm, 118, 22: 'The stone which the builders rejected, is become the head stone of the corner' (Vygotsky 1927/1997b, 233), which he also chose as the epigraph to his manuscript on the crisis of psychology.

chology of 1844' (cf. Raeithel 1983). Seen from this vantage point the 'coincidence of the changing of circumstances and human activity or self-change' seems to be a more general framework than 'revolutionary praxis' understood as political activity in the narrow sense. It is a characterisation of human activity in a general sense — and a strong argument against the contemplative point of view.

This interpretation is not too far from Marx's intentions in the *Economic and Philosophical Manuscripts* — because he is writing about private property and industry as revolutionary forces that have been changing human nature.

'The coincidence of the changing of circumstances and human activity', then, is the place where the actor is 'woven into' the web of practical activity, to use a term that Michael Cole (1996) coined to address the question of the role of praxis in cultural psychology. Given this focus on self-change that arises from the preceding analysis, it would be important to know what the coincidence of changing circumstances and self-change mean psychologically.

Praxis and Self-Control through Higher Mental Functions

In the following I shall examine some points from Vygotsky's well-known treatment, taken from his *History of the Development of Higher Mental Functions*, of the concept of self-control or mastering one's own behaviour. I will show that this concept is a central motive in Vygotsky's work.

The theme of the 'mastery of one's own behaviour' is part of Vygotsky's (1931/1997a) attempt to formulate a fundamentally new approach to the study of 'higher forms of higher mental functions' as the history of higher mental function. This approach unites three basic concepts: *'the concept of higher mental function, the concept of cultural development of behavior, and the concept of mastery of behavior by internal processes'* (p. 7).

In elaborating this conception, Vygotsky uses two metaphoric examples throughout his analysis. The one, already mentioned, is the famous example of tying a knot in a handkerchief; the other one is the no less famous picture of Buridan's ass caught between two equally attractive heaps of hay.

The example of tying knots is used in the argumentative context of the emergence of signification as a phylogenetically and ontogenetically new regulatory principle. For Vygotsky, it is situated within the overarching fundamentality of the stimulus-response principle.

In contrast to Lewin, we attempt to provide for the concept of mastery of one's own behavior a completely clear and precisely determined content. We proceed from the fact that the processes of behavior represent the same kind of natural processes subject to the laws of nature as all other processes. Neither is man, subjecting processes of nature to his will and intervening in the course of these processes, an exception in his own behavior. But a basic and very important question arises: how does he represent the mastery of his own behavior to himself?

... Just as mastery of one process or another in nature, mastery of one's own behavior assumes not a change in basic laws that control these phenomena, but subjection to them. We know that the basic law of behavior is the law of stimulus-response; for this reason, we cannot master our behavior in any other way except through appropriate stimulation. The key to mastery of behavior is mastery of stimuli. Thus, *mastery of behavior is a mediated process* that is always accomplished through certain auxiliary stimuli. (Vygotsky 1931/1997a, 87)

Of course, it gives one a strange feeling to read from the founder of the cultural-historical approach about the fundamental importance of the stimulus-response principle. If we think about the stimulus-response principle in terms of artifacts, it seems to make more sense: it is more like the S-R principle is serving as a basic metaphor for the flow of energy or movement as a general presupposition to mental or psychological functioning. There is an undertone in this quote towards a rather 'vulgar' form of materialism, but the question is formulated to the point: how do humans represent self-regulation to themselves?

Vygotsky gives some hints to an answer to the question.

First, human self-regulation follows what he called the 'general genetic law of cultural development' (Vygotsky 1931/1997a, 106) stating that psychological functions develop ontogenetically from the outside to the inside, from the social to the individual level:

Initially, the sign is always a means of social connection, a means of affecting others, and only later does it become a means of affecting oneself. ... In general, we could say that the relations between higher mental functions were at one time real relations between people. I relate to myself in the same way that people relate to me. (p. 103)

The ontogenesis of the semiotic control structures, then, in this view presents no secret. I control my behaviour very much in the same way I have seen other people control their behaviour, preferably people that are in my zone of proximal development. Another quote, however, illustrates that the whole process might not be so benign.

Of what do the basic changes consist? They consist in that at the higher stage of development, man begins to control his own behavior, subjects his own reactions to his own control. Just as he controls the actions of outside forces of nature, he also controls his own processes of behavior on the basis of the natural laws of be-havior. Since the basis of natural laws of behavior are laws of stimuli–responses, a reaction cannot be controlled as long as the stimulus is not controlled. Con-sequently, a child controls his own behavior, but the key to this lies in controlling the system of stimuli. The child controls arithmetic operations, having mastered the system of arithmetic stimuli.

Precisely in this way, the child masters all other forms of behavior, having mas-tered the stimuli, but the system of stimuli is a social force presented to the child from outside. (pp. 112-13)

'Social force' seems to be a strong word. But it indicates that there is a boundary for the otherwise constructive spirit in the whole picture of the indi-viduals mastering stimuli and in this way mastering their own behaviour.

To get a clearer picture of the possible meaning of 'mastering the system of stimuli presented as a social force', it is necessary to introduce the issue of 'sense and meaning' (see the last chapter of Vygotsky's *Thinking and Speech* 1934/1987, or the more elaborated version in Leontiev 1959/1981). Leontiev showed that the *meaning* of activity or objects always involves a societal dimension to the extent that these meanings represent the interindividual or — as Vygotsky put it — the interpsychological. In contrast, *sense* is the intra-individual meaning, which the historically and practically situated individ-ual interprets as meaning, 'as a social force'.

Having considered Vygotsky's view of self-control, we can now show how self-regulation can be understood in the previous discussion about the-ory and praxis and psychological knowledge as a mediating artifact.

The recursive image of self-application was shown to be central in Vy-gotsky's analysis of the development of higher mental functions. If praxis is the cornerstone of psychology, its meaning within the system of psychology is self-regulation through artifacts. The 'coincidence of changing circum-stances and human activity or self-change' can serve as a paradigm example for the type of change in a societal praxis that psychology has to deal with.

Just like context and event are interwoven into the cultural web, so theory and praxis are two threads woven together. If I should make an attempt to formulate the object and the goal of psychology, I would say that it is the production of tertiary artifacts that have as their object the use of secondary artifacts in the context of a specific activity, of the relation of subject ↔ artifact ↔ object.

Consequences of the Theory-Praxis Complementarity

What are the consequences of this view on theory-praxis complementarity for my own work as a psychological researcher in the field of learning? I would like to mention three consequences: one relates to the question of the future orientation of the research field, another to a more general question about change and the role of contemplation and action, and the last to the question of the reflexive nature of knowledge gathered in my research.

An important consequence for my own research is that praxis is leading my activity in the dual sense of offering the totality of the practical situation as a springboard for an integrative approach and of necessitating reflexive steps both in the sense of self-application and in the sense of taking the reflexivity of the subjects into account.

Another important consequence is related to the question of the nature of change that a praxis-oriented research perspective deals with. I am very sympathetic here with Seth Chaiklin's extension of Marx's eleventh thesis on Feuerbach: 'The point is not to interpret nor change the world, but to live in it' (Chaiklin 1993, 398). Of course, this is not the whole picture, in my view. It is true that there is one important strand in social life where it is more important to understand and live and let live — that is, especially, as regards the question of the diversity of cultures and life-styles that make up societal praxis. But as regards the production of social life through the large trusts and conglomerates, it would be a terrible mistake to 'just live it'. Here, the need to change the conditions of living which lead to living a better life is obvious.

I see the clearest consequence to my own work in the fact that everything I think can count as knowledge in my research area, knowledge I have gained through empirical research or through conceptual analysis, must also be applicable to myself and my own activity. In other words, there is no knowledge, at least not in principle, that is only applicable to 'them', but is not equally valid for me.

Concluding with Open Questions

Many questions have to be left open. I would like to briefly mention some that I find especially noteworthy.

If we approach the theory-praxis issue from the perspective of self-regulation, of constructing and adopting tertiary artifacts that mediate secondary artifacts, the question must arise: What is the self (e.g., in the sense of something that stays identical across diverse situations)? Questions about identity and authenticity might arise connected to ideas about the self deeply rooted in everyday psychology. I am far from even trying to give an answer to that question, but I want to point to an interesting aspect of self-regulation as a core element of the relation of theory and praxis.

It is a common understanding that theory-praxis interactions, interactions between researchers and practitioners or 'just plain folks' ('jpfs' in Jean Lave's 1988 choice of acronyms), carry with them multiple sources of misunderstandings, difficulties to communicate and to understand each other. Here, the problem is to find a coordination between different selves, between researcher and jpfs, and so on. Susan Leigh Star (1989) has shown how 'boundary objects' can be conceived of as mediating between different selves with different lifeworlds consisting of different objects and subjects. They mediate these different worlds because they dwell, so to speak, on the threshold between these worlds and activity systems, creating an overlapping that can coordinate efforts and understanding.

This problem of coordination, however, does not only occur between the selves of members of larger societal groups, but also within the self of one individual person as a conflict or coordination of the different selves of that individual (cf. Peterson 1998). For example, my personal theory-praxis problem could be the coordination and conflict between my self as researcher and psychologist and my self as father. These conflicts can lead to dead ends, if they are not reconciled, but they can also trigger a deepened understanding of what I am doing as a father as well as a researcher. But the actual situation is not that balanced. In one case, I would experience behaviour deviating from what I consider a decent way of behaving, of learning, of living one's life. Would I really look for support in the scientific literature or do my own studies with other subjects? I guess I would not do it because I am in doubt that this will do any good. The other case is that I manage to rephrase my life — including my life in my family and with my children — in terms of a psychological theory that I have adopted. Now, there is a homogeneous theoretical layer extending from the books, my work to my family and my friends. In the first case, we find an ambient personal theory-praxis conflict in the form of a role conflict between the researcher and the father, in the second case we have the perfect researcher-father.

Both cases are equally dissatisfying. The personal theory-praxis issue, in my case and view, has very much to do with getting wise as a lifelong learning task. Here, I find Kessels and Korthagen's (1996) call for contemplation perfectly in place.

I have mentioned the problem of a 'personal' theory-praxis problem not so much because its discussion would give me the opportunity to present my private philosophy. I wanted to point to a problem following the emphasis on the situatedness of practical and theoretical activity, a problem that deserves some attention. If theory and praxis are looked at from the perspective of their situatedness, one can possibly lose the idea of what connects them and what makes them two parts of a complementarity. 'Situatedness' tends to emphasise the 'relativistic' nature of theoretical and practical activity, relativistic in the sense that its respective meaning is interpreted as related to a theoretical or practical situation. While this makes sense in relation to explaining (e.g., meaning-making as being tied to certain situations), it may create problems in relation to ethical questions. For instance, are the ethical norms only valid for a certain situation or is there something like a more general horizon? Can one claim that what one does in praxis does not touch what one does in theory, or, that what one does in praxis *A* does not touch what one does in praxis *B*? Given the growing expansion of the situatedness-stance, the need to answer these open questions will become acute.

Summing up, we can now formulate some results of our discussion:

- the complementarity of theory and praxis is an essential feature of meaning making in the social sciences;
- the basis of this complementarity is reflexivity in a double sense: in the sense of self-application of theoretical/research results and in the sense of the necessity to take the reflexiveness of the subjects into account;
- praxis is guiding theory (e.g., through requiring that the totality of the situation be grasped in a theoretical/scientific analysis).

As mentioned before, many questions have to remain open. Let me conclude with a quote from one of Charles Sanders Peirce's late manuscripts illustrating the quantity of problems still to be tackled. In passing, I should note that the issue of self-regulation was also for Peirce a major motive for the development of his system of signs (cf. Bernstein 1971; Colapietro 1989; Raeithel 1992).

In a manuscript on existential graphs, Peirce (1906) writes about the number of open problems:

My classification of signs is not yet fully matured. I have been at work upon it, or at least have kept in mind since 1863, but still confidently expect important improvements in it. If I live to complete it, it will be the contribution to exact logic that has cost me the most labor, and it will be recognized by exact logicians as a very positive and indisputable contribution to exact logic even if I should leave it in its present imperfect state. There remain many hundreds of difficult questions yet to be considered, though the majority of them have received an examination which cannot justly be called careless or summary. *Lest it should be suspected that I exaggerate in saying that there are many hundred questions I will say that the exact number, so far, is 205 billion 891132 million 94619. But these are not all independent. From the answers to some the answers to others can be deduced. The total number of really independent and really difficult questions, requiring each some days of laborious consideration is only 1073 million 741794. So that if I should have the good fortune to live 82 or 83 million years longer I might hope to exhaust the subject.* It is not to be expected that I should live long enough to answer them all with positive assurance.[9]

Happily enough, I do not feel to be in the position to be able to number the quantity of open problems in the theory-praxis issue. The degree of interdependence of the problems is definitely much higher than in Peirce's problem space. They might well lead back to one central problem, as Vygotsky (1927/1997b, 306) put it, how 'practice reforms the whole methodology of science'. The solution of the theory-praxis issue is, however, not primarily a theoretical problem:

It is apparent how the resolution of *theoretical* antitheses is possible *only* in a *practical* way, only through man's practical energy, and hence their resolution is in no way merely a problem of knowledge but a *real* problem of life which *philosophy* could not solve because it grasped the problem as *only* theoretical. (Marx 1844/ 1967, 310)[10]

9. My thanks to Michael Hoffmann for showing me this quote. The asterisk * indicates Peirce's own insertion.
10. The original German quote expresses more clearly that Marx thought of the resolution as a 'task for life', a *Lebensaufgabe* where social as well as individual life is meant: 'ihre Lösung daher keineswegs nur eine Aufgabe der Erkenntniß, sondern eine wirkliche Lebensaufgabe ist, welche die Philosophie nicht lösen konnte, eben weil sie dieselbe als nur theoretische Aufgabe faßte.' (Marx 1844/1982, 394)

References

Anscombe, G.E.M. (1957). *Intention*. Oxford: Blackwell.

Bateson, G. (1972). *Steps to an ecology of mind*. New York: Ballantine.

Bernstein, R. (1971). *Praxis and action: Contemporary philosophies of human activity*. Philadelphia: University of Pennsylvania Press.

Bourdieu, P. (1977). *Outline of a theory of practice* (R. Nice, trans.). Cambridge: Cambridge University Press. (Original work published 1972)

Caplan, N., & Nelson, S.D. (1973). On being useful: The nature and consequences of psychological research on social problems. *American Psychologist, 28*, 199-211.

Cassirer, E. (1980). *Substanzbegriff und Funktionsbegriff. Untersuchungen über die Grundfragen der Erkenntniskritik*. Darmstadt: Wissenschaftliche Buchgesellschaft. (Original work published 1910)

Chaiklin, S. (1993). Understanding the social scientific practice of *Understanding practice*. In S. Chaiklin & J. Lave (eds.), *Understanding practice: Perspectives on activity and context*. Cambridge: Cambridge University Press, 377-401.

Cochran-Smith, M., & Lytle, S.L. (1990). Research on teaching and teacher research: The issues that divide. *Educational Researcher, 19*(2), 2-10.

Colapietro, V.M. (1989). *Peirce's approach to the self: A semiotic perspective on human subjectivity*. Albany, N.Y.: State University of New York Press.

Cole, M. (1996). *Cultural psychology: A once and future discipline*. Cambridge, Mass.: Harvard University Press.

Engeström, Y. (1987). *Learning by expanding*. Helsinki: Orienta-Konsultit Oy.

Goswami, D., & Stillmann, P.R. (1987). *Reclaiming the classroom: Teacher research as an agency for change*. Upper Montclair, N.J.: Boynton/Cook.

Groeben, N., & Scheele, B. (1977). *Argumente für eine Psychologie des reflexiven Subjekts: Paradigmawechsel vom behavioralen zum epistemologischen Menschenbild*. Darmstadt: Steinkopff.

Habermas, J. (1968). *Erkenntnis und Interesse*. Frankfurt: Suhrkamp.

Jensen, U.J. (1999). Categories in activity theory: Marx's philosophy just-in-time. In S. Chaiklin, M. Hedegaard, & U.J. Jensen (eds.), *Activity theory and social practice: Cultural-historical approaches*. Aarhus, Denmark: Aarhus University Press, 79-99.

Kedrov, B.M. (1966/67). On the question of the psychology of scientific creativity: On the occasion of the discovery by D.I. Mendeleev of the periodic law. *Soviet Psychology, 5*(2), 18-37.

Kessels, J.P.A.M., & Korthagen, F.A.J. (1996). The relationship between theory and practice: Back to the classics. *Educational Researcher, 25*(3), 17-22.

Lacan, J. (1994). *The four fundamental concepts of psycho-analysis* (J.-A. Miller, ed.; A. Sheridan, trans.). London: Penguin Books. (Original work published 1964)

Lave, J. (1988). *Cognition in practice: Mind, mathematics and culture in everyday life.* Cambridge: Cambridge University Press.

Leontiev (Leont'ev), A.N. (1981). *Problems of the development of the mind* (M. Kopylova, trans.). Moscow: Progress. (Original work published 1959)

Lewin, K. (1935). *A dynamic theory of personality: Selected papers.* New York: McGraw-Hill.

Lobkowicz, N. (1967). *Theory and practice: History of a concept from Aristotle to Marx.* Notre Dame, Ind.: University of Notre Dame Press.

Lukács, G. (1954). *Die Zerstörung der Vernunft.* Berlin: Aufbau-Verlag.

Marcuse, H. (1964). *One dimensional man: Studies in the ideology of advanced industrial society.* Boston: Beacon Press.

Marx, K. (1967). Economic and philosophic manuscripts. In L.D. Easton & K.H. Guddat (eds. and trans.), *Writings of the young Marx on philosophy and society.* Garden City, N.Y.: Anchor Books, 283-337. (Original work written 1844)

Marx, K. (1982). Ökonomisch-philosophische Manuskripte (Zweite Wiedergabe). In K. Marx & F. Engels, *Gesamtausgabe* (MEGA), Band 2. Berlin: Dietz Verlag, 323-438.

Marx, K. (1983). Theses on Feuerbach. In E. Kamenka (ed. and trans.), *The portable Karl Marx.* New York: Penguin Books, 155-58. (Original work written 1845)

Mercken, H.P.F. (ed.) (1973). *The Greek commentaries on the* Nicomachean Ethics *of Aristotle.* Leiden: Brill.

Miller, G.A. (1969). Psychology as a means of promoting human welfare. *American Psychologist*, 24, 1063-75.

Most, G.W. (1999). *Raffael — Die Schule von Athen. Über das Lesen der Bilder.* Frankfurt: Fischer.

Nelson, B. (1969, September 12). Psychologists: Searching for social relevance at APA meeting. *Science*, 165, 1101-4.

Peirce, C.S. (1906). On the system of existential graphs considered as an instrument for the investigation of logic. In *The Charles S. Peirce papers* [MS 499, 499s]. Cambridge, Mass.: Harvard University, The Houghton Library.

Peterson, P.L. (1998). Why do educational research? Rethinking our roles and identities, our texts and contexts. *Educational Researcher*, 27(3), 4-10.

Raeithel, A. (1983). *Tätigkeit, Arbeit und Praxis — Grundbegriffe für eine praktische Psychologie.* Frankfurt: Campus.

Raeithel, A. (1992). Semiotic self-regulation and work: An activity-theoretical foundation for design. In C. Floyd, H. Züllighoven, R. Budde, & R. Keil-Slawik (eds.), *Software development and reality construction.* Berlin: Springer, 391-415

Raeithel, A. (1998). *Selbstorganisation, Kooperation, Zeichenprozess. Arbeiten zu einer kulturwissenschaftlichen, anwendungsbezogenen Psychologie.* Opladen: Westdeutscher Verlag.

Scribner, S. (1984). Studying working intelligence. In B. Rogoff & J. Lave (eds.), *Everyday cognition: Its development in social context*. Cambridge: Cambridge University Press, 9-40.

Scribner, S. (1992). Mind in action: A functional approach to thinking. *Quarterly Newsletter of the Laboratory of Comparative Human Cognition*, 14, 103-10.

Schatzki, T.R. (1996). *Social practices: A Wittgensteinian approach to human activity and the social*. Cambridge: Cambridge University Press.

Smith, M.B. (1973). Is psychology relevant to new priorities? *American Psychologist*, 28, 463-71.

Schön, D.A. (1983). *The reflective practitioner: How professionals think in action*. New York: Basic Books.

Star, S.L. (1989). The structure of ill-structured solutions: Boundary objects and heterogeneous distributed problem solving. In L. Gasser & M.N. Huhns (eds.), *Distributed artificial intelligence* (vol. 2). London: Pitman, 37-54.

Tobach, E. (1999). Evolution, genetics and psychology: The crisis in psychology — Vygotsky, Luria, and Leontiev revisited. In S. Chaiklin, M. Hedegaard, & U.J. Jensen (eds.), *Activity theory and social practice: Cultural-historical approaches*. Aarhus, Denmark: Aarhus University Press, 136-60.

Tobach, E., Falmagné, R.J., Parlee, M.B., Martin, L.M.W., & Kapelman, A.S. (eds.) (1997). *Mind and social practice: Selected writings of Sylvia Scribner*. Cambridge: Cambridge University Press.

Vygotsky, L.S. (1987). Thinking and speech (N. Minick, trans). In R.W. Rieber & A.S. Carton (eds.), *The collected works of L.S. Vygotsky: Vol. 1. Problems of general psychology*. New York: Plenum Press, 38-285. (Original work published 1934)

Vygotsky, L.S. (1997a). In R.W. Reiber (ed.), *The collected works of L.S. Vygotsky: Vol. 4. The history of the development of higher mental functions* (M.J. Hall, trans). New York: Plenum Press. (Original work written 1931)

Vygotsky, L.S. (1997b). The historical meaning of the crisis in psychology: A methodological investigation (R. van der Veer, trans.). In R.W. Reiber & J. Wollock (eds.), *The collected works of L.S. Vygotsky: Vol. 3. Problems of the theory and history of psychology*. New York: Plenum Press, 233-343. (Original work written 1927)

Walker, E.L. (1969). Experimental psychology and social responsibility. *American Psychologist*, 24, 862-68.

Wartofsky, M.W. (1979). *Models: Representation and the scientific understanding*. Dordrecht: Reidel.

3 Family Interactions as a Source of Being in Society: Language-Games and Everyday Family Discourse Genres in Language Construction

Roxane Helena Rodrigues Rojo

Discourse genres are — in Vygotskian and Bakhtinian terms — 'mega-instruments' (Schneuwly 1994) for language construction or language acquisition. Descriptions of the social and interactional process by which this construction takes place can also broaden our understanding of the construction of acting and belonging in society.

According to Vygotsky (1925/1976) and to Volosinov/(Bakhtin) (1929/1981),[1] the study of the intersection between social and individual practices requires an investigation of how the forms of human social action and interaction (language activities or discourses) are able to multiply and reproduce themes and forms of discourse, which in turn reflect and refract possible themes or forms in determined social, political and ideological scenarios.[2]

Research on language acquisition and on the ontogenesis of discourse genres is crucially involved in the answer to these questions. However, traditional research on language acquisition focuses mainly on the order of appearance of morphological and syntactic-semantic linguistic categories, rather than on discursive ones, and even in interactional approaches the focus is essentially on interactional processes and procedures.

So, to begin to investigate and explain 'how the forms of human social action and interaction are able to multiply and reproduce themes and forms of discourse', we must first reinterpret concepts and categories involved in language construction explanations and point out their links with discourse genre building.

1. When I mention Volosinov, I refer to the ideas from the Bakhtinian circle to which Volosinov contributed deeply in the early 1930s. To indicate this, I sometimes follow the Brazilian practice of referring to Volosinov as Volosinov/(Bakhtin).
2. It is important to notice here that these early ideas of Volosinov/(Bakhtin) (1929/1981) are related to the latest theory of discourse genres in Bakhtin's (1979/1985b) work.

Trying to reach this aim, the main goal of this chapter is first to bring the Bakhtinian 'theory of discourse genres' into this Vygotskian discussion. In other words, to reinterpret Bakhtinian concepts — like discourse genres, utterances, and social conditions of utterance — in relation to the social interactive activities[3] involved in language construction. Secondly, to test empirically this analytical framework with a specific data collection (child-family language use), in a specific context (everyday family interaction).

Viewing 'language acquisition' as part of the process of 'acquiring' society, I will discuss how different language constructions between parents and their children (family interactions) reflect their social histories, determine differences in terms of language, action and person construction and possibly have an impact on child social development.

The main question raised here is: What are the differences — in terms of language, action and person construction — among children who come from different social-cultural traditions of practice, especially if they participate in different language-games or activities in a distinct manner?

To answer this question, I will analyse everyday family interactions for two Brazilian children, Helena and Priscilla,[4] both two years old, but from different social-cultural traditions of practice, with social histories based on different language activity patterns.

Both children are integrated in a family situation that includes careful and attentive mothers. However, they differ in the way their interactions are enacted. Priscilla is very active and always moves her body, but does not talk much. Helena, in turn, asks, demands, disagrees, comments and makes other people do things for her. In other words, she is often in control of actions and situations. As a way to explain these initial differences, I will examine the (everyday family) patterned language activities (formatted language-games) related to the discourse genres that make up the girls' interactions.

In the rest of the chapter, I first clarify and relate central concepts from the Bakhtinian circle and from Wittgenstein to construct a framework for analysing language interactions; then explain the research context and methodology of data collection and analysis; followed by a discussion of some of the data collected about Priscilla's and Helena's language activity. Finally, I comment on some implications of these results for a Bakhtinian-inspired approach to studying language construction.

3. Here interpreted in a Wittgensteinian way ('language-games' and language activities).
4. These are invented names.

Activity Patterns, Language Activities, Language-Games and Discourse Genres

In a cultural-historical perspective, the social construction of language and action is essentially determined by the social history of the interactions and the language-patterned activities in which subjects under constitution are and were immersed. Different patterns of language activities (Schneuwly 1988), linked to the building of discourse genres, will have various effects on the constitution of action forms and on the ways of speaking about them (Bronckart 1997).

Although the previous statement may seem trivial in relation to a cultural-historical research model in sociology, psychology or linguistics, it involves some basic aspects worked out by different approaches: the relation between action, language and thought; the intersection between social and individual practices; the process of appropriation of social practices by an individual who is being constituted by those practices.

Both Vygotsky (1925/1976) and Bakhtin's circle (Bakhtin 1981b, 1979/1985a, 1979/1985b, 1975/1988; Volosinov 1929/1981, 1929/1993) have mentioned the notion of social corps psychology (Plekhanov 1922) viewed as an analysis sphere that lies between sociology and psychology, and represents the process and product of reproduction and refraction of the macrosocial on the micropsychological level. Both Vygotsky and Bakhtin identify a different level between the economic relations of the infrastructure (productive forces and social-political situation) and the different ideologies that reflect and refract these infrastructures at the superstructure, namely the psychological context of social man (Vygotsky 1925/1976) or the ideology of everyday life (Volosinov 1929/1981). They both see the need of a social psychology to analyse the human dynamics for the perpetuation and change of social structures and to describe the process of appropriation by the human individual of social practices (*die Praxis*). Finally, both view social interaction (through words or signs) as the material basis for this social device.

But how can one describe 'social interactions' in terms of discursive interchanges without losing their relations to social contexts or social practices?

Bakhtinian concepts of utterance and of communicative situation or social conditions of utterance production (Bakhtin 1981b, 1979/1985b, 1975/1988; Volosinov 1929/1981, 1929/1993) — closely related to the concept of discourse genres — can lead us to describe social interaction or language activities as discourse or utterances, without losing their relations to cultural patterns or social positions. Defining an *utterance* as a unique, unreproducible piece of discourse, the Bakhtinian circle ascribed this uniqueness to the specific context or communicative situation in which it is generated.[5] The social conditions of utterance production is related to the role or social position of the participants (speaker/audience), the social-historical time and place in which the utterance takes place, the goals of interaction, and so forth. In other words, the utterance depends on the social sphere of activity in which it takes place and on the types of relations in social communication it determines.

Volosinov/(Bakhtin) (1929/1993, 247)[6] distinguishes five types of relations in social communication, by means of which we can classify discourse genres: artistic relations, production relations, business relations, strict ideological relations (in science, philosophy, the press, school, propaganda, etc.), and everyday life relations. Each of these spheres of social activity has its specific forms (and themes) of action, interaction and discourse genres that in turn are related to and sometimes determine possible forms and themes of utterances in these spheres.

Three of the five types of social communicative relations (or spheres of social activities) mentioned above — namely, production relations, business relations and ordinary everyday life relations — take place in the sphere of social corps ideology or everyday life ideology and, because of it, they can feed, reproduce and create strict ideological relations and products.

Also inspired by Bakhtinian ideas, Schneuwly (1988) formulated this idea as a necessary articulation between activities and social relationships. Social activity patterns (Sève 1974, cited in Schneuwly 1988) — viewed as determining social forms and contents of individual activities — are the necessary link between social and individual reproduction and the functioning of social relationships. Different types of activities — language activities among them — are formatted by social patterns of activities and on the individual level are viewed as actions. In this approach, social activity patterns are the concrete forms in which a social corps psychology can be formulated.

In my view, language activities taken as being organised by social activity patterns have two theoretical advantages for concretising any discursive anal-

5. In this sense, an utterance can be materialised in any traditional linguistic unit — word, phrase, sentence, period, turn, episode, text, etc. The Bakhtinian meaning of utterance refers to any piece of discourse that, in a given specific context, makes sense.
6. See also Bakhtin (1929/1981a, 289).

ysis: they presuppose a social subject (and not merely a psychological one) and they link the social situation of utterance production to a specific language activity and its discursive format (discourse genres). Therefore, we can expect that social activity patterns (or interactional patterns) in everyday family relations and interactions will be responsible for specific and context dependent utterances.

The methodological procedures indicated by Volosinov/(Bakhtin) (1929/1981) are to study and describe these utterances first by interpreting:

- The forms and types of verbal interaction in connection with the concrete conditions in which it takes place.
- The forms of distinct utterances, of isolated speech acts, in strict relation to the interaction of which they are elements (e.g., the categories of speech acts in everyday life and in ideological creation which are determined by verbal interaction).
- From this, the examination of linguistic forms in its current interpretation. (p. 124) [my translation]

Inspired by this analytical method, I will first examine here the verbal interaction in connection with its communicative situation, which I will call *activity patterns*; then discuss the types of verbal interaction that are relevant and determined by these contexts (*language activities*) and their *format*; and finally relate them with the discourse genres being constructed in/by these interactions.[7]

When this analytic method is applied to examine child language construction, then an additional problem appears, because the child has not yet constructed or appropriated the primary or everyday discourse genres (e.g., questions and orders)[8] that circulate in the child's everyday family interaction. We cannot yet speak about discourse genres in child speech. So, we need an intermediate category to treat children's utterances in everyday family interactions.

7. See the analytical pattern presented later in Figure 3.1.
8. Bakhtin (1979/1985a) distinguishes between primary and secondary discourse genres, with primary genres being more simple and adopted in everyday practices, often oral and dialogical ones. Secondary discourse genres appeared later historically, in the most complex sociohistorical situations, frequently related to writing or public contexts. Bakhtin's analysis of secondary discourse genres is notable because these genres often transform and absorb primary discourse genres.

In my view, we can use Wittgenstein's (1953) notion of language-game as the intermediate category that can be understood as a transition to the Bakhtinian concept of primary and secondary discourse genre.[9] In section 7 of *Philosophical Investigations*, Wittgenstein introduces the main notion of language-game — using an example of a primitive language that he presented in section 2, and to which he refers as (2).[10] Wittgenstein stresses the following points that are important to the analysis conducted in this chapter:[11]

– the term language-game is used primarily to refer to the complex consisting of activity and language-use;[12]
– the training activity antecedent to the language-game, mentioned in (2), is itself a language-game;[13]
– the use of language as portrayed in (2) can be considered as a model of initial language-learning;
– the distinction between word and sentence is drawn by reference to use. We can distinguish between ordering (in the building activity) and naming or repeating (in the learning activity). So 'slab' is a word in the naming activity and an imperative sentence in the building activity;
– the context of the game is constituted by: (a) the participants (builder and assistant; adult and learner); (b) the essential activities without which the game cannot be played (building or teaching-learning activities); (c) the essential objects (building or language materials);
– that the game is to be considered as a whole.

9. See also Bronckart (1992, 20-21) about this point.
10. 'Let us imagine a language … meant to serve for communication between a builder A and an assistant B. A is building with building-stones: there are blocks, pillars, slabs, and beams. B has to pass the stones, and that in the order which A needs them. For this purpose they use a language consisting of the words "block", "pillar", "slab", "beam". A calls them out; — B brings the stone which he has learnt to bring at such-and-such a call. — Conceive this as a complete primitive language.' (Wittgenstein 1953, 3e)
11. See also Baker and Hacker (1980).
12. 'In the practice of the use of language (2) one party calls out the words, the other acts on them.' (Wittgenstein 1953, 5e)
13. 'We can also think of the whole process of using words in (2) as one of those games by means of which children learn their native language. I will call these games "language games" and will sometimes speak of a primitive language as a language-game. … I shall also call the whole, consisting of language and the actions into which it is woven, the 'language-game.' (Wittgenstein 1953, 5e)

So, the Wittgensteinian concept of language-game can be used as:

– the material, historical and monist unit of language analysis as a practice or activity;
– dialogical practices;
– formatted practices;[14]
– a concept that specifies both the difference and the relation between learning language-games and ordinary language-games.

By taking language-game as a category of analysis of the child language construction process, we can infer the relations between the different language-games in a diachronic view of development (intergame relations) and the relations of different language-games within a complex language-game in a synchronic view of development (intragame relations).[15] These relations and movements of language-games are viewed here as the driving force of language development dynamics as discourse genres construction.

Briefly, in my opinion, the building of language by the child and the dialogic everyday family genres (Bakhtin 1979/1985a) — viewed as learning/ everyday language-games — would be responsible for both the constitution of action forms (teleological action), and their normalisation (normative action) (Bronckart 1992, 1997). Also, they would determine the emergence of other primary and secondary discourse genres, by means of inter- and intragames relations.[16]

14. Although Wittgensteinian language-games are not mentioned, the concepts of language-games and format (as a linguistic form) can be found in the interactionist approach to analysing language acquisition. See, for instance, Bruner (1975), Brant de Carvalho (1989), Brant de Carvalho-Dauden (1993), Fernandes (1995), de Lemos (1988), Lier (1985), and Rojo (1992, 1994b, 1998). In this chapter, I point out some typical, frequently-used formats that characterise different language-games and that are reorganised in primary discourse genres.
15. For an example of an inter- and intragames relation functioning in language construction, see the example from Helena's sample (02;03;13) on pages 77-78, where the adult, through name-games and tell-games (an intergame relation) functioning inside a major tell-game (intragame relation), will construct — conjointly through dialogue with the child — a report of the book pictures, reorganising the child's language and discourse genre.
16. For a detailed description and deeper discussion about the role of these inter- and intragames relations in narrative discourse genre construction, see Rojo (1992, 1994a, 1994b, 1994c, 1995, 1996a, 1996b, 1998).

Finally, included in the theoretical point of view sketched above — and important to my data analysis — is the fact that, in more advanced moments of language constitution, different narrative genres will unfold — in particular, reports of situated sequences of actions, stories and fairy tales. Because of their relatively early constitution by the children and the fact that they are focused on actions in different manners — conjunctive and disjunctive referentiality (Bronckart, Bain, Schneuwly, Davaud, & Pasquier 1985) — these normative genres should play an important role in the social construction of discourses about the action and, therefore, in its awareness.

Research Context, Data, and Methodology of Analysis

As mentioned before, the second objective of this chapter is to test empirically the analytical framework constructed in the previous section in a specific data collection of everyday family interactions showing two different processes of child language construction.

The main research questions were: (a) what are the differences — in terms of language, action and person construction — between two children who come from different social-cultural traditions of practice? (b) did they participate in a distinct manner in different social activities, language activities and learning language-games? (c) can we find different discourse genres and linguistic structures being constructed? (d) can we predict an impact of these differences in language, action and person construction for these two children's social development?

Before discussing these questions in the following sections, I will first explain the research context and the methodology of data collection and analysis.

Two girls, Helena and Priscilla, were observed and videotaped every two weeks (for about 45 minutes) from age 02;01 to 03;01, while they were involved in family interactions.

Priscilla is the first daughter of a housemaid and a butcher. The family lives on the outskirts of São Paulo — Brazil's largest city — and includes the child, her mother and father, the grandparents, two adolescent uncles and a sister born within the period of the research project, all living together in the same house. The dynamics of the family is wholly embedded in its community. In all the recordings there are often relatives, friends and neighbours present, but mainly and regularly other children from the neighbourhood. Although the adults can read and write, we did not observe any reading or writing activity in this family during the research period, indicating that although the family is literate, literacy activities are not functional for them. Priscilla does not go to school and the mother says that the girl will not go to school until she is seven years old.[17]

Helena is the youngest child of two college professors (philosophy and linguistics). She has three brothers and a sister, whose ages during the research period ranged from 7 to 12 years. All of them go to school regularly, including Helena, who has been going to nursery and preschool since she was 8 months old. Writing and reading activities occur frequently in this family, and involve all literacy domains including reading and telling stories to the children.

In this chapter, I have selected three observation sessions for each child — chosen at the beginning, the middle and the end of the research period. In these three recorded sessions, each child is respectively 02;02, 02;07 and 03;01 years old. In the analysis perspective adopted here, the criterion of chronological age is arbitrary, because, as we will see, children at the same age can have different interactional histories and are already constituted as differentiated persons.

As mentioned before, the analysis will examine the (everyday family) patterned language activities (formatted language-games) related to the discourse genres that make up the girls' interactions. These categories show the kind of activity and the social situation of utterance production for a specific language activity linked with its discursive format being built (discourse genres).

The raw data (i.e., the utterances) are described by their formats (see Figure 3.1, fourth column). Formats are specific instantiations of learning language-games, which are specific to each language. The formats listed in the third column of Figure 3.1 are specific to Brazilian Portuguese translated into English. Learning language-games are a kind of language activity (second column) — which in turn reflects social activity patterns (first column). There are two main kinds of language activity: teleological and normative. Teleological activity shows how actions and action reporting are developed; nor-

17. In Brazil, obligatory schooling begins at age seven, but typically, children are not left at home until they are seven years old. In the middle and upper socioeconomic classes, children begin schooling earlier in private nurseries or preschools. Working class families bring their children to public preschools or to daycare facilities provided by their employers. It seems that in Priscilla's family the community organisation substitutes for schooling.

Activity Patterns	Language Activities	Learning Language-Games	Formats	Primary/Everyday Family Discourse Genres under Construction*
Teleologicals	Teleological ('make them do')	**Order-Game** ('make them do')	• Imperative V (+X). • 'Let's + Infinitive V (+ X)?' • 'Want X!'	to order them to do something
		Role-Play-Game ('pretend to do')	• 'Let's + Infinitive V (+ X)?' • Imperative V (+X)	to order them to do something
		Name-Game ('make them speak – to name')	• 'What's X?/Who's X?' • 'Where's X?'	to name
		Tell-Game ('make them speak – to tell')	• 'Tell me X'. • Indicative V (+X)?	to tell Secondary genre: stories or fairy tales reporting
Normatives	Normative ('may/can/let them do')	**Deontic-Game** ('may/can/let them do')	• 'May I X?' • 'You can (not) do X'	to order them to do something to request
	('can/cannot do')	**Epistemic-Game** ('can/cannot do')	• '(I/you) (not) be able to do X' (?) • '(I/you) (not) know how to do X'. (?)	to request

* Except for tell-games, where some secondary genres appeared in Helena's sample.

Figure 3.1. Analysis pattern used to code utterances in family language interactions.

mative activity shows how actions and action reporting will be regulated and controlled (Bronckart 1992, 1997). The last column refers to the relation between those activities and the girls' way of reporting the action and/or telling stories[18] that will also be taken into account, with special emphasis on the analysis of different shapes of transitivity and thematic roles being constructed.[19]

The learning language-games are listed in order of decreasing frequency.[20] The language games and their associated formats that were most frequently observed in my data sample are listed in the third and fourth columns of Figure 3.1. These games (e.g., name-games) tend to disappear[21] during development, absorbed by other complex games and discourse genres through inter- and intragame relations. Others remain almost unchanged because they constitute primary or simple everyday discourse genres, such as order-games will constitute orders. It means that the same analysis pattern can be applied, without these two columns, in samples where learning is not in question (e.g., everyday family genres as interaction).

The unit of analysis was the utterance, in Bakhtinian terms, instead of turns or episodes.[22] For each session for each child, the utterances were categorised according to the type of learning language-game where it was contextualised. The frequencies of occurrence for the different learning language-games are plotted on a graph for ease of comparison.

The results show two distinct processes of language construction. For Priscilla, her language acquisition process is based mainly on the construc-

---

18. In this case, secondary discourse genres.
19. As we know, linguistically, transitivity and thematic roles are two main syntactic-semantic aspects of action discourse construction. As such it will be a special focus of the data analysis to see what formal properties of language the children are constructing.
20. Note that the role-play-game is a complex category. Although it is not a learning language-game — in Wittgensteinian terms — it must be considered here, because within it (intragames relation) there are other learning language-games (name-game, order-game, tell-game, etc.), but functioning in a disjoint context.
21. Or, in some contexts, they will specialise and become canonised (see Bakhtin 1981b).
22. As discussed in the second section of this chapter, an utterance can be materialised by any traditional linguistic unit, including turns and episodes. They can even be constituted by actions or other semiotic ways of communication (gestures, drawings, paintings, etc.). An utterance, in Bakhtinian terms, is defined by its 'responsibility' (e.g., the capacity for internal, actional or linguistic external response by the partner in the interaction). In this sense, most of the utterances in my data were empirically coincident but not conceptually equivalent to turns.

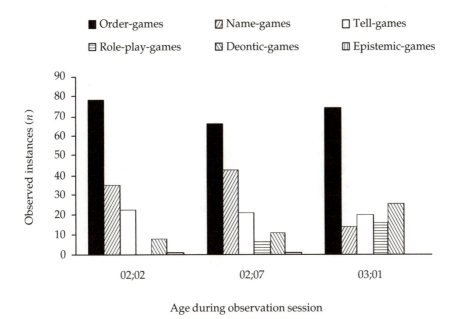

Figure 3.2. Frequency of different learning language-games in Priscilla's sample.

tion of dialogic primary genres, while narratives are almost absent. This fact also presents a relevant interface both with the situated sequence of action reports and the role-play-games. However, the construction of ways of speaking about action (transitivity and thematic roles) is slower and more limited in Priscilla's case.

The opposite is revealed in Helena's process. Her language construction is based mainly on narratives and fairy tales. It means that during the research period her process was centred on only a few forms of action and their normalisation. The intense tutorial negotiation of the ways she reports action on the discursive plan of the utterance for the disjoint narrative leads to a more complex and thematic construction of transitivity and thematic roles.

The two next sections describe in detail these results for Priscilla and Helena, respectively. We will look initially at the relative occurrences of the different language-games in the two samples, to see which ones are emphasised more in the everyday family interactions; then, we will focus specifically on 'tell-games' to discuss how discourse genres that report and re-create actions (reports, stories and fairy tales) are being constructed and the effects these constructions have on acquisition of sentence syntactic-semantic relations of transitivity and thematic roles.

Priscilla and the Construction of Action, Order, and Obedience

Figure 3.2 shows the observed frequency of different learning language-games in Priscilla's sample. The interesting results are found by comparing the relative frequency of occurrence of different learning language-games within a particular session, and the increase or decrease in the frequency of a particular game across sessions.

A closer look at Figure 3.2 shows that for all three recorded sessions, the most frequent teleological language activity is the order-game, formatted as an imperative verb of action (+X) or as 'Let's' + an infinitive verb of action (+X) in adult language and as 'Want X' in child language. Here is an example that shows the typical format of the episodes, where the imperative verbal form is repeated several times, with or without the vocative. The adult utterances are normally followed by a child's actions (also an 'utterance' in Bakhtinian terms). The discourse genre under construction is clearly what Bakhtin (1979/1985a) named *primary everyday family genres*, by means of order-games.

Context: Priscilla (C), V (grandmother) and L (a neighbour child) are playing outside the house; her mother (M) and the researcher (R) watch the game and sometimes interfere:

> V: Kick, Pri! Kick the ball to her! C'mon luv! Kick the ball! C'mon kick! Kick!
> C: (Kicks the ball).
> M: Gooaaal! C'mon run! Go and get the ball!
> C: (Runs to get the ball).
> V: Kick! Kick!
> M: Let's score a goal now! C'mon let's do that! C'mon score a goal!
> C: (Kicks the ball). Gooaal!!!
> M: Kick! Kick! Kick the ball over there!
> C: (Kicks the ball).
> M: Good! Like this! …

C: (Picks up the ball and moves backwards).
M: Come here, look! L has got the ball.
C: (Falls over with the ball in her hands).
C: Ouch!
L: (Sits beside R).
M: Let's score a goal, Pri! C'mon luv!
C: (Keeps on kicking the ball on the wall).
C: Hold ... Hold?

Another language-game that occurred frequently in the three analysed sessions is name-game, formatted as 'What is X?/Who is X?', followed by an action of naming an object or a person, or as 'Where is X? It's here' with a pointing gesture. According to Bronckart, it is a designation pattern of language activity. In Priscilla's sample the frequency of name-games is explained by a recursive practice during the research period: to leaf through a family photo album, recognising and naming her relatives in the photos.

The data shown in Figure 3.2 also document the emergence and increase of role-play-games in the episodes recorded at 02;07 and at 03;01. In these learning language-games we recognise again the format order/action-obedience, but with an increasing disjunction provided by the fictionalisation in role-play-games. As shown in the next example, although there is a fictional role-play-game, in terms of language and action construction, what is being negotiated here linguistically is the structure of order (imperative verb of action), followed by a child action. In these sessions, the child is in a more symmetric or reciprocal situation to the order because of the other children's participation. Also, the adult utterances are more modalised, often appearing as a conjoint action of 'invitation' rather than an order, which the child can reject or negotiate.

Context: Priscilla (C) is sitting in the garden, holding a toy telephone.

M: Ring daddy, c'mon! Sit here with S. [another neighbour child]
C: Sit here! C'mon luv! [to S]
S: (Looks around).
C: Look, here! Look!
S: (Sits beside C).
C: Look, luv. Here, look. Take. (Gives the telephone to S).
S: (Remains silent).

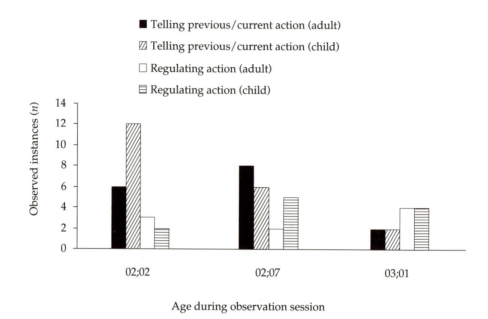

Figure 3.3. Frequency of tell-games in Priscilla's sample.

C: Hello?
S: (Playing with a plastic duck).
M: Talk to him, c'mon luv!

These data also show that in the one-year span of Priscilla's development, the recorded interactions were essentially focused on the construction of action and the primary everyday family discourse genre 'order/obey', except for the construction of designation (name-games).

Normative language activities also increased in those episodes, essentially constituted by deontic language-games focused on what 'we can (not)/may (not) do'. Again, the basic format is the modalised order/obedience one.

Tell-games occur third-most frequently in these three sessions, and with almost identical frequency. To analyse them closely, we must differentiate the kinds of tell-games that appeared in Priscilla's sample. The tell-games involved either telling about a current sequence of actions or regulating them. Either the child or the adults could perform this tell-game, hence four

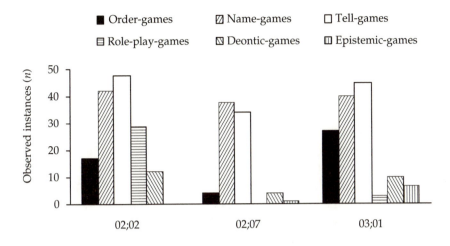

Figure 3.4. Frequency of different learning language-games in Helena's sample.

different kinds of tell-games. The frequency of occurrence for these four kinds of tell-games is shown in Figure 3.3.

The tell-games shown in Figure 3.3 reflect productions in which forms of reporting action are constructed. Either the adult or the child tells about a previous or, more often, a current action or they regulate a current action. In the case of regulating action, the utterance functions as an instruction rather than a report.

Note that over the three observation periods, the frequency of Priscilla's telling previous/current action decreases greatly. At the same time, the relative number of tell-games observed from the adults and the child become progressively balanced, with an increase in instructional or regulating current action language-games versus a relevant decrease in reporting language-games. This reflects the fact that the adults stop asking the child to tell about lived experiences and engage mainly in instructing or regulating the child's current action. As a result, the construction of a discourse that is not directly dependent on the actual world is progressively abandoned rather than increased, as would be expected.

Because Priscilla did not have the opportunity to co-construct reports that are disjoint from the actual world, then linguistic forms of action sentences are not negotiated. As a result, neither transitivity nor thematic roles are constructed effectively in the language construction of action discourse in this production situation.

Helena and the Construction of Action Discourse

In Helena's sample (see Figure 3.4), in contrast to Priscilla's, tell-games are emphasised rather than order-games. However, in a process apparently similar to the one in Priscilla's sample, name-games are the second most frequent. Order-games are not altogether absent in Helena's sample, occurring third-most frequently in the second and third analysed sessions, while the role-play-game (in which we can see functioning order-games, tell-games and name-games, i.e., intragame relation) was the third-most frequent in the first session (02;02).

In the following example, we can see that most of these language-games appear in a very different way (family production situation) in Helena's sample. In the order-game case, Helena is already in a reciprocal situation with the adult in this language-game. In contrast to Priscilla's sample, most of the order-games that occur in this first example are from the child, who is giving orders or demanding something ('Want X!') in an exclamation form, which in most situations is 'obeyed' by the mother.

Context: Helena (C) and her mother (M) are dressing C's doll after bathing it. They are playing a role-play-game; the researcher (R) records the game:

C: I wanna dress her! I wanna dress her!
M: OK. She is wearing trousers.
C: No! I wanna dress her!
M: To put the dress on her? (Gives the dress to C).
C: Dress?
M: (Takes the doll from C and dresses it). Let's put the dress. Like thiiisss ... all right?
C: Lovely dress, baby! [to the doll]
M: (Keeps on dressing the doll). OK! Baby looks lovely! Is the baby going to the party?
C: (Takes the doll). Party of ... of ... Trousers fall down.

M: Yes, her trousers are too big!

R: Look, here's the small trousers! (Gives the other pair to C).

C: (Takes the pair). The small trousers! This is the small trousers. Small trousers … (Tries to dress the doll with the small pair).

M: Whose party is she going to?

C: Tuddy's.

M: Whose?

C: I wanna dress her. Mummy, wanna dress her. (Hands the doll and the trousers to her mother).

M: Let's try to dress her up for the party? (Dressing the doll).

C: She's going to the party!

M: Whose party?

C: Buddy's.

M: Who is going to the party?

C: The girl.

M: The little girl? Whose party is she going to?

C: (Takes the other doll and the mirror). I wanna dressss heeer!

M: There you go … She is all dressed up!

C: Really?

M: Is she going to the party?

C: She is going to … party … Helena is going to party too!

M: Really? Is Helena going to the party too? Whose party is it?

C: Helena …

M: Raphael's party?

C: Raph's … party … (Looks at the doll in the mirror).

M: Oh, I see! Raphael's party!

C: Buddy's party … Raph … . Look! Beauuutiful! (Shows the doll to R in the mirror).

R: Lovely!

M: Yes, she is! Look at her in the mirror!

C: (Looks at herself in the mirror). She wanna lipstick. (Points at the doll).

M: Lipstick on her? She is a baby. Babies don't wear lipstick.

The main intervention on the mother's part in this role-play-game episode is not to give orders, instruct or orient the child's action, but rather to negotiate tell-games, where the child must either report and project actions and experiences or tell about her current action, often by orienting herself in the said action by means of a 'planner speech' (Vygotsky 1934/1987, chap. 2).

As illustrated in the next example, Helena's name-game is less limited or specialised to a canonical context than Priscilla's, which is ritualised in situations of 'see-and-name' relatives in photos. The name-game here occurs either to designate new unfamiliar objects, thus expanding the child's vocabulary, or guide the recognition of needed objects to perform a current action in a role-play-game.

Context: Helena (C) and her mother (M) are looking at picture books in the bedroom. The researcher (R) records the interaction:

> M: Who is under the carpet?
> C: (Opens the door in the picture).
> R: Who is this?
> M: What animal is this?
> C: It's aaaaa … aaa … aaa … aaa … baby frog.
> R: It's a baby frog? … (Everyone laughs). It's a turtle!
> C: Yes, a turtle.
> R: Turtle.
> C: It's a turtle, mummy. It is not a baby frog.
> M: No, it isn't! It isn't a baby frog, is it?
> C: (Turns the page).
> …
> R: And how about this? What is this?
> M: Hi … ppo … po …
> C: pu.
> M: No, my darling! It's hippopotamus!
> C: … potamus.
> The bird is eating … seed (Points at the picture in the book).
> M: Birdseed.
> C: Birdfeed.
> M: (Everyone laughs). Birdfeed.
> C: Bird is asleep too. (Turns the page).
> M: Ugh, is it?

In Helena's sample we can find the real designating function of learning name-games, that is to learn the designation or recognition of new unfamiliar objects (such as turtle, hippopotamus, birdseed). In the last part of this session, we can also see a symmetrical or reciprocal situation in which the

■ Telling current action (adult)   ▨ Telling current action (child)

□ Orienting action (adult)   ▤ Orienting action (child)

▨ Story telling (adult)   ▥ Story telling (child)

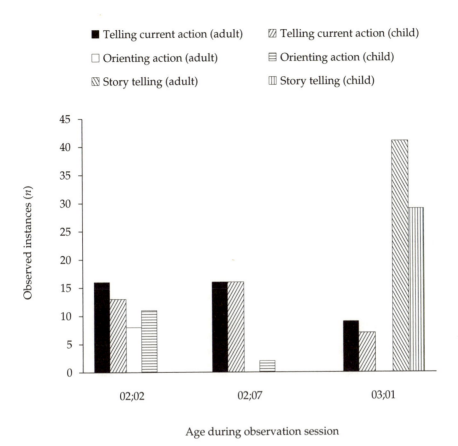

Figure 3.5. Frequency of tell-games in Helena's sample.

child is performing a tell-game that reports the action of the character in the picture ('Bird is sleeping too'). It is exactly this language activity that results in the tell-game having the most frequent occurrence in Helena's sample.

Order- and deontic-games were also observed, but much less frequently than name- or tell-games, and they focused mainly on the action of leafing through a book and its regularisation (i.e., norms related to the direction, continuity, and manner for 'leafing through a book').

In the last session (03;01), the main teleological language activity is to tell stories, usually fairy tales. As a result, the graph in Figure 3.4 shows a high frequency of tell-games for this session, with name-games also occurring frequently because they are used to designate the main characters in the story or essential objects in it such as Snow White, the hunter, the Seven Dwarfs, the mirror, the witch, and so forth. The relative frequency of order-games reflects the interaction of orienting and normalising the current action of leafing through the book or telling the story. It also shows epistemic-games, which are focused on the power to tell, based on 'know how to tell' the story.

When we examine the details of the tell-games in Helena's sample (see Figure 3.5), we can see another configuration of the construction of the forms of speaking about actions, which is a consequence of this language activity of telling stories or fairy tales previously heard. In particular, apart from a more symmetric situation between child and adults in proposing these games, there is also a decrease or disappearance of tell-games that report current action and orienting actions, and the unfolding of a new language activity (story telling), mediated by all others types of learning language-games (intragame relations) and related to the secondary discourse genres construction (stories and fairy tales).

Comparing Priscilla's and Helena's Samples

In short, in Priscilla's sample the main objects under construction were action, its normalisation and the interactive pattern order/obedience, while in Helena's sample we observe forms of reporting action through tell-games focused on reporting, projecting or telling current actions and experiences, or on reporting ('reading') stories or fairy tales previously heard. Tell-games reporting a current action have a double function in Helena's sample: they either report the current action in real life or pictures in the book by constructing ways to talk about action, or they orient the current action in a hetero- or autoregulation ('planner speech').

Thus, regarding the construction of the ways of reporting action we have identified two inverse movements in the interactional histories of Priscilla and Helena:

- Priscilla's interactions focus on instructing current actions, while in Helena's sample these instructions decrease and are specialised, thus becoming relevant only to role-play-games;
- reports of experienced or current action decrease significantly in Priscilla's interactions, while in Helena's sample they remain mainly in action reports based on book pictures and constitute the framework to

report fairy tales previously heard, thus conveying an exercise in secondary discourse genres;

– No evidence for secondary discourse genre construction was found in Priscilla's sample, while in Helena's sample, a new social practice that constitutes progress in the construction of secondary discourse genres may be identified, namely reporting stories or fairy tales.

This last aspect is particularly relevant to the theoretical framework presented here. It shows clearly how dialogic language activities — based on primary everyday family genres such as name-games, tell-games of current action to report or orient them, order-games, deontic-games to normalise actions — will be absorbed and operate effectively in the construction of language activities in a secondary discourse genre, presented in a monological way — like fairy tale reports — as proposed in the Bakhtinian works.[23]

These new secondary practices are important for the child's construction of a language and grammatical system because they convey transitivity and, as a consequence, thematic roles are often negotiated and constructed. To better illustrate the process, here is a clear example taken from Helena's sample (02;03;13):

Context: The mother (M), the child (C) and her sister (J) in the bedroom. There are several books around them.

M: (Points at a picture in the book). What's this animal?
C: It's … a … baby bear …
M: It's about to eat.
C: It's about to eat … this.
M: Yes … It is sitting and it's about to eat. What is it going to eat? Here, what is this? (Points at the picture).
C: It's gonna eat. (Points at the picture).
M: And here, what is this? (Points at the picture).
C: It's, it's, it's … Jacket.
M: No! It's an egg!
C: It's an egg.

23. Ninio and Bruner (1978), Ninio (1980), Pflaum (1986), Teale (1982, 1984) among others, also identify naming and reporting book pictures as an important framework for constructing fairy tale reports, narrative discourse and literacy.

M: An egg. It is going to eat an egg. Yum-yum … it's such a yummy egg! … (Turns the page). And now what? What's the bear doing now? (Points at the picture in the book).

C: I see it.

M: No! It's drinking water. It's drinking juice. (Turns the page). Is it eating here? (Points at the picture).

C: It is eating.

M: What? What is this? (Points at the picture on the book).

C: It's a ball.

M: No! It's an apple.

C: It's an apleeee!

M: Yes! It is eating an apple.

C: It is eating an apple.

In this interaction, we can find again the format 'What is this?', typical of primary name-games, by means of which the mother negotiates morphology (new items) and syntax.

Figure 3.6 shows this negotiation by graphically representing the movements of changing in paradigmatic and syntagmatic axes through the negotiation that linguistically constitutes a conjoint episode of story telling. As we can see, at the system level, through the format of name-game ('What is this?'), the mother negotiates the nominal phrase subject of the sentence (agentive thematic role). When the child shows symmetry[24] to this language-game, the adult immediately goes on to choose a format of tell-game ('What is it doing/about to do?'), where the verbal paradigm is set up. When the child stabilises and starts 'reporting the action', we have another 'new game' functioning again through a name-game format which negotiates, on the system level, the nominal phrase object (objective thematic role), its designation and acceptability, which allows the child to construct an action discourse conjointly with the adult.

Conclusions

The data analysed here show the differences between two children who construct action and language in the universe of different sociocultural

---

24. For example, the child is able to complement the meaning negotiated by the adult, answering their questions in an appropriate manner.

What is this? (NG)	What is it doing/ about to do? (TG)		What is this? (NG)	
The baby bear	is about to	eat		
	is sitting to	eat		
	is gonna	eat	~~jacket~~	
			an egg	
it	is going t o	eat	an egg	
			a yummy	egg
it	is	drinking	water	
			juice	
	is	eating	~~a ball~~	
			an apple	
it	is	eating	an apple	

Figure 3.6. Scheme of the changes in paradigmatic and syntagmatic axes during the interaction between Helena and her mother.

traditions of practice. The data also show how speech operates and becomes functional in everyday life — what Marxist authors named 'social corps psychology' or 'everyday life ideology'. In Bakhtinian terms,

this sphere of exterior and interior speech, disorganised and not fixed in a system, that goes with each of our gestures or actions, in each one of our states of consciousness. (Volosinov 1929/1981, 118) [my translation]

In the beginning of this chapter, the question was raised about how to interpret and evaluate such distinct social developments. I proposed that Priscilla plays, acts, obeys, moves about, makes others act but does not utter many words; Helena, in turn, plays, demands, gives orders, disagrees, comments, makes others act and is in control of other people's actions and situations.

Instead of dealing with a single social corps psychology, we may have several different social corps psychologies here. These data support the interpretation that differentiated, deep-rooted types of interaction can be observed among families in different sociocultural traditions of practice: In Priscilla's case, the child learns especially to act, to obey and also to order; in

Helena's case, the child learns to order, to report actions and stories, and talk about different worlds. Obviously, Helena also learns to act and to lead others to act, but she resists obeying. These different constructions of social acting, accentuation and values, and language capacities can reflect the different social places and behaviours of the girls in society: a person who is 'built' to act and obey, and a person who is 'built' to order and 'talk about'.

Of course, we might interpret these differences as simply idiosyncrasies of the family interactions, family relationships, or mother-child relationships in these two particular families. Alternatively, these regularly-patterned activities may belong to different social groups or classes in Brazil. These possibilities can only be resolved by carrying out more of this type of contrastive research among the various Brazilian social groups and segments.

Furthermore, although the focus of this chapter has been on language acquisition, there are also important implications for thinking about societal development in general. If acquiring language is part of 'acquiring' society, and schooling is understood as participating in the child's language construction, then it is clear that schooling has an influence in these societal development processes. In any case, literacy and educational research shows that schools prefer the language capacities constructed by children like Helena (e.g., talk about disjoint worlds, report experiences, and tell stories) more than the ones constructed by children like Priscilla.

Finally, these results reinforce two of my main positions. First, that a 'psychology (and a linguistics) of everyday life', is perfectly feasible by following the root of Bakhtinian and Vygotskian works, without missing the links to a sociocultural tradition of practice. Second, the discourse genre theory, as presented in the Bakhtinian works, is a powerful instrument for understanding and explaining this social-construction process. If we view primary everyday discourse genres (like learning language-games) as mega-instruments to secondary discourse genres construction (Schneuwly 1994), the methodology of analysis adopted in this research process and their results may contribute to elaborate categories and analysis patterns in the field of language acquisition which can be used to relate linguistic levels (e.g., morpho-syntactic level) of language acquisition to its discursive levels, like genre and language activities construction.

References

Baker, G.P., & Hacker, P.M.S. (1980). *An analytical commentary on Wittgenstein's* Philosophical Investigations, *Vol. 1.* Chicago: University of Chicago Press.

Bakhtin (Bakhtine), M.M. (1981a). La structure de l'énoncé. In T. Todorov, *Bakhtine: Le principe dialogique.* Paris: Seuil. (Original work published 1929)

Bakhtin, M.M. (1981b). *The dialogic imagination: Four essays by M.M. Bakhtin* (M. Holquist, ed. and trans.; C. Emerson, trans.). Austin, Tex.: University of Texas Press.

Bakhtin (Bajtín), M.M. (1985a). El problema de los géneros discursivos (T. Bubnova, trans.). In M. Bajtín, *Estética de la creación verbal.* México City: Siglo XXI, 277-326. (Original work published 1979)

Bakhtin (Bajtín), M.M. (1985b). *Estética de la creación verbal* (T. Bubnova, trans.). México City: Siglo XXI. (Original work published 1979)

Bakhtin, M.M. (1988). *Questões de literatura e de estética: A teoria do romance* (A.F. Bernardini, J. Pereira, Jr., A. Góes, Jr., H.S. Nazário, and H.F. de Andrade, trans.). São Paulo: Hucitec. (Original work published 1975)

Brant de Carvalho, A.T. (1989). O desenvolvimento do discurso narrativo: A relação interjogos na emergência das narrativas orais e escritas. *Estudos lingüísticos, XVIII — Anais de Seminários do GEL.* São Paulo: University of São Paulo, Linguistics Studies Group.

Brant de Carvalho-Dauden, A.T. (1993). *A criança e o outro na construção da linguagem escrita.* São Paulo: Pancast Editor.

Bronckart, J.-P. (1992). El discurso como acción: Por un nuevo paradigma psicolingüístico. *Anuario de Psicología,* 54(3), 3-48.

Bronckart, J.-P. (1997). *Activité langagière, textes et discours: Pour un interactionisme socio-discursif.* Neuchâtel: Delachaux & Niestlé.

Bronckart, J.-P., Bain, D., Schneuwly, B., Davaud, C., & Pasquier, A. (1985). *Le fonctionnement des discours: Un modèle psychologique et une méthode d'analyse.* Neuchâtel: Delachaux & Niestlé.

Bruner, J.S. (1975). The ontogenesis of speech acts. *Journal of Child Language,* 3, 1-19.

Fernandes, M.T.O.S. (1995). Desenvolvimento do discurso narrativo: A emergência das diferentes vozes. Unpublished masters thesis, Catholic Pontifical University of São Paulo, Brazil.

de Lemos, C.T.G. (1988). Prefácio. In M. Kato (ed.), *A concepção da escrita pela criança.* Campinas, Brazil: Pontes, 9-14.

Lier, M.F.A.F. (1985). O jogo como unidade de análise. *Série estudos: Vol. 11. Aquisição da linguagem.* Uberaba, Brazil: F.I.S.T.A, 45-55.

Ninio, A. (1980). Picture-book reading in mother-infant dyads belonging to two sub-groups in Israel. *Child Development,* 51, 587-90.

Ninio, A., & Bruner, J.S. (1978). The achievement and antecedents of labelling. *Journal of Child Language*, 5, 1-16.

Pflaum, S.W. (1986). *The development of language and literacy in young children* (3rd ed.). Columbus, Ohio: Charles E. Merrill.

Plekhanov, G.V. (1922). *Osnovnye voprosy marksizma* [Fundamental problems of marxism]. Moscow: Gosudarstvennoe Izd-vo.

Rojo, R.H.R. (1992). 'Espelho, espelho meu': O jogo de papéis e a constituição da narrativa e do letramento. *Anais do II encontro nacional sobre aquisição da linguagem*. Porto Alegre, Brazil: Catholic Pontifical University of Rio Grande do Sul, CEAAL, 225-45.

Rojo, R.H.R. (1994a). Du dialogue au monologue: parole lettrée et la lecture des livres enfantins aux interactions scolaires. In *Actes du XVè Congrès International des Linguistes* (vol. 3). Québec, Canada: Les Presses de l'Université de Laval, 525-28.

Rojo, R.H.R. (1994b). Turning points: Emergent literacy in socio-historical approaches. In J.V. Wertsch & J.D. Ramírez (eds.), *Explorations in socio-cultural studies: Vol. 2. Literacy and others forms of mediated action*. Madrid: Aprendizaje S.L., 197-202.

Rojo, R.H.R. (1994c). Book reading in classroom interaction: From dialogue to monologue. In N. Mercer & C. Coll (eds.), *Explorations in socio-cultural studies: Vol. 3. Teaching, learning and interaction*. Madrid: Aprendizaje S.L., 153-59.

Rojo, R.H.R. (1995). Interação e discurso oral: Questões de aquisição de linguagem e de letramento emergente. *Revista D.E.L.T.A.*, 11(1), 65-90.

Rojo, R.H.R. (1996a). A emergência da 'coesão' narrativa: 'E daí' em narrativas infantis. *Revista D.E.L.T.A.*, 12(1), 57-86.

Rojo, R.H.R. (1996b). 'Miroir, mon beau miroir', qui suis-je moi? — Les effets du récit dans la constitution du langage et du sujet. *Abstracts of the 2nd Conference for Socio-Cultural Research*, 107.

Rojo, R.H.R. (1998). O letramento na ontogênese: Uma perspectiva socioconstrutivista. In R.H.R. Rojo (ed.), *Alfabetização & letramento: Perspectivas lingüísticas*. Campinas, Brazil: Mercado de Letras, 121-72.

Schneuwly, B. (1988). *Le langage écrit chez l'enfant: La production des textes informatifs et argumentatifs*. Neuchâtel: Delachaux & Niestlé.

Schneuwly, B. (1994). Genres et types de discours: Considerations psychologiques et ontogénétiques. In Y. Reuter (ed.), *Les interactions lecture-écriture*. Bern: Peter Lang, 155-73.

Sève, L. (1974). *Marxisme et théorie de la personalité*. Paris: Editions Sociales.

Teale, W.H. (1982). Toward a theory of how children learn to read and write naturally. *Language Arts*, 59, 555-70.

Teale, W.H. (1984). Reading to young children: Its significance for literacy development. In H. Goelman, A.A. Oberg, & F. Smith (eds.), *Awakening to literacy*. Exeter, N.H.: Heinemann, 110-21.

Volosinov (Volochínov), V.N./(Bakhtin, M.) (1981). *Marxismo e filosofia da linguagem* (M. Lahud, Y.F. Vieira, L.T. Wisnik, & C.H.D.C. Cruz, trans.). São Paulo: Hucitec. (Original work published 1929)

Volosinov (Voloshínov), V.N./(Bajtín, M.) (1993). La construcción de la enunciación (A. Bignami, trans.). In A. Silvestri & G. Blanck (eds.), *Bajtín y Vigotski: La organización semiótica de la consciencia*. Barcelona: Anthropos, 245-76. (Original work published 1929)

Vygotsky, L.S. (1976). *La psicologia dell' arte* (A. Villa, trans.). Roma: Editori Riuniti. (Original work written 1925)

Vygotsky, L.S. (1987). *Pensamento e linguagem* (J.F. Camargo, trans.). São Paulo: Martins Fontes. (Original work published 1934)

Wittgenstein, L. (1953). *Philosophical investigations* (G.E.M. Anscombe, trans.). Oxford: Blackwell.

4   The Origins of Activity as a Category in the Philosophies of Kant, Fichte, Hegel and Marx

Charles W. Tolman

Activity theory takes its inspiration from the philosophy of Karl Marx. The contributions of Vygotsky and Leontiev are rightly seen as the further development of fundamental insights contained in Marx's thought. Like Marx, they took as their premises 'real individuals, their activity and the material conditions under which they live, both those which they find already existing and those produced by their activity' (Marx & Engels 1846/ 1970, 42). This was manifest in Marx's writings in the centrality that labour took in all his analyses. What was central to the economics of *Capital*, was equally central to psychology: 'The history of *industry* and the established *objective* existence of industry,' wrote Marx (1844/1964), 'are the *open book of man's essential powers*, the exposure to the senses of human *psychology*' (p. 142). Moreover, the essentially social nature of the category was always foremost:

Activity and mind, both in their content and in their *mode of existence*, are *social*: *social* activity and *social* mind. The *human* essence of nature first exists only for *social* man; for only here does nature exist for him a *bond* with *man* — as his existence for the other and the other's existence for him — as the life-element of human reality. (p. 137)

There can be no question of the pivotal position of the category of activity in Marx's thought. The very power of his theoretical insight rests upon that category. Likewise, the strengths of Vygotsky's and Leontiev's theories about psychological processes stem from the priority they gave to activity and its development.

Where did this category come from? Marx did not invent it, nor was he the first to understand its importance. The category, in short, has a history. Indeed, the history is a very long one. It can reasonably be argued that some form of activity has been presupposed by all philosophies, including the earliest pre-Socratic ones. What is important for our present purposes, however, is that the activity central to virtually all philosophies up to the time of Kant was *theoretical* activity, that is, the activity of the mind as constituting both objects and selves. This is plainly evident in the thought of Descartes and the empiricist philosophers such as Locke and Hume. A revolutionary shift in the concept of activity took place in the philosophy of Immanuel Kant. Although the move is incomplete, there is a distinct shift there from the primacy of theoretical activity to that of *practical* activity.[1]

Practical activity was important to Kant because he was concerned about our moral capacity to freely and responsibly determine our own actions. As he noted in his preface to the *Critique of Practical Reason*, 'all of reason proves its own reality and that of its concepts only in the deed' (1788/1990, 3). The moral law could thus not be expressed in the abstract but only as an admonition to *act* rightly: 'act such that the maxim of your will can at all times count simultaneously as a principle of general law' (p. 36). Indeed, at one point Kant was compelled by his own deliberations to conclude that 'pure practical reason' had to assume priority over the 'pure speculative reason' and could not be otherwise because 'all interest is ultimately practical, even that of the speculative reason is conditional and only complete in practical application' (p. 140).

Despite these insights, however, practical activity did not achieve the status for Kant of a fundamental category. Instead, the entire critical philosophy remained effectively committed to the primacy of speculative — that is, theoretical — reason and to the absolute separation of the intelligible and natural worlds.[2] As John Macmurray (1957) observed:

Through every stage of the progressing argument Kant proceeds as if reason were primarily theoretical; as if the *cogito* and the standpoint it establishes were ade-

1. The reader may wish to compare the account of the history of the notion of activity given by Lektorsky (1999). It appears to me that by choosing to emphasise the 'subjectivism' of the German idealist philosophy, Lektorsky fails, in my view, to sufficiently highlight Kant's revolutionary shift from theory to practice, which, in the long run, was far more important historically than any lingering subjectivism in his system.
2. The predicament that Kant (1781/1913) had created for himself with respect to activity is painfully obvious in the brief section late in the *Kritik der reinen Vernunft*, entitled 'Von dem letzten Zwecke des reinen Gebrauchs unserer Vernunft'. He is forced by his own logic to assign practical activity to the realm of nature, leaving it effectively out of the reach of reason or intelligible knowledge.

quate. The conclusion, that reason is primarily practical, takes us beyond this premiss, and involves its qualification from a more comprehensive standpoint. But there is this difference from all earlier stages, that the discovery of the primacy of practical reason is a final conclusion, and not the starting-point of a new stage. Kant goes no further. Our acceptance of practical reason and its categorical imperative remains a matter of faith. (p. 69)

Activity — that is, practical activity — appears in Kant's philosophy as a conclusion and as a logical necessity, but never as a determining category, never as a starting point, and never as a premise. It can be taken as a failure of Kant not to have revised his philosophy in light of his conclusions about the practical, and there are grounds for thinking that this failure lay at the bottom of many of the difficulties that continued to trouble the critical philosophy.

Partly in response to these difficulties in Kant's account of practical reason, both Fichte and Hegel began to take practical activity more seriously, and in a way that would solve many of Kant's problems and would have, it can be argued, far-reaching effects later in the social sciences through their influence on Karl Marx.

The philosophy of Johann Gottlieb Fichte was, according to its author, simply a further development of Kant's critical philosophy, but with two significant differences. The first was Fichte's outright rejection of the thing-in-itself together with its implied dualism. We need not dwell upon this move here except to note that it will appear to be entirely consistent with the second difference, from which it might even have flowed as an implication. This second move was to accept Kant's primacy of practical reason, as Kant did not, and to attempt consistently to work out a philosophy in accordance with it. Fichte admitted that the primacy of the theoretical was supported by strong intuitions, but these, he urged, would on adequate reflection prove to be wrong. The argument is close to the one that led to Kant's original conclusion about the relation between the theoretical and the practical:

it will appear ... that it is not in fact the theoretical faculty which makes possible the practical but on the contrary, the practical which first makes possible the theoretical (that reason in itself is purely practical, and only becomes theoretical on application of its laws to a not-self that restricts it). (Fichte 1794/1982, 123)

What makes the theoretical appear to come first is that practical principles are first encountered by reflection in their thinkability. But objects that can be thought represent an achievement that results from practical *striving* by the self to make things conform to itself. This constituted for Fichte the proof of reason's fundamental practicality:

This demand that everything should conform to the self ... is the demand of what is called — and with justice — practical reason. Such a practical capacity of reason has been postulated hitherto, but not proved. The injunctions issued now and then to the philosophers, to prove *that* reason is practical, were therefore fully justified. — Now such a proof must be carried out agreeably to theoretical reason itself, and the latter should not be ousted from the case by mere decree. This can be achieved not otherwise than by showing that reason cannot even be theoretical, if it is not practical; that there can be no intelligence in man, if he does not possess a practical capacity; the possibility of all presentation [*Vorstellung*] is founded upon the latter. And this proof has now just been effected, in showing that, without a striving, no object is at all possible. (Fichte 1794/1982, 232-33)

It is a fair assessment that Fichte proceeded to do just that, to show that there were no objects such as we know them without human striving or, in more up-to-date language, such that are not constituted in our practice with them. But the acts that Fichte emphasised in his philosophy were (ironically, it seems) largely *mental* acts like striving and positing. It is also a fair assessment to say that his notion of practice was mainly mental and that real social practices were included only by implication. Moreover, the social relations in which the self, others, and objects were constituted were interpersonal, not the societal relations in which we would expect to find social practices. On this basis, the common charge against Fichte of subjective idealism would appear to be at least partially justified.[3]

This was overcome to some extent, though by no means completely, by Hegel. In his *Phänomenologie des Geistes*, Hegel (1807/1967) presents his account of the development of consciousness and self-consciousness. He finds over and over again that the self is complicit in what it knows. The problem of knowledge emerges as a problem of the self. As he says, 'not merely is consciousness of a thing only possible for a self-consciousness, but ... this self-consciousness alone is the truth of those attitudes [of consciousness toward things]' (p. 212). But: 'Self-consciousness exists in itself and for itself, in that,

---

3. Subjective idealism stresses the constitution of objects and events by the mental, reducing the apparently objective to the subjective. It is a position that is ultimately both solipsistic and self-contradictory. Although this is widely regarded as a consequence of Fichte's philosophy, it does not appear to have been his intention.

and by the fact that it exists for another self, another self-consciousness' (p. 229).

It is at this point that Hegel turns to his allegory of masters and bondsmen to explain how self-consciousness arises. By his account, this begins when humans begin to desire, that is, to assert themselves, though before they are conscious of the self they are asserting. People can desire objects, but by doing so they make themselves 'thingish'; such desire does not make them *selves*. Only by asserting themselves against others, by negating the selves of the others can they become conscious of themselves as selves in the assertion. Thus the initial 'social practice' in which self-consciousness is constituted is one of attempted mutual annihilation.

But most potential selves are less motivated to assert themselves in this way than others. Loving life more than they do themselves, they allow themselves to become bondsmen to the successful asserters. The irony in all of this is that the bondsmen have the greater benefit from the arrangement in at least three important respects. First, the masters cannot have the bondsmen's recognition without recognising them. But the bondsmen's recognition of the masters is impoverished in value because bondsmen have no choice in the matter. The masters have a choice, so their recognition of the bondsmen is of greater value. Thus the selves which the bondsmen realise in the relationship, without seeking to realise it, has higher quality than anything the masters can attain.

Second, the masters have nothing to fear from the bondsmen, whereas the bondsmen live in a constant state of fear and trembling. But it is this very fear and trembling that yield for the bondsmen what Hegel calls *reines Für-sichsein* [pure being-for-itself] and regards as an essential ingredient in the development of full self-consciousness.

Third and perhaps most important, by having to provide for all the masters' needs, the bondsmen must come to master the physical world through labour. In Hegel's (1807/1967) words:

Through work and labour ... this consciousness of the bondsman comes to itself. In the moment which corresponds to desire in the case of the master's consciousness, the aspect of the non-essential relation to the thing seemed to fall to the lot of the servant, since the thing there retained its independence. Desire has reserved to itself the pure negating of the object and thereby unalloyed feeling of self. This satisfaction, however, just for that reason is itself only a state of evanescence [*Ver-schwinden*], for it lacks objectivity or subsistence. Labour, on the other hand, is desire restrained and checked, evanescence delayed and postponed; in other words, labour shapes and fashions the thing. The negative relation to the object passes into the *form* of the object, into something that is permanent and remains; because it is just for the labourer that the object has independence. ... The consciousness that toils and serves accordingly attains by this means the direct apprehension of that independent being as its self. (p. 238)

Thus we arrive at the self as constituted in the activity — that is, in the social practice — of labour. This is clearly more concrete an account than Fichte's, but it remains abstract to a yet significant degree. Two aspects of its abstractness are noteworthy. First, the account is fictional. It is not derived from any study of concrete, historical practice. Second, it presumes that the social relations of the constituting practice are naturally or even normatively oppressive. This runs directly counter to ordinary common sense, which would expect loving and supporting relations to be the more constitutive.[4] But there is no theory about relational quality in Hegel's account: at most, there is a distinction between dominant and submissive.

Marx's account improved considerably upon the general understanding of activity in at least two substantially important ways. First, as already noted earlier, his account was based upon an analysis of real human practical activity. Second, he was motivated from the start not only by an interest in self and agency, but also by a concern for the quality of the human relations and activity that constitute us as human persons. The pertinent theoretical aspects of Marx's anthropology were his understandings of need, species being, and alienation.

It was clear to Marx that human needs were not going entirely unsatisfied, even under the worst of societal circumstances. No society could continue to function if some needs were not being regularly satisfied at some functional level. These most basic needs that had to be met if people were to continue to survive as biological beings, he called 'subsistence' or 'reproductive' needs. Such needs are not distinctive of us as human beings, although the ways in which we satisfy them are distinctively human. In that sense subsistence needs are still human in a minimal sense, especially as they become expressed as the need to participate in the human modes of satisfying needs, that is, in social practice.

---

4. It also runs counter to some persuasive philosophical accounts of the self, such as the one given by John Macmurray (1961) in his *Persons in Relations*.

More distinctive of human beings are the needs that develop historically and that are not met just to sustain physical existence but have more to do with the quality of life. These are needs that are satisfied for their own sakes, not for the sake of something else. These human needs are most closely linked to the realisation of our selves as persons.

The capacity for human needs and their satisfaction Marx called 'species-being'. It is our 'natural being' that is served by the satisfaction of subsistence needs. And our natural being is certainly human, though just barely so. 'Species-being' referred to our capacity to maximise human individuality and self-consciousness in social practice, according to the historically conditioned possibilities for such development.

What hindered the maximal realisation of the societal potential for 'species-being' was alienation. Workers were alienated, for instance, by the relations of capitalist production from the products of their labour. The goods they produced were not theirs to dispose of for any kind of satisfaction. Rather, the workers were engaged in producing wages for the satisfaction of, at best, their own subsistence needs. They were thus also alienated from the very activity of labour itself, which they were now prevented from enjoying for its own sake. These distortions of the labour process thus focussed all attention upon subsistence of the natural being; in this way, the worker was alienated from his own species being.

In his work, therefore, he does not affirm himself but denies himself, does not feel content but unhappy, does not develop freely his physical and mental energy but mortifies his body and ruins his mind. (Marx 1844/1964, 110)

An important result of this was further alienation from others: first, from the owners and consumers of his/her products; then, second, from his/her fellow workers and family in that he/she becomes for them only a means to their own survival.

In an argument that echoes Kant's insistence on [the] human being as an end not a means, Marx maintains that from the perspective of the owner of the means of production, the worker represents no more than a potential source of profit, not a human being valuable as an end in himself. In the same way, even within the working class, people tend to relate to one another as expendable units in the productive process, but not as real human beings. The result is a generalized estrangement in all human relations. (Rockmore 1980, 42)

In Marx's account, the category of practical activity achieved a highly concrete conceptualisation, fully situated both in human needs, natural and cultural, and in the societal relations of historically conditioned social practices. Moreover, activity was conceived as constituted by societal relations, and thus as constituting the individual, but also as individuals' means of constituting societal relations, and thus also of constituting themselves. Both the distortions in relations and the means of correcting them are thus embraced by the theory.

We can see, however, that Marx did not extract his theoretical ideas about activity from thin air. The groundwork for such a theory was put in place by Kant and Fichte and given significant elaboration by Hegel. Marx's contribution can be understood as completing the philosophical shift, initiated by Kant, from the primacy of theoretical activity to the primacy of practical activity by giving a fully concrete account of the latter. Marx's was a philosophy of practice in which individual human activity had become the central category. It would be left to Leontiev and others to develop the psychological implications of this category.

It is important to understand that practical activity is not just one among many possible focuses for philosophy or for psychology. It is rather the fundamental category from which all others are derived. The problem with virtually all previous philosophy and psychology is that their proponents have assumed — or have acted as if they assumed — that human beings think themselves into existence by means of what is effectively theoretical activity. The history of philosophy plainly does not sustain this thesis. We are constituted instead by our practical activity, in particular by our participation in social and historical practices. It is only in collectively organised practical activity that all objects and concepts of philosophical and psychological interest emerge. It is vital for us today to understand that Kant's assertion of the primacy of practice was a necessary assertion, the profound implications of which we are still in the process of discovering.

References

Fichte, J.G. (1982). Foundation of the entire science of knowledge. In P. Heath & J. Lachs (eds.), *J.G. Fichte: The science of knowledge*. Cambridge: Cambridge University Press, 89-287. (Original work published 1794)

Hegel, G.W.F. (1967). *The phenomenology of mind* (J.B. Baillie, trans.). New York: Harper & Row. (Original work published 1807)

Kant, I. (1913). *Kritik der reinen Vernunft*. Leipzig: Felix Meiner Verlag. (Original work published 1781)

Kant, I. (1990). *Kritik der praktischen Vernunft*. Hamburg: Felix Meiner Verlag. (Original work published 1788)

Lektorsky, V.A. (1999). Historical change of the notion of activity: Philosophical presuppositions. In S. Chaiklin, M. Hedegaard, & U.J. Jensen (eds.), *Activity theory and social practice*. Aarhus, Denmark: Aarhus University Press, 100-113.

Macmurray, J. (1957). *Self as agent*. London: Faber and Faber.

Macmurray, J. (1961). *Persons in relation*. London: Faber and Faber.

Marx, K. (1964). *The economic and philosophic manuscripts of 1844* (D.J. Struik, ed.; M. Milligan, trans.). New York: International Publishers. (Original work written 1844)

Marx, K., & Engels, F. (1970). *The German ideology* (C.J. Arthur, ed.; W. Lough, C. Dutt, and C.P. Magill, trans.). New York: International Publishers. (Original work written 1846)

Rockmore, T. (1980). *Fichte, Marx, and the German philosophical tradition*. London: Feffer & Simons.

5   The Idea of Units of Analysis: Vygotsky's Contribution

René van der Veer

Introduction

Throughout the history of Western thought philosophers have dealt with the problem of how to understand complex wholes. A major approach has been to break down the complex whole into its constituent parts, which are supposedly easier to grasp. The nature of the complex whole is then explained on the basis of an understanding of these parts (e.g., Verbeek 1992). This analytic approach has always had its critics. They suggested that a complex whole cannot be fully explained from its constituent parts, that the relationships between parts are crucial, that so-called emergent properties exist, and so on. The nature of a society, for example, cannot be explained on the basis of the properties of the individuals that make up that society, these critics claimed. This viewpoint has been called the holistic view. The debate between adherents of an analytic approach and adherents of a holistic approach in philosophy has been less outspoken at times but has never really left us.

Psychology has not been able to avoid this debate. Human behaviour is a complex phenomenon and psychologists have tried to understand it by turning to its 'basic elements'. Reactologists, to name but a few currents, opted for the 'reaction' as the fundamental unit of behaviour, reflexologists choose the unconditional or conditional 'reflex', and associationists selected the 'sensations' (Zinchenko 1985; Zinchenko & Morgunov 1994). Reflexologists claimed, for example, that all human behaviour could in principle be fully explained on the basis of unconditional and conditional reflexes. However, the representatives of other major currents in psychology, of which the Berlin school of Gestalt psychology is the most well-known, argued that such an approach was inadequate or at best incomplete. In their view, the whole (i.e., human behaviour) was more than the sum of its parts (i.e., reflexes).

The principal figure of this chapter, Lev Vygotsky, was exquisitely aware of these discussions. He felt quite close to the Gestalt movement and made a major effort to disseminate its tenets in the Soviet Union (van der Veer & Valsiner 1991). At the same time, while sympathising with the nonreductionist, holistic approach of the Gestalt school, he argued that the Gestalt psychologists lost sight of the genetic, historic dimension of mental phenomena. According to Vygotsky, the issue is not just to identify proper levels of analysis. We must also address the issue of what counts as a unit and this requires attention to historical and relational aspects. Here, Vygotsky was influenced by the evolutionary thinking of Darwin and the historicist tradition of Marxism (cf. Bronckart 1996). He was also influenced by the notions of the then-current *Ganzheit* psychology.

In what follows I wish to discuss Lev Vygotsky's reflections about proper units of analysis in psychology. I will first follow Vygotsky's reasoning and then show that this reasoning was congruent with the emphasis on holistic thinking in the German language[1] psychology of that time, notably with *Gestalt* psychology and *Ganzheit* psychology. I will then take one of Vygotsky's lesser-known examples of a unit of analysis, to wit the concept of *perezhivanie* or *emotional experience*,[2] which he advanced as the proper unit to analyse the complex relationship between child and environment. I have chosen this concept not because it was particularly well elaborated and resistant to any criticism but because it was rooted in Vygotsky's practical activities and because it combined the aspects he found relevant in an instructive way.

I will try to show that this concept of *perezhivanie* has several merits and roughly meets Vygotsky's own requirements for a proper unit of analysis given below. Finally, I will venture the conclusion that Vygotsky's concept is consistent with the continental European emphasis on integral wholes and that such concepts are still badly needed in psychology. Human behaviour, especially the so-called higher mental processes, is a highly complex phenomenon and in trying to understand it we cannot avoid the question of proper units of analysis.

1. The holistic approaches I have in mind were advanced by psychologists writing in German but not necessarily by Germans. That is why I sometimes speak about the 'German language psychology', sometimes about the 'continental' tradition. Each label has its inadequacies.
2. In Vygotsky (1934/1998), *perezhivanie* is translated as 'experience'. I prefer the translation 'emotional experience', as explained in van der Veer and Valsiner (1994, 354, fn. 1).

The Study of Higher Mental Processes: Analysis in Units and Analysis in Elements

The issue of psychological analysis was one of Vygotsky's main concerns throughout his career as a psychological researcher. A particularly clear discussion of proper analysis in psychology is found in chapter 3 of *The History of the Development of the Higher Mental Functions,* written as an attempt to clarify his and Luria's thinking about the right methodological approach in psychology. His other discussions of the topic of analysis either largely overlap (Vygotsky 1935, chap. 2), or more clearly serve a polemical goal (e.g., in his treatment of the crisis in psychology, Vygotsky 1927/1997c).

In *The History of the Development of the Higher Mental Functions,* Vygotsky (1931/1997a, 67) mentioned that the representative of *Ganzheitspsychologie,* Hans Volkelt, distinguished between integral or holistic analysis — which retains the properties of the whole — and analysis into elements — which reduces the whole to its smallest particles, elements, or atoms that no longer have anything in common with the whole. He immediately posited that the second type of analysis (characteristic of associationism) was obsolete and clarified his own position while referring to contemporary psychologists (Volkelt, Koffka, Werner) whose ideas concerning this issue he more or less shared.

Let us follow Vygotsky's reasoning for some moments. He advanced three different but interconnected requirements for proper analysis (Vygotsky 1931/1997a, 68-78).

Analysis of Things versus Analysis of Process

According to Vygotsky, we must distinguish the analysis of things from the analysis of processes. Mental functions are not fixed things, do not form a mosaic of hard and immutable parts, but are processes that undergo development. Here Vygotsky referred both to Koffka, who coined the term 'mosaic' in this connection, and to Heinz Werner. Like Werner, Vygotsky believed that we must introduce the genetic viewpoint (i.e., to try to lay bare the genesis of mental processes) and that development can sometimes be called forth in the laboratory. Thus, we must artificially create the process of development in the laboratory, so to speak, and re-create the separate moments of the mental process. It is obvious that Vygotsky's method of double stimulation (cf. Valsiner & van der Veer 2000; van der Veer & Valsiner 1991) was meant to aid this reconstruction of the developmental process. By forcing subjects to externalise or exteriorise part of their actions the researcher is able to trace the early stages in the development of some skill or mental process.

Explanatory versus Descriptive Analysis

We must furthermore distinguish between explanatory and descriptive tasks of analysis. Here Vygotsky (pp. 68-69) linked up with the well-known discussion about the respective advantages and disadvantages of description and causal explanation in psychology and clearly opted for causal explanation (van der Veer & Valsiner 1991). Drawing heavily on Kurt Lewin's theoretical analyses (cf. Lewin 1931/1981a, 1927/1981b), Vygotsky explained that we must try to lay bare the causal, dynamic links of the phenomena. Lewin had shown that explanatory concepts in biology had replaced descriptive concepts and that, prior to Darwin, biological phenomena were classified according to their phenomenal characteristics — the examples he used were the botanist's classification of leaves according to their form and the zoologist's classification of animals according to their morphology. Classifications based on phenomenal characteristics led researchers to consider the whale to be a fish, a classification that we no longer make. So Lewin (e.g., 1931/1981a, 234) claimed that biology was essentially descriptive before Darwin, while after Darwin phenomena were classified on the basis of their origin. Darwin was able to lay bare the genotypical differences behind the superficial phenotypical similarities, because he took the genesis of species into account. Here we see, incidentally, how the requirement to lay bare the conditions that lead to certain phenomena (their causal explanation) is linked to the genetic viewpoint discussed in the section on analysis of things versus analysis of process. A good analysis would not accept phenomenal similarities between processes at face value, rather one must analyse the origin of these phenomenally similar processes, which may lead to the conclusion that these processes are fundamentally different. As you may recall, Vygotsky's favourite example of the hazards of exclusive reliance on phenomenal similarities was that of conceptual thinking in children and mental patients: the similarities that one may see in their thinking are real enough, but they are like the similarity between two trains departing in different directions (cf. Vygotsky 1930/1997b, 101-2).

Uncovering the Genesis of Behaviour

Finally, Vygotsky observed that we often meet what he called fossilised behaviours, that is, behaviours that no longer change. His favourite example here was that of behaviours that have become automatic because they have been repeated so many times. In order to understand the true nature of such processes (e.g., typewriting) it is often advisable to go back to their early stages of development. In this context, Vygotsky spoke about the need to 'liquefy' the fixed behaviour. He discussed (Vygotsky 1931/1997a, 71-78) the then-current reaction-time research and criticised the habit of discarding pilot trials in this type of research. It is exactly these pilot trials — traditionally used to familiarise the subject with the experimental task and ignored in the analysis of the results — which give us important information about the genesis of behaviour. Vygotsky suggested to study these pilot trials and to delay and externalise the subjects' reactions by giving them instruments to use, that is, he proposed his method of double stimulation as a method to lay bare the genesis of actions (p. 78). It is clear, then, that this third point is again connected with the genetic viewpoint discussed in the section on analysis of things versus analysis of process.

Genetic Analysis

These are the interrelated requirements for proper analysis in psychology that Vygotsky advanced in *The History of the Development of the Higher Mental Functions*. Vygotsky did not elaborate the point that we need to retain the properties of the whole while analysing complex mental processes. But the point that we must try to capture the development, the history, or the genesis of mental processes was elaborated in several, interconnected ways, because analysis was primarily genetic analysis for Vygotsky. As indicated in the introduction, both points were made repeatedly in the psychology of the beginning of the 20th century. A brief look at some of the more vocal psychologists of Vygotsky's time will allow us to see the embeddedness of his thinking in the psychology of that period more clearly.

German Holistic Thinking

We have seen that Vygotsky referred repeatedly to such thinkers as Volkelt, Werner, and Lewin, and we know that he was very familiar with the work of Gestalt theorists such as Wertheimer, Koffka, and Köhler (van der Veer & Valsiner 1991). Each of these German-speaking thinkers had outspoken ideas about the proper way to analyse complex phenomena (Valsiner 1998; Valsiner & van der Veer 2000). It is probably fair to say that the common feature in their views was an emphasis on the dominance of the whole over its parts and a focus on the relationships between the parts and the whole. The core issue of all holistic perspectives is the decision to recognise qualitative differences between different levels of organisation of phenomena. Because organisms consist of hierarchically-organised levels that are qualitatively different, we cannot fully reduce the organism to its constituent elementary components. With this nonreductive view, these researchers differed from the mainstream of Anglo-Saxon researchers who emphasised the reduction to and association of elements.

The nonreductive, anti-associationist focus of the Gestalt psychologists can be traced back further in the history of German psychology. Wilhelm Wundt — in his *Völkerpsychologie* — argued that many mental phenomena defy experimental analysis and emphasised the complex, developmental nature of the higher mental processes. His division of psychology into lower, simpler phenomena amenable to experimental analysis, on the one hand, and more complex, higher phenomena amenable to description, on the other, has been criticised but now draws renewed attention (see Cole 1996). We can also think of the work of von Ehrenfels that led to Gestalt psychology as it is usually known, that is, to the Berlin school of Gestalt psychology with Köhler, Wertheimer, Lewin, and others (Fabian 1997; Sarris 1997; Sprung & Sprung 1997). Less known but equally important was the rival school of *Ganzheitspsychologie* in Leipzig. There too, we find the emphasis on nonreducible wholes and development that so appealed to Vygotsky. Significant in this respect are the writings of Felix Krueger, Wundt's successor, and the leader of the Second Leipzig school. In arguing for an explicitly developmental sociogenetic theory, Krueger (1913) claimed that:

It seems to me one of the most general and important results of experimental analysis that every psychic phenomenon, even the most simple, depends not only upon actual conditions, but also upon the after-effects of determinable *past* experience.

Thus already the classical methods of psychological experimentation them-selves are leading to the systematic limitations of experimental psychology.

The ever changing genetic conditions of all psychic processes and the inti-mate fusion of their effects with those of actual circumstances, constitute a char-acteristic trait of all psychic life. Herein lies the essential reason why the psychic cannot be reduced to constant and qualitatively equal elements such as physical atoms ... / ... the comparative psychological study of the human mind must be carried on at all stages of mental and cultural development. The genetic structure of human consciousness is really an historical one, that is to say, fundamentally dependent upon every individual's interrelations with other individuals and upon the past of their civilisation. These social-genetic or cultural conditions admit less of experimental method than do those of the individual. (pp. 260-61)

Again we see the core elements of a genetic holistic approach, the empha-sis on both the developmental, historical character of phenomena and the impossibility to reduce them to the smallest elements or atoms. Elsewhere, Krueger (e.g., 1915, 97-102) elaborated his viewpoint, arguing against atom-ism, pleading for a comparative approach (that, characteristic for his time, involved the comparative study of animals, non-Western people, children, and adults),[3] and opposing Wundt's bifurcation of psychology into experi-mental psychology and nonexperimental *Völkerpsychologie*. In contradistinc-tion to his former teacher, Krueger did see a role for the experimental approach in genetic comparative investigations of more complex mental pro-cesses. In fact, it can be argued that Krueger anticipated Lewin's conditional-genetic analysis by several decades. His tradition was carried forward by Volkelt, Sander, and others (cf. Valsiner & van der Veer 2000).

It seems quite clear, then, that we can situate Vygotsky's concern with units of analysis in a German, or rather European continental tradition of holistic thinking, a tradition that was antithetic to British associationism, American behaviourism, and so on. Against this background it should not come as a surprise that Vygotsky's own attempts at finding units of analysis have this same flavour. Most well-known is his concept of word meaning, but in this chapter I would like to pay attention to one of his lesser known proposed units, the concept of *perezhivanie* (*Erlebnis* in German), or *emotional*

3. Krueger's writings (together with those of Heinz Werner) formed the principal source of inspiration for Vygotsky's own comparative approach (e.g., Vygotsky 1930/1993). The merits and shortcomings of Vygotsky's comparative approach have been the sub-ject of intense discussion (see Scribner 1985; Wozniak 1996).

experience. This concept has the merits of being simple and instructive at the same time. It also had a practical background: it was meant to help us understand how children of different ages cope with identical or very similar environmental circumstances.

Emotional Experience as a Unit of Analysis

Shortly before his death, Vygotsky advanced the concept of *perezhivanie* in his classes taught at the Herzen Pedagogical Institute in Leningrad during the academic year 1933-1934. In various lectures he criticised the current practice of considering the child and its environment as two mutually exclusive factors that interact in a purely external fashion (Vygotsky 1935/1994, 1934/1998). His interest in this topic was not just theoretical: throughout his career Vygotsky worked as a clinician in various outpatient clinics. In this capacity he saw numerous children, tried to assess their condition and the influence of the environment on their behaviour. Many of these children grew up in deprived homes or belonged to the army of *bezprizorniki* (homeless children) who roamed the country without their parents as a result of the atrocities of the revolution and different wars (Stevens 1982). Others suffered from congenital diseases or deformities. In order to assess the possibilities of these children (e.g., their learning potential), it was vital to be able to make some educated guess about the influence of the environment on the child's character and capacities, if only because the authorities were considering the advisability of removing these children from their homes.

No easy answers were available here. Vygotsky soon realised that one cannot conceive of the child's behaviour and condition at a specific moment as being the result of a simple summation of his or her innate abilities and his or her environmental background. The timing of environmental events is crucial. That is why the study of absolute characteristics of the environment (e.g., socioeconomic status, housing) is misleading if we take them as determining factors per se. As Vygotsky (1934/1998) argued:

the essential difference between the child's environment and that of an animal is that the human environment is a social environment, that the child is part of a living environment and that the environment never is external to the child. (p. 293)

It is crucial, Vygotsky argued, not to consider the environment per se, but to consider the environment through the prism of the child's intellectual and emotional understanding. We have to take into account how the child experiences the environment, we must study the child's *perezhivanie*, the way the environment is reflected or refracted in the child's mind.

The child's *perezhivanie* is that most simple unit about which we cannot tell what it is — environmental influence on the child or a property of the child itself; *perezhivanie* is the unity of personality and environment as represented in development. [my translation, see Vygotsky 1934/1998, 294]

Thus, the environment determines the development of the child via the (emotional) experience of that environment and this is one reason why we cannot simply take objective indicators of the environment, add them to the child's innate abilities, character and so on, and make our predictions about psychological consequences such as the child's future emotional state of mind, or his or her cognitive development. This implies that the same environment may have different consequences for children of different age groups, different temperament, intelligence, and other characteristics.

Applying Perezhivanie

To clarify Vygotsky's notion of *perezhivanie* and see what it entails for the analysis of child-environment dialectics, I will discuss it in somewhat more detail. The discussion is meant to clarify the implications of Vygotsky's view but rests on my own interpretation.

First, it is obvious that as time goes by both the child and the child's environment will change: the child will grow older, the environment may grow 'older' — insofar as it consists of persons — or become larger, or simply different. But in addition, the child's experience of the environment (as Vygotsky argued) and the environment's experience of the child changes as well. Let us take a look at several of the possibilities:

–   The physical environment may remain exactly the same in a sense but become available for the first time when, for instance, the child begins to move around, exploring the room, house, and garden. The bookshelf with books now comes within reach. In essence, then, the child's available physical space is enlarged.

–   The physical environment remains exactly the same but becomes interpreted or experienced by the child differently. With a little bit of help from his friends, the child becomes able to identify the objects on the bookshelf as books, certain forms as letters, etc. The environment becomes, in other words, imbued with (different) meaning, becomes symbolic in a sense. One might also say that the child's 'semantic space' is created or enlarged (Rodríguez & Moro 1999). With the exception of rare cases of pathology, such cases of newly acquired meaning cannot be undone. Vygotsky's (e.g., 1934/1998, 290-91) favourite example in this context was that of chess players of different strength who literally come to see different things on a chessboard. The experienced player is no longer able to perceive the position on the chessboard in a naïve way. In the same way, normal adults cannot fail to see that certain objects are books, others cars, and so on.

- The surrounding persons also change for the child, as they become more understandable, interpretable, and predictable. For example, the child learns to understand speech, and acquires useful knowledge of the characters, habits, and preferences of significant adults. In this process, these significant adults become distinguishable from the multitude of others. In other words, what at first were just persons now have become special persons, a process that was described beautifully in Saint-Exupéry's *Little Prince*.

- The surrounding persons also change objectively in different ways. Not only do they grow older and may change character, they also may gradually begin treating the child differently. As the child gets older, parents may make other demands, requiring the child to behave more adult-like and so on. They also may behave differently towards the child as they learn to know the child's character and to know which approaches are likely to be the most successful or preferred by the child.

Evaluating Vygotsky's Perezhivanie Unit

My simple observations show that Vygotsky had a good point in arguing that we cannot simply add inherited characteristics and environmental properties in a mechanistic fashion. What we lose then is what I would like to call the dimension of time. It makes a big difference, for example, whether a child is struck by some mishap (e.g., the loss of a parent) at age three or at age seven, because the child will interpret this event differently at age seven than at age three. If we take this dimension of time into account it becomes obvious that we must look at the child-environment relationship as it unfolds over time. Crucial in this relationship is that the environment exerts its influence on the child through the child's continually shifting interpretation of that environment and vice versa (insofar as the environment consists of persons).

Vygotsky's lectures on the concept of environment lead us to say that the environment changes both objectively, as seen from the outside, and in its meaning for the child. Children of different age can interpret objectively equivalent or identical behaviour differently. The concept of *perezhivanie*, or 'environment-as-experienced' (vs. 'environment per se') was meant to capture this aspect of the child-environment dialectics. It expresses a simple, perhaps even trivial, fact about child development which, I feel, is nevertheless still being overlooked at times and this fact needs to be emphasised. Child development is not A + B, but perhaps A times B times A' times B' etc.

Can we say that Vygotsky's concept of *perezhivanie* meets his requirements for good units of analysis? I think that in a general sense we can. The concept of *perezhivanie* captures the idea of analysis in units rather than elements. Vygotsky emphasised that we cannot artificially separate subject and environment, but need to address both in their unity. The concept of *perezhivanie* also captures the idea of development by insisting on the ever-changing character of interpretations or emotional experiences (which are also dependent on changing word meaning, another of Vygotsky's units of analysis). In doing so, this concept reflected a major trend in continental European psychology: the urge to respect the properties of the whole and to study the history of behaviour.

Conclusions

We have reviewed Vygotsky's discussion of the requirements that units of analysis in psychology should ideally meet. It was shown that his discussion borrowed much from the holistic trends of Gestalt psychology and *Ganzheit* psychology in European psychology. To illustrate his ideas, I then took Vygotsky's own example of *perezhivanie* as a unit of analysis, elaborated it somewhat, and concluded that it met his requirements.

My purpose in discussing this part of Vygotsky's work was not just historical. It is my claim that the problem of selecting a proper unit of analysis in psychological work still exists even when it may often be ignored in empirical research. What should we take as proper units of analysis when analysing perception and memory? Fodor's modules? Selfridge's demons? Neurons? And which requirements should these units meet? These are still unsolved problems and in reading classical psychological literature we realise how little theoretical headway has been made in the last half of the 20th century.

This is not to say that the psychologists of the first half of the 20th century knew the answers or that there are easy recipes for finding proper units of analysis in understanding complex psychological processes. But the writers of that time did show a sensitivity to such methodological issues. Modern developmental psychology cannot permit itself to ignore the topic of the unit of analysis and does well to take the ideas of that period seriously. Fortunately, there seems to be a renewed interest in the work of classic psychological thinkers (e.g., the work of Wundt). If studying the work of sociocultural thinkers such as Lev Vygotsky makes us aware of the important traditions in the history of psychology that still deserve to be studied in detail, then much has been gained. And for developmental psychology it will mean a change for the better.

References

Bronckart, J.-P. (1996). Units of analysis and their interpretation: Social interactionism or logical interactionism? In A. Tryphon & J. Vonèche (eds.), *Piaget-Vygotsky: The social genesis of thought*. Hove, England: Psychology Press, 85-106.

Cole, M. (1996). *Cultural psychology: A once and future discipline*. Cambridge, Mass.: Harvard University Press.

Fabian, R. (1997). The Graz school of Gestalt psychology. In W.G. Bringmann, H.E. Lück, R. Miller, & C.E. Early (eds.), *A pictorial history of psychology*. Chicago: Quintessence, 251-55.

Krueger, F. (1913). New aims and tendencies in psychology. *Philosophical Review*, 22, 251-64.

Krueger, F. (1915). *Über Entwicklungspsychologie: Ihre sachliche und geschichtliche Notwendigkeit*. Leipzig: Verlag von Wilhelm Engelmann.

Lewin, K. (1981a). Der Übergang von der aristotelischen zur galileischen Denkweise in Biologie und Psychologie. In C.F. Graumann (ed.), *Kurt-Lewin-Werkausgabe: Band 1. Wissenschaftstheorie 1*. Bern: Hans Huber, 233-78. (Original work published 1931)

Lewin, K. (1981b). Gesetz und Experiment in der Psychologie. In C.F. Graumann (ed.), *Kurt-Lewin-Werkausgabe: Band 1. Wissenschaftstheorie 1.* Bern: Hans Huber, 279-320. (Original work published 1927)

Rodríguez, C., & Moro, C. (1999). *El mágico número tres: Cuando los niños aún no hablan.* Barcelona: Paidós.

Sarris, V. (1997). Gestalt psychology at Frankfurt University. In W.G. Bringmann, H.E. Lück, R. Miller, & C.E. Early (eds.), *A pictorial history of psychology.* Chicago: Quintessence, 273-76.

Scribner, S. (1985). Vygotsky's uses of history. In J.V. Wertsch (ed.), *Culture, communication, and cognition: Vygotskian perspectives.* Cambridge: Cambridge University Press, 119-45.

Sprung, L., & Sprung, H. (1997). The Berlin school of Gestalt psychology. In W.G. Bringmann, H.E. Lück, R. Miller, & C.E. Early (eds.), *A pictorial history of psychology.* Chicago: Quintessence, 268-72.

Stevens, J.A. (1982). Children of the revolution: Soviet Russia's homeless children (*bezprizorniki*) in the 1920s. *Russian History/Histoire Russe, 9,* 242-64.

Valsiner, J. (1998). *The guided mind: A sociogenetic approach to personality.* Cambridge, Mass.: Harvard University Press.

Valsiner, J., & van der Veer, R. (2000). *The social mind: Construction of the idea.* Cambridge: Cambridge University Press.

van der Veer, R., & Valsiner, J. (1991). *Understanding Vygotsky: A quest for synthesis.* Oxford: Blackwell.

van der Veer, R., & Valsiner, J. (eds.) (1994). *The Vygotsky reader.* Oxford: Blackwell.

Verbeek, T. (1992). *Descartes and the Dutch: Early reactions to Cartesian philosophy, 1637-1650.* Carbondale: Southern Illinois University Press.

Vygotsky, L.S. (1935). *Osnovy pedologii* [Foundations of pedology] (M.A. Levina, ed.). Leningrad: Gosudarstvennyj Pedagogicheskij Institut Imeni A.I. Gertsena, Kafedra Pedologii.

Vygotsky, L.S. (1994). The problem of the environment (T. Prout, trans.). In R. van der Veer & J. Valsiner (eds.), *The Vygotsky reader.* Oxford: Blackwell, 338-54. (Original work published 1935)

Vygotsky, L.S. (1997a). Analysis of higher mental functions (M.J. Hall, trans.). In R.W. Rieber (ed.), *The collected works of L.S. Vygotsky: Vol. 4. The history of the development of higher mental functions.* New York: Plenum Press, 65-82. (Original work written 1931)

Vygotsky, L.S. (1997b). On psychological systems (R. van der Veer, trans.). In R.W. Rieber & J. Wollock (eds.), *The collected works of L.S. Vygotsky: Vol. 3. Problems of the theory and history of psychology.* New York: Plenum Press, 91-107. (Original work written 1930)

Vygotsky, L.S. (1997c). The historical meaning of the crisis in psychology: A methodological investigation (R. van der Veer, trans.). In R.W. Rieber & J. Wollock (eds.), *The collected works of L.S. Vygotsky: Vol. 3. Problems of the theory and history of psychology.* New York: Plenum Press, 233-343. (Original work written 1927)

Vygotsky, L.S. (1998). The crisis at age seven (M.J. Hall, trans.). In R.W. Rieber (ed.), *The collected works of L.S. Vygotsky: Vol. 5. Child psychology.* New York: Plenum Press, 289-96. (Original work written 1934)

Vygotsky, L.S., & Luria, A.R. (1993). *Studies on the history of behavior: Ape, primitive, and child* (V.I. Golod & J.E. Knox, trans.). Hillsdale, N.J.: Erlbaum. (Original work published 1930)

Wozniak, R.H. (1996). Qu'est-ce que l'intelligence? Piaget, Vygotsky, and the 1920s crisis in psychology. In A. Tryphon & J. Vonèche (eds.), *Piaget-Vygotsky: The social genesis of thought.* Hove, England: Psychology Press, 11-24.

Zinchenko, V.P. (1985). Vygotsky's ideas about units for the analysis of mind. In J.V. Wertsch (ed.), *Culture, communication, and cognition: Vygotskian perspectives.* Cambridge: Cambridge University Press, 94-118.

Zinchenko, V.P., & Morgunov, E.B. (1994). *Chelovek razvivaiushchiisia: Ocherki rossiiskoi psikhologii* [Developing man: Sketches of Russian psychology]. Moscow: Trivola.

6 Contextual, Interactional and Subjective Dimensions of Cooperation and Competition: A Co-Constructivist Analysis

Angela Uchoa Branco

The complexities involved in the study of cooperation and competition in human relationships require a theoretical approach that takes into account the multidimensional and interdependent aspects of the phenomena from a systemic perspective. A necessary starting point, from my perspective, is to integrate contextual, relational and subjective dimensions (or levels of analysis) of the phenomena usually conceptualised as cooperation or competition, particularly what takes place within structured contexts such as the school. In schools, teachers and educators do not traditionally give the same attention and careful planning to the development of social goals as they do for cognitive goals. In this secondary role, child social development has become primarily an issue of the so-called 'hidden curriculum' of schools (Branco 1998; Branco & Mettel 1995; Giroux & Purpel 1983) rather than a special educational goal requiring well-designed activities.

Despite the ideological backgrounds that certainly contribute to concealing social aspects of child development, the fact remains that social development occurs whenever a child participates in a schooling activity, from literacy training to mathematics problem solving. If teachers are going to give special attention to promoting the attainment of specific social goals in the classroom, then they must be continuously aware of every detail regarding the structure of the activity as well as the quality of the dynamics in teacher-student and student-student interactions.

The objectives of this chapter are threefold: First, to present a conceptual analysis of cooperation and competition from a co-constructivist framework, which aims to integrate the multidimensional characteristics of such patterns of social interactions and relationships. Second, to illustrate how the framework can be used, I present some data from an experiment carried out in Brasilia where we analysed the effects of cooperative versus competitive structured contexts on children's social interaction patterns (Branco 1998; Branco & Valsiner 1992). Third, to contextualize the issue of social motivation within educational settings, discussing some of the aspects related to the achievement of specific social goals. The idea is to provide some suggestions and strategic guidelines that might facilitate the promotion of social development goals within the school environment.

Cooperation and Competition from a Co-constructive Viewpoint

From a sociohistorical co-constructivist framework (Branco & Valsiner 1997; Valsiner 1994, 1997), human development is considered as a constructive sociogenetic process through which change is promoted at interindividual (interactional) and intraindividual (subjective) levels. This framework emphasises the dialectical interplay between the active individual and the canalising functions of culturally-structured contexts. As the development process proceeds within the semiotic context in which the person is embedded, she/he co-constructs her/his own particular version of the culture (characterised by Valsiner, 1994, as the 'personal culture'). Co-constructed personal cultures are dialectically integrated to what Valsiner designates as 'collective culture', formed by meanings jointly constructed and shared by the social group.

The co-construction of meanings at both individual and collective levels has a fundamental role in co-constructivism. From my perspective, though, such a co-constructive approach must be integrated with a systemic framework conceptualised along the lines of a 'developmental systems theory' (Fogel 1993; Ford & Lerner 1992), together with a special emphasis on the fundamental role played by emotions in the co-construction of subjective meanings. As the individual develops, dynamic motivational systems are constantly being co-constructed as a result of the interplay between inter- and intra-subjective psychological processes.

Cooperation and competition are conceptualised as different ways to co-ordinate the goal orientations of individuals in interaction. The concept of goal orientations refers to the dynamic nature of an individual's goals, and can be defined as a kind of internal constraining system, semiotically mediated, that, by projecting into the future, constrains actions, feelings, and thoughts in the present time (Branco & Valsiner 1997, 50).

The term goal orientation represents the existence of a flexible direction towards a desirable process or outcome. As each person is usually motivated by many goals, depending on numerous and varied factors like context, subjective conditions etc., her/his motivational system is permanently constructed by an ever-changing organisation of goal orientations, each one assuming specific priorities as the person-context relationships also change. Therefore, depending on the situation, a person's goal orientations can be coordinated cooperatively (same goals) or competitively (opposite goals).

However, cooperation and competition, being two of the most relevant aspects of social interdependence, need to be analysed to the full extent of their complexity. Here I propose that cooperation and competition are diverse aspects of the same psychological domain, which has to be investigated from a 'inclusive separation' perspective (Valsiner & Cairns 1992) at three different levels, namely, the *contextual*, the *relational* and the *subjective* levels.

Cooperation and competition are ideologically-framed concepts used in social and psychological sciences that point at some important relational aspects of human social phenomena. The issue of social interdependence has a significant impact over individual development as well as over the organisation and dynamics of human social life. Cooperation is usually defined as the association of a number of people in an enterprise for mutual benefits or profits. The existence of a common goal is recognised in the definition of *cooperative*: 'to act or work together with another or others for a common purpose' (*Webster's New World College Dictionary* 1996, 306).

On the other hand, competition is traditionally defined as rivalry or opposition in a contest or match, or in situations where the available supply of a desired object is somehow limited. According to the dictionary definition: 'competition denotes a striving for the same object, position, prize, etc., usually in accordance with certain fixed rules' (p. 284).

Concepts like cooperation and competition, drawn from commonsense terminology, have polysemic characteristics that make it difficult to investigate them as psychological phenomena. Researchers who try to define cooperation and competition within their theoretical framework usually diverge concerning the semiotic dimension of those constructs (Feger 1991). Slavin (1991), for example, uses the term *cooperation* to describe students' joint efforts to achieve shared goals within the classroom, whereas Boyd and Richerson (1991) apply the concept to designate self-sacrifice, that is, to die for the benefit of the group. Polysemic constructs, thus, demand researchers' efforts to constrain or to make explicit the scope and framework within which such terms should be interpreted. According to Feger (1991, 299) there exists no theory dominating the field of cooperation research, and even a commonly accepted terminology is in its first stages of development.

Traditionally, cooperation and competition are pictured as antithetical concepts. From a co-constructivist approach, however, the 'exclusive partitioning' of classical logic in the definition of psychological constructs has been criticised (Valsiner & Cairns 1992). A better analytical approach is the 'inclusive separation of the partitioned parts' of a whole phenomenon. The idea is to preserve the systemic organisation of the whole (in our case, the systemic organisation of social interdependence), while recognising that it is differentiated, but interconnected parts. Thus, cooperation and competition do not emerge as antithetical constructs, rather they are transitory results of a continuous dynamic that reflects specific states of coordination of individuals' goal orientations as they interact with each other.

Morton Deutsch, in his paper entitled 'A Theory of Cooperation and Competition' (1949), refers to cooperation when there are 'promotively interdependent goals' between the individuals, and to competition when 'contriently interdependent goals' are found. Cooperative and competitive social interdependence rules can be objectively structured within the context itself, namely, by implicit or explicit rules establishing the way individuals' behaviours should relate to each other. In cooperation, individuals are expected to coordinate their conduct to accomplish a common goal, whereas in competition, the more one person approaches a goal the further away the other person is driven from that goal.

Deutsch (1949) made an interesting distinction between different perspectives from which individuals' interdependence can be analysed. He posed the existence of an 'objective-subjective' dimension, 'objective' probably meaning context structure, while 'subjective' refers to an individual's representations. That these two levels are frequently interrelated (i.e., it is more likely to find competitive attitudes within competitively structured activities, Johnson & Johnson 1989; Slavin 1991) does not entail that all individuals will necessarily show such propensities. The structure of the activity usually induces corresponding goals at the psychological level, that is, cooperatively organised contexts tend to promote cooperative goal orientations and so on (Branco & Valsiner 1993; Johnson & Johnson 1989). However, individual actors can bring unexpected goals into the situation when they actively introduce their particular goal orientations (which belong to the person's subjective world). For example, in one of our projects (Branco & Mettel 1995) we found the teacher, who thought of herself as an active promoter of pro-social behaviour in the classroom, struggling to prevent five-year-old kids from helping each other within a game-like structured activity!

Deutsch (1949) also stressed the pluralistic nature of social interdependence acknowledging situations that involve both cooperation and competition at the same time, at different levels. Within a group, for example, members cooperate while competing against another group (Harcourt 1992; Triandis 1991). Also, group members may compete with each other, the end result being a mix of cooperation and competition within the group. Despite numerous examples of such puzzling situations, the complexities of the dynamic interactions occurring between individuals' goal orientations (Branco & Valsiner 1997) and the structural arrangements of specific activities are acknowledged only by a few investigators (Johnson & Johnson 1989).

Depending on the theoretical framework adopted, the definition of constructs such as cooperation or competition may emphasise perceptual, behavioural, relational or context-structural components of social interdependence (e.g., Hinde & Groebel 1991; Johnson & Johnson 1982, 1989; Slavin 1991). Consequently, diverse aspects of human social interdependence must be considered, such as an individual's perception, social interaction, and cultural organisation. This focus on diversity is necessary for linking together all parts of the whole, thereby providing a more productive picture of the phenomenon.

A conceptual appraisal of the meaning of social interdependence inevitably leads, at a more general level, to discuss the meaning of culture as an organising construct. In many cross-cultural studies, culture is still approached as a variable to be investigated. From a co-constructive perspective, however, culture is invested with a special significance, because of its constitutive power concerning human development. Taking into account the complexities and heterogeneity of cultural contexts, co-constructivism shows how naïve it is to establish a clear-cut opposition between psychological constructs such as self versus other, individualistic versus collectivist, or cooperation versus competition (Branco 1996). Hence, the attempts to categorise social interdependence into predetermined and simplistic classes turn out to be meaningless.

Let us take the concept of self as an illustration. According to a sociogenetic perspective, the cultural context plays a central role in the construction of self identity, which emerges from the continuous dialogical interaction of the person and the social other. Along the process of identity construction, the notions of 'self' and 'other' are progressively co-defined in a complementary way, and such notions significantly change across cultural contexts and over time. Thus, it is almost impossible to specify personal goals concerning exclusively the 'self' or exclusively the 'other' as though self and other were universal constructs. In some cultures, or for some people in any culture, the accomplishment of somebody else's goals may be an important part of the individual's goals. How then can one assert the generality of such constructs?

By the same token, the substantial degree of heterogeneity found within cultural contexts does not recommend the classification of cultures into such categories as individualistic or collectivist (Branco 1996). However, specific contexts and activities can still be analysed in terms of their typical structures, which may be facilitating either cooperative-convergent or competitive-divergent coordination of the social conduct of individuals. The developing person is an active, constructive agent of the culture, moving within a highly heterogeneous landscape filled with diversities, inconsistencies, and contradictions. However, social messages conveyed by collective culture can be reasonably redundant in order to provide semiotic constraints that canalise the person's development to some extent towards specific directions. Social development may, thus, be canalised into convergent or divergent interactive patterns that, for their part, help create more and more situations or activities that are cooperatively or competitively structured.

On the other hand, microgenetic analysis of social interactions reveals an interplay between convergence (compatibility of goal orientations), divergence (incompatibility of goal orientations), and negotiation that resembles a ceaseless dance interlacing the fabric of social relationships under the rhythm of metacommunication frames. Moreover, the functional roles of conflicts and negotiations in the construction of convergent interactions of qualitatively different kind have been observed in many studies and deserve a further analysis (Branco & Valsiner 1993).

Considering the existence of different and successive levels of analysis of interactive phenomena (Hinde & Groebel 1991), namely, the interaction, the relationship, and the group sociocultural structure, Branco (1989) discusses how the same event can be interpreted diversely depending on which level of analysis is in focus at a certain moment. A husband who helps his wife, doing everything for her (and therefore is thought of as a cooperative and nice man), might behave like that just to have full control over the situation by keeping his wife absolutely dependent on him. Also, to hurt someone's feelings by telling her the truth about her attitude in a specific situation, could, instead of being nasty behaviour, actually represent an instance of friendship which is meant to help the other person who is perhaps about to make a bad choice in her life.

Taking a perspective that transcends the interaction allow us to identify the qualitative frame characterising the relationship between the individuals. Such frames result from the coordination of goal orientations in the history of interactions between people, and play an important metacommunicative role in allowing for the interpretation of signs exchanged between them. Together with relational frames, another important factor contributing to the co-construction of social interdependence lies at the intraindividual or subjective dimension.

When speaking of inter- and intraindividual levels, though, we have to keep in mind that those levels do not represent a dichotomy but rather two different perspectives of a unique system related dialectically to each other. The subjective level concerns the structures of goal orientations, constructed out of a system that integrates affect and cognition such as values and beliefs. It addresses the psychological domain of motivation expressed by intentionality and hidden motives that accompany every action, playing a significant role in weaving the coordination of goal orientations held by individuals within a certain context.

In the next section, I will illustrate the way we have been investigating patterns of interdependence such as cooperation and competition. We use conceptual tools such as convergence, divergence and negotiation to analyse the social interactions that occur when different social frames are co-constructed by the participants of the projects (Branco 1998; Branco & Valsiner 1997).

Coordination of Goal Orientations in Social Interactions: An Empirical Approach

In many of the projects developed at the Laboratory for the Microgenetic Study of Social Interactions at the University of Brasilia, Brazil (Branco 1998; Branco & Mettel 1995; Branco & Valsiner 1993, 1997; Fogel & Branco 1997; Mugnatto & Branco 1998), we are investigating the processes involved in the co-construction of diverse social interactive frames as they are dynamically structured over time. Moreover, we verified the power of cultural canalisation processes acting both at the structural level of the activities and at the semiotic level in interactions among teachers and students and among adults and children.

In the projects, we are developing methodologies that allow for a micro-genetic analysis of child-child and adult-child interactions. Conceptual tools drawn from a co-constructivist framework (Branco & Valsiner 1997; Valsiner 1987, 1997) — such as convergence, divergence, negotiation and ambiva-lence — have been used to designate different patterns of interaction. Other constructs are taken from Valsiner's theory (1987, 1997, 1998), such as *zone of promoted action* (ZPA) and *zone of free movement* (ZFM). ZPA refers to the con-strained field (physical and/or psychological) within which a person tries to promote specific actions by others. ZFM indicates the domain (also at both levels) within which the person allows the other to move around.

In one study designed by Branco and Valsiner (1992) to examine the microgenetic development of social interactions in structurally different sit-uations among three-year-old children, two triads (two boys and one girl) were organised. Triads (as opposed to dyadic or polyadic social groups) were used so that there were plenty of opportunities for interpersonal coalitions or confrontations in task-oriented contexts, without being too complex for analysing social conduct.

Both triads participated in six experimental sessions (twice a week for three weeks). Each session lasted about 25 minutes, during which the children, together with an adult supervisor, were free to play with each other, using materials provided during the sessions (e.g., blocks, a family-doll set, puz-zles, bowling game). The materials were varied to sustain the children's interest, and to afford coordination of different kinds of goal orientations. For one triad, the adult supervisor tried to intervene to encourage the children to play cooperatively. For the other triad, the supervisor tried to create con-ditions that would encourage competitive play.

The children came from middle-class families and attended the same preschool. Prior to the experiment, ten hours of free-play interactions in the preschool were videotaped. Based on these observations, children were selected who did not demonstrate excessive social inhibition or dominance, and placed in a triad where they were familiar with each other, but were not preferred playmates. The six experimental sessions were followed by a test situation. All the experimental and test sessions were conducted in a room at the children's preschool. These sessions were fully videotaped and super-vised by a young female adult (the research assistant).

In the *cooperation* context, children were asked (and reminded) by the supervisor to interact with each other in order to build a unique structure from small pieces of a same material. For example, they were invited to work together to build only one construction with wooden blocks, or they were asked to play together with different objects, such as little dolls. In the *competitive* context, children were asked to work/play alone and they were told from the start that their performances would be compared. For instance, the children were told that the adult would take photographs of their constructions (as in the example of constructing something with wooden blocks), and that later the preschool staff would choose the best one. On other occasions, the adult marked, on cardboard, children's individual scores during competitive games. In the last case, little stars were put on the cardboard next to each child's name, so that everybody was able to acknowledge the results and praise the best players by the end of the session.

During the test situation, both triads were instructed to perform the same task. They had to carry a big doll, which was supposed to be ill, undress her, pretend to bath, dry, and dress her again, then carry the doll to the 'hospital', where she would be examined and medicated, and finally bring her back 'home'.

For both groups, the social interactions among the four participants (triad plus research assistant) in the test situation were analysed in the following way. A graphical representation was created for each person, showing the interactive or noninteractive patterns for that person over the time course of the test session. The categories of interaction patterns were:

- *individual activity* (no interaction at all)
- *social attention* (characterised by eventual observations and/or indicators of awareness of the other's activity, without any mutual regulation)
- *convergence* (compatible, but not necessarily identical, goal orientations, for at least two of the children; *cooperation* is a special case in which two or more children have the same goal orientation.)
- *divergence* (incompatible goal orientations)
- *negotiation* (behavioural efforts to move from divergence to convergence)

The results of the experiment clearly indicated the occurrence of cultural canalisation processes. The test situation was a task that was designed so that it could be accomplished easily by the adoption of cooperative strategies. For the triad that experienced cooperative rules during the six experimental sessions, there were convergent interactive patterns (with at least two of the children) for 95% of the test session (81% in cooperation). On the other hand, for the triad that engaged in the competitively-structured experimental sessions, two or more children spent only 12% of the test session in convergent interactions (8% in cooperation).

The way that the children in the competitive triad regulated their behaviour, avoiding true social exchanges with each other, was quite amazing. One child, for example, repeatedly waited until the other gave up a certain activity in order to engage in the same activity.

After concluding that the differences detected in the test session were strong enough to support the canalising effects of specifically structured contexts, we developed a way to analyse co-constructive processes, based on the interpretation of the participants' goal orientations.

To show the analytic approach adopted in the study, I will now present a transcript of a short sequence of events taken from the first experimental session with the 'cooperative' triad.

Before the sequence of events transcribed below, W and F (the boys) were struggling over a specific wooden block from among a few that had a shape of a clock. The girl (G) was playing by herself nearby with some blocks, and the supervisor (S) was trying to get the three children to cooperate in making one construction together. W intentionally knocks down F's construction. The following two and a half-minute interaction ensued. Actions are described in parentheses. Our commentary is in square brackets. Session times are shown in minutes and seconds in the curly brackets.

{18.52}
(S throws down W's construction.) [S's intervention can be seen as retaliation for the 'act of aggression' by W against F's construction. De facto it amounts to a coalition formation with F, and can be viewed as a step towards S's goal to unite all blocks into a pile from which all three children could construct a joint structure. The ZPA stems from S's own goal orientation in this context; her intervention can also be considered as a divergent movement in relation to W.]

W: (screams) No! No! No! [active verbal resistance to the demolition act by S, W is visibly emotionally upset. The divergent goal orientation between W and S is clearly established here.]

S: Look here! [redirection of attention, by ZPA formation; she tries to diffuse W's frustration.]

W: I don't want it!

S: Look at what I have here! (She picks up another block in the shape of a clock, and shows it to W.) [S now shows W the same kind of block that W was previously quarrelling about with F. She continues to create a ZPA including that block, in the hope that W will engage in joint action with others.]

W: I didn't want it, I didn't want it, you are mixing everything up!

{19.06}

S: But it belongs to everyone! Your name isn't written on it, is it? (She manipulates some blocks.) [S continues to assert, verbally and in manipulating the blocks, the 'joint ownership' concept, in challenge to W's previous assertion of his 'ownership' over the blocks, and expropriation of his construction.]

(W grabs some blocks with his arms and pulls them towards himself.)

W: I'm taking everything again! [reassertion of the divergence claim, reinstatement of the previous division]

(S takes one block from the pile.)

{19.20}

S: Look, it's here! Let's start again. [Another effort to unite children in joint construction activity.]

(W, F, and G each grab a part of the blocks.)

S: Folks (she smiles), what have you done? [Commentary upon the children's joint refusal to accept her suggestion. At this moment, the children converge in their actions of divergence to S's goal orientations. The content of the verbalisation resets the ZPA by a negative evaluation, but nonverbal cues such as smiling and the accepting intonation of her voice try to create a metacommunicative frame that will maintain her communicative channels with the children, along the lines of a possible future convergence.]

W: I won't let him take these from me!

F: Neither will I!

{19.34}

S: (asks W) But why? Isn't he your friend? [S tries to promote convergence by the semiotic use of the general concept 'friend', leaving its meaning unspecified.]

W: No, I'm not his friend because he's taking, he doesn't let me take his clock …

S: But you also have a clock!

W: Where is the clock?

S: (picks up F's clock) What if we have a clock here and we make a church? [S changes her strategy. She gives up the persuasion effort with W, and turns to expropriate F's block, suggesting a new theme for joint construction.]

{19.53}

F: (takes his clock back from her) No! [F sets a ZFM for her and the other children, on the basis of 'ownership'.]

W: Oh, where is my clock?

S: It's not yours, it belongs to everyone, W! [Another assertion of common ownership, in a situation where the blocks are now actually divided between children.]

W: Where is my clock that was here?

(F looks at W.)

S: I don't know …
    (W looks for his block clock.)
S: F could help you! He could lend you the clock and then you'd make some-
    thing very big here. (She points to the centre of the cardboard.) [Again, pro-
    motion of the theme of 'helping', with de facto accepting that F 'owns' a block
    that he could 'lend'. By doing this, she tries to become an ally with F and also
    W, hoping to bridge the gap between an individualistic goal orientation and
    cooperation, using the semiotic marker 'help', which acknowledges the tran-
    sitory existence of a kind of ownership rule.]
    (F holds firmly his block 'clock' with both hands.)
W: (to F) So you lend it to me … [Accepting S's suggestion for F to help him, not
    vice versa, and demanding it from F; a convergent movement, but in coordin-
    ation with his own individual interests.]
{20.27}
F: (moves towards G's construction) Look what we have here! (He picks up a
    block-'clock' in G's construction and gives it to W, who takes it. G looks at
    them.) [F converges towards W: a new coalition with W, along the lines of S's
    suggestion, but with the modification that he expropriates G's block and gives
    it to W.]
W: (to G) Give it to me! That's what I was looking for, this clock … [W immedi-
    ately joins in, constructing a new coalition with F, which follows along the lines
    of S's suggestion.]
S: But this belongs to everybody! (She now picks up F's clock.) We can put two
    clocks if we do just one thing! [S intervenes again, using her adult power role
    by expropriating F's block_'clock' and verbally suggesting a modified con-
    struction where two clocks can be utilised if all children build 'just one thing'.]
{20.46}
F: (takes his block back immediately) OK, but this is mine! [Renegotiation of the
    suggestion introduced by S; again he sets the ZFM for the others.]
S: Hmmm …
W: This belongs to him! Nobody can take it, isn't that right, F? This is mine (he
    holds his) to build something like this, and nobody will get inside my build-
    ing. I have to put all here, or they'll get lost [W joins F, and further co-con-
    structs with F a convergent frame, by defending F's possessions and reassert-
    ing the 'ownership' of building materials and constructed outcomes.]
{21.08}
S: W is not going to help G? She's starting to do it, it's turning into a very nice
    job! [S cleverly distracts W and F from the ownership issue, and again reintro-
    duces the topic of 'one child helping the other', as a possible bridge towards
    cooperation.]

W: (moves towards G) Do you want me to help you? [W accepts the suggestion, and his convergent move towards G also includes a convergence towards S.] (W picks up a block that lies in front of G's construction and puts it on her construction.) [W finally 'helps' G by a convergent building on her construction.]

S: OK, that's it! [Immediate positive feedback comes.]

W: (to S) Like this. It's a good idea, isn't it?

S: Good idea! [This little sequence denotes, through W's acknowledgement and positive evaluation of the 'doing together' idea, S's success for the moment concerning the core of her ZPA. Her effort to promote cooperation between the children, at least at this point, allowed for convergence between S's and W's goal orientation, indicating the possibility of further developments in that direction involving the three children.]

{21.22}

It is important to notice that before the conflict or divergence between W and F started, the children were not interacting with each other. They were oriented to their individual activities. Therefore, we can speculate about the functional role of relatively long episodes of conflict interactions in an experimental session for the emergence of prosocial and cooperative conduct. This fits the suggestion, already discussed in the theoretical presentation of a co-constructivist framework, that cooperation and competition should be conceptualised as different aspects of a same phenomenon, according to the notion of 'inclusive separation' (Valsiner & Cairns 1992).

The dynamics between divergence and convergence of goal orientations, represented in the preceding example, illustrates the complex mechanisms involved in social interaction. It seems that the most productive way to analyse such dynamics is to use a microgenetic approach.

Through a continuous negotiation over the rules, the adult succeeds in eliciting active negotiations among children, which ends up in a convergent interaction between them. The child, W, who had first stated that F was not his friend, less than a minute later defended F's possessions and helped G with her construction, arguing that, indeed, it was a 'good idea'!

Many examples of this kind can be identified from videotaped sequences of peer interactions. Such findings point to the dynamic nature of social processes, and render as meaningless all efforts to categorise social interactions into specific classes of behaviour (like cooperative patterns as opposed to competitive ones). Another interesting conclusion here is the possibility of identifying and analysing, from a different perspective, the functional dimension of episodes of conflict or competition in the co-construction of convergent and cooperative interactions between children.

In sum, both cultural canalisation processes and the person's active role within structured contexts must be taken into account in understanding the permanent reconstruction or re-organisation of social interactions or interdependence. This means that within a cooperative context, the emergence of divergence and subsequent negotiations can very likely be observed. In a competitive situation, on the other hand, the agreement over the rules frequently induces some forms of cooperation, in the sense of facilitating the occurrence of expected actions.

We should always keep in mind the complexities involved in social interaction phenomena, and prevent the creation of dichotomies and over-generalisations at both theoretical and empirical domains of investigation. An interesting topic for further study, for example, could be the functional analysis of divergent and negotiation processes that promote the introduction of novel elements both in the realms of information and relationship constructions.

Social Interdependence within Educational Contexts

With the aim of helping educators achieve their objectives, I will now focus attention on preschool and school contexts, indicating some specific points which I think are of central interest to those who research such settings. In the literature, there are many examples of research showing how cooperatively or competitively structured activities promote different results concerning students' performance and psychological characteristics. Almost all studies demonstrate how cooperation seems to be the best choice to promote improved performance and healthier psychological attributes in our students (Johnson & Johnson 1989; Slavin 1991).

It seems to me that a priority should be assigned to unravel the structural arrangements and the particular dynamics supported by such structures for each and every school activity. Such investigation would shed light on important aspects of the hidden curriculum underlying specific activities, and allow for the choice of those arrangements that better fit certain educational objectives.

The hidden curriculum not only plays a fundamental role in children's social development, but it also has a strong impact over knowledge construction, learning processes and personality development (Giroux & Purpel 1983; Maciel, Branco, & Valsiner, in press; Valsiner 1998).

By providing an analysis of the structure and dynamics of the activity, researchers could make explicit the social interdependence domains of each learning context. Investigations of the interplay between the teacher's and the students' goal orientations, as well as the functional role of conflicts and negotiations within activities could help educators to better plan and organise their work.

Moreover, the communication and metacommunication processes that take place in the course of human interactions within schools needs to be fully investigated (Fogel & Branco 1997). The need to carry out research projects aiming at identifying and analysing such processes cannot be overestimated, for they consist of the way we can best have access to the sociogenetic mechanisms involved in human development (see also, Santamaría, this volume).

Processes and products of educational efforts are profoundly engendered by social and individual motivations. The network of relationships that are permanently being co-constructed within everyday activities between the teacher and students, and between students themselves, are of central importance to create a positive motivational context that may facilitate learning and development. Communication and metacommunication patterns of interactions give rise to qualitatively different relationships that provide the basis for the necessary motivation to successful teaching-learning experiences.

In McDermott's view (1977), the construction of a trust relationship between the teacher and her/his students is the privileged ground for the attainment of any educational goals. As subject-matter learning is definitely not in opposition or conflict with social goals, that opens up a whole new perspective for effectively integrating and promoting children's academic and social development. With good psychological research that analyses both the learning activities and the relationship networks within school settings, educators would be able to design special activities that actively promote the kind of social interdependence implied by the social objectives drawn from the school philosophy.

References

Boyd, R., & Richerson, P.J. (1991). Culture and cooperation. In R.A. Hinde & J. Groebel (eds.), *Cooperation and prosocial behavior*. Cambridge: Cambridge University Press, 27-48.

Branco, A.U. (1989). Socialização na pré-escola: O papel da professora e da organização das atividades no desenvolvimento de interações sociais entre crianças. Unpublished doctoral dissertation, University of São Paulo, Brazil.

Branco, A.U. (1996). Constraints on the universality of psychological constructs [Review essay]. *Culture & Psychology, 4*, 477-84.

Branco, A.U. (1998). Cooperation, competition, and related issues: A co-constructive approach. In M.C.D.P. Lyra & J. Valsiner (eds.), *Child development within culturally structured environments: Vol. 4. Construction of psychological processes in interpersonal communication*. Stamford, Conn.: Ablex, 181-205.

Branco, A.U., & Mettel, T.P.L. (1995). O processo de canalização cultural das interações criança-criança na pré-escola. *Psicologia: Teoria e Pesquisa, 11(1)*, 13-22.

Branco, A.U., & Valsiner, J. (1992, July). Development of convergence and divergence in joint actions of preschool children: The emergence of cooperation and competition within structured contexts. Paper presented at the meeting of the Twenty-Fifth International Congress of Psychology, Brussels.

Branco, A.U., & Valsiner, J. (1993, July). Dynamics of social interaction strategies among young children. Paper presented at the biennial meeting of the International Society for the Study of Behavioural Development, Recife, Brazil.

Branco, A.U., & Valsiner, J. (1997). Changing methodologies: A co-constructivist study of goal orientations in social interactions. *Psychology and Developing Societies, 9(1)*, 35-64.

Deutsch, M. (1949). A theory of cooperation and competition. *Human Relations, 2*, 129-52.

Feger, H. (1991). Cooperation between groups. In R.A. Hinde & J. Groebel (eds.), *Cooperation and prosocial behavior*. Cambridge: Cambridge University Press, 281-300.

Fogel, A. (1993). *Developing through relationships: Origins of communication, self, and culture*. Hempstead, England: Allyn & Bacon.

Fogel, A., & Branco, A.U. (1997). Meta-communication as a source of indeterminism in relationship development. In A. Fogel, M. Lyra, & J. Valsiner (eds.), *Dynamics and indeterminism in developmental and social processes*. Hillsdale, N.J.: Erlbaum, 65-92.

Ford, D.H., & Lerner, R.M. (1992). *Developmental systems theory: An integrative approach*. London: Sage.

Giroux, H.A., & Purpel, D. (1983). *The hidden curriculum and moral education: Deception or discovery?* Berkeley, Calif.: McCutchan.

Harcourt, A. (1992). Cooperation in conflicts: Commonalities between humans and other animals. *Politics & the Life Sciences,* 11, 251-59.

Hinde, R.A., & Groebel, J. (eds.) (1991). *Cooperation and prosocial behavior.* Cambridge: Cambridge University Press.

Johnson, D.W., & Johnson, R.T. (1982). Effects of cooperative, competitive, and individualistic learning experiences on cross ethnic interaction and friendship. *Journal of Social Psychology,* 118, 47-58.

Johnson, D.W., & Johnson, R.T. (1989). *Cooperation and competition: Theory and research.* Edina, Minn.: Interaction Book Company.

Lawrence, J.A., & Valsiner, J. (1993). Conceptual roots of internalization: From transmission to transformation. *Human Development,* 36, 150-67.

Maciel, D., Branco, A.U., & Valsiner, J. (in press). Bi-directional process of knowledge construction in teacher-student relations: A microgenetic analysis. *Infancia y Aprendizaje.*

McDermott, R. (1977). Social relations as contexts for learning in school. *Harvard Educational Review,* 47, 198-213.

Mugnatto, A., & Branco, A.U. (1998, July). Mother-child interactions within a structured situation: Influences of mother's literacy. Paper presented at the biennial meeting of the International Society for the Study of Behavioural Development, Bern, Switzerland.

Slavin, R. (1991). Synthesis of research on cooperative learning. *Educational Leadership,* 48(5), 71-82.

Triandis, H.C. (1991). Cross-cultural differences in assertiveness/competition vs. group loyalty/cooperation. In R.A. Hinde & J. Groebel (eds.), *Cooperation and prosocial behavior.* Cambridge: Cambridge University Press, 78-88.

Valsiner, J. (1987). *Culture and the development of children's action.* Chichester: Wiley.

Valsiner, J. (1994). Culture and human development: A co-constructivist perspective. In P. van Geert, L.P. Mos, & W.J. Baker (eds.), *Annals of theoretical psychology* (vol. 10). New York: Plenum, 247-98.

Valsiner, J. (1997). *Culture and the development of children's actions* (2nd ed.). New York: Wiley.

Valsiner, J. (1998). *The guided mind: A sociogenetic approach to personality.* Cambridge, Mass.: Harvard University Press.

Valsiner, J., & Cairns, R. (1992). Theoretical perspectives on conflict and development. In C.U. Shantz & W.W. Hartup (eds.), *Conflict in child and adolescent development.* Cambridge: Cambridge University Press, 15-35.

Webster's New World College Dictionary (3rd ed.). (1996). New York: Macmillan.

Wertsch, J.V. (1993). Commentary [on Lawrence & Valsiner]. *Human Development,* 36, 168-71.

7 The Concept of Role as Unit of Analysis of Young Peers' Interactions and Cultural Learning

Zilma de Moraes Ramos de Oliveira

A challenging task faced presently by human development research is how to explain the way individuals share some culturally elaborated fields of consciousness that are in constant transformation and, by doing that, construct their psychological development. Nevertheless the study of human action as socially and historically embedded has a long tradition in developmental psychology (Baldwin 1895; Janet 1929; Mead 1934; Vygotsky 1934/1986; Wallon 1942, 1959, 1973) and has been reemphasised in new ways during the last decades (Berger & Luckmann 1966; Bronckart 1992; Cole 1985; del Río & Álvarez 1994; Doise & Mugny 1984; Du Preez 1991; Levine & Resnick 1993; Newman, Griffin, & Cole 1989; Rogoff 1990; Shotter 1989, 1993; Smolka, Goes, & Pino 1997; Tudge 1990; Valsiner 1987; Wertsch 1985).

From a sociohistorical perspective, human development is a joint and reciprocal task occurring in semiotic contexts with their culturally modulated forms of social relationships. The investigation of human social interactions created in concrete circumstances is therefore the basic point for the comprehension of the ontogenesis of psychological processes. However, a methodological limit in many studies about human interactions is the lack of truly interactional categories.

The semiotic character of all human behaviour has to be taken as the constitutive factor in human thought and action. To understand the co-construction of mind and self, we must not adopt a perspective that isolates the individual's performance from his/her partners' actions. The investigation has to capture the ongoing nature of the interactional process because both the individual and his/her environment are constantly changing and creating singular situations. Furthermore, nonrational aspects of behaviour have to be considered.

Elsewhere I have proposed the concept of *role* as a unit of analysis for human interactions (Oliveira 1988, 1998; Oliveira & Rossetti-Ferreira 1996; Oliveira & Valsiner 1997). That concept was elaborated from observational studies of interactions among one to six year-old children in Brazilian daycare settings.

The concept of role was formulated originally in the sociogenetic tradition (Baldwin 1895; Bergson 1889/1948; Guillaume 1925; James 1890; Janet 1929; Mead 1934; Moreno 1953; Royce 1901/1988). It was also considered by Vygotsky and Wallon who have taken the idea of role as a cultural model related to social resources for the construction of culturally specific ways of psychological functioning. For Vygotsky (1989) and Wallon (1959), human development would occur in the core of interpersonal dramas created in semiotic contexts where certain forms of social relationships, that is, roles, are present (see also Harré 1979; Shotter 1993).

Inspired by that tradition, I start with the assumption that psychological inquiry should focus on the daily experience of individuals in ideologically-organised social matrices. The child is inserted in these matrices from birth. A baby and his or her human environment create dynamic situations. Some meanings are attributed to the baby's actions by his or her partners' actions as they interpret the situation as having certain goals and/or different intentions and representations. These framed behaviours constitute roles that are assumed by the child and his or her partners in the interactional process. In an interactional situation, the confrontation of needs, senses and ideas related to the roles being played leads the child and his/her partners to continuously negotiate the meanings they attribute to themselves and to the situation as a whole in order to construct and attain their frequently antagonistic goals and motives. The study of human interactions, from this perspective, has to capture this confrontation process and to follow it from a developmental viewpoint.

The Concept of Role as a Methodological Device: An Empirical Study

To discuss the value of the role perspective as a unit of analysis of social interaction and its effects on child development, I will present some empirical data to point out the processes young children use to coordinate the roles they play in the situations they create together in a daycare centre. That task implies that the researcher must apprehend how the partners negotiate the meanings implied in the roles they play in the ongoing situations and to identify changes in their pattern of role coordinations.

I decided to privilege the study of child-child interactions, as the major emphasis of developmental research on adult-child interaction has created a bias that prevents us from seeing the mediation of the baby's own activity toward an age peer and vice-versa (cf. Bruner 1999). Additionally, I agree with the sociohistorical research tradition that views the study of children's symbolic play as an important source for understanding psychological development. In play, the child shifts from one situation to another by affective movements in the abstract field of meaning as he or she submits his or her behaviour to the rules created in the situation, thus acting in a more advanced level of development.

In this chapter I will make some commentaries about the analysis of some episodes around a certain theme extracted from the transcriptions of 10 free play sessions of approximately 15 minutes each of a group of six children. The children were 21 to 23 months old at the beginning of the research, and the observations were video-recorded over a 12 month period in the children's Brazilian public daycare centre for low-income families.

Most of the children lived in slums or in other poor housing in São Paulo City. Their parents worked in unskilled jobs. Their mothers usually worked as domestic helpers; half of them were single mothers. The children attended the daycare centre from 7 a.m. to 6 p.m. in groups of 18 children with one caretaker for each six-hour period. All the caretakers were female and had no specific professional training for developing educational activities with the children.

For each session a microgenetic transcription of the continuous flow of each participant's behaviour was prepared with a detailed description of their gestures, postures, verbalisations, and also objects and aspects of the physical symbolic environment involved. Each tape was transcribed independently by two trained observers and their disagreements were discussed by reviewing the scenes and jointly describing them with more detail.

Cultural Repetition and Innovation: A Key for Development

The contextual, transactional analysis of all the sessions allowed me to recognise that through role coordinations, action and meaning adjustments reorganise each child-environment relationship and promote development. This point will be presented by the analysis of some episodes.

When the children are younger, role coordination is mediated especially by the affective sphere: they explore lived situations mainly through emotive-postural channels. Their coordination of roles, that is, of the proposals that can be apprehended in their gestures, postures and verbalisations, occurs as sequences of actions that are collectively created through the synchronisation of expressive gestures, as shown in Episode 1.

Episode 1

Two girls, Telma (23 months) and Vania (21 months) are seated side by side, playing with some wooden blocks. At a certain moment, Vania, with a serious face, carefully rubs one block on another, as if rubbing a bar of soap on a bath sponge. She takes one of the blocks and rubs it several times in all directions in Telma's hair, as if washing it. Vania stops for a while and then rubs the block carefully, from the front to the back, in Telma's hair, in a gesture similar to combing hair. Putting her face quite close to Telma's, she asks, while smiling and nodding her head affirmatively: *Bom, né?* [Beautiful, isn't it?].

This episode shows the segmentation and integration of fragments of the children's previous experiences reproduced in contexts of activity presently constructed. Two interrelated scripts involved in their daily activities are interwoven in the children's actions: hair washing (the gesture of rubbing a soap or sponge in the peer's hair) and hair combing (the gesture of rubbing a small wooden block from the front to the back of her peer's hair). Their gestures act as effective signals for initiating the activities in which their emotional expressions and postural adjustments create a kind of language that model their actions while they interact.

This collage of experiences created through the confrontation of interpersonal boundaries would explain the syncretic character of children's representations in very short periods of gesture complementation around a common theme.

The analysis of this episode allows us to notice that the children's gestures reproduce quite well the postures, expressions and verbalisations related to some roles constitutive of their cultural environment, in this case mother/caregiver and child. The representational process is mediated by the fact that the children take some starters — in this case, some small wooden blocks and the partners' close presence — as support for their actions in a here-and-now frame. The starters' culturally attributed characteristics allow

the re-creation of past experiences in the play situation through highly imi-
tative gestures reproduced in ways increasingly related to postural adjustments and to the appropriation of sociocultural discourses.

That last point is crucial for the comprehension of the semiotic character
of all role coordinations. The children, besides using gestures, integrate the
roles they assume in their interactions through the use of verbal expressions
that are part of well-known daily scripts with their basic characters ('Beautiful, isn't it?') and their ideological meanings.

On the other hand, as the children develop, their reproduction of past experiences increasingly differentiates the original elements that are brought
into the present situation. These elements are transformed together with the
evolution of their role coordination, as it is possible to apprehend from the
next episode.

Episode 2 (one month later)

Vania (22), smiling, combs her own hair with a comb she found on the
floor among other toys and objects while she walks toward Vivi (22), who is
playing with some toys, and, brushing her hair, says to her: *Qué?* [(Do you)
Want?], *Tá bom?* [Is it okay?]. As soon as Vania starts to brush her hair, Vivi
starts to cry. Vania stops her brushing gesture and asks, with a serious face:
Dói? [Does it hurt?] to Vivi, who looks at the researcher and says in a weeping tone: *Oh, tia!* [Oh, teacher!].

In Episode 2 there is a real comb, which probably facilitates the scripts'
differentiation and a better definition of the theme. The gestures are now
more clearly defined and the expressive language shows with more detail
how memory in action mediates the children's play.

It is possible to recognise from Episodes 1 and 2 that the young children
assume different cultural attitudes in order to attribute some meanings to the
actions they are creating jointly. In Episode 2 Vania interpreted Vivi's cry as
a pain sign, although other interpretations could be used in the situation. It
is interesting to notice how Vania plays a sensitive caregiver role when she
asks Vivi if it hurt to comb her hair.

On the other hand, as the partners test the appropriateness of each others'
actions through the use of diverse cognitive-affective psychological instruments, their actions have to fit with the singularity of the on-the-spot situations in which shared semiotic fields of actions are expanded or constricted.
That point will be illustrated in the next episode.

Episode 3 (six months later)

Telma (now 30 months) walks around the room, combing her own hair with a comb she found in a toy box. She stops behind Vivi (28) and, standing up, rubs the comb on Vivi's hair. Vivi, who is handling some objects, cries *Ai* [Ouch!] and, looking at the researcher, says, in a weeping tone: *Tia …* [Oh, teacher! …] Telma starts to comb Vivi's hair again and looks at the researcher, who says to Vivi: *Dói o cabelo?* [Does it hurt?] Vivi leaves the comb on the floor and goes to manipulate other objects. Eight minutes later, she picks up the comb from the floor and combs Alexandre's (30) hair. Alexandre continues to manipulate a little pot in silence, even when Vivi carefully passes her right hand through his hair, moves back a little bit, points at his hair and states firmly, looking at him: *Qué tebêlo!* [(You) want hair!] She then combs his hair again while saying in an authoritarian tone: *Fica quieto, Alexandre!* [Keep quiet, Alexandre!]. She stopped combing Alexandre's hair and started to explore other objects that were on the floor. Almost two minutes later, Vivi, standing still, opens both arms and with the tips of her fingers pointing down to the floor, looks around, and says with a worried expression: *Não tá. Onde tá? Onde está o tebêlo, tia?* [It's not here! Where is it? Where is the hair, teacher?], looking at the researcher. She walks up to Alexandre and asks him: *Alexandre, cadê o tebêlo?* [Alexandre, where is the hair?], and then moves away looking all over the floor.

The reproduction of some rituals created in daily experiences at home and in the daycare centre's instructional activities, and expressed by gestures and oral language, as in Episode 3, allows the children's performance to occur without any trouble. There is role complementation and a clearer subordination to the rules involved in the situation being created by the children. When Vivi approaches Alexandre and makes a combing gesture through his hair, she is proposing a joint activity to him. She then states firmly: '(you) want hair!', thereby taking an authoritarian adult role or replying to an imaginary question whether he wanted to have his hair combed. After that, she scolds him: 'keep quiet!' while combing his hair.

On the other hand the confrontation of the roles being negotiated by the children's actions, more explicit in Episode 3, gives rise to some tensions that continuously change the context (i.e., its rules, meanings and values) they create. The gestures and words already established by the children are instantiated from their previous meanings, and used to open new possibilities for their interactions.

As some signs help the children make new differentiations in their behaviours, while they attribute some meanings to their partners' actions, there is a process of recombination of the different cultural meanings circulating among the partners' actions and capturing them in very interesting ways. For instance, in Episode 3 one can observe that Telma alternates between the gestures of combing her own hair and combing the other girl's hair. There is also a differentiation between who combs (i.e., Telma) and thus causes discomfort to the other and who screams in protest (i.e., Vivi).

From the analysis of the three episodes, it is possible to point out at least two aspects. First, the children become increasingly acquainted with the changes in the roles that can be assumed according to the situations and are ingenious in passing alternatively from one role to another. Second, by being authoritarian, polite, nice, worried, seductive and so on, in the interpersonal relationships they create, the young children can navigate through different social masks modelling human sensibility and creating the *persona* (in the ancient Greek sense).

On the other hand, the analysis of the episodes around the same theme extracted from further sessions showed that a linguistic differentiation, denotative of a more elaborate process of representation by the children, is gradually achieved thanks to role differentiation occurring in daily joint experiences. This more elaborate process will be discussed in the next episode.

Episode 4 (three months later)

Vivi (31 months), who is walking around the room, stops in front of the researcher and asks: *Cadê o pente?* [Where is the comb?] The researcher replies: *Pente? Eu não tenho nenhum pente!* [Comb? I don't have any comb!] John (33), who is observing the scene, asks the researcher: *O pente, tia?* [The comb, teacher?] She answers: *Sim* [Yes!]. John passes his right hand through his hair while saying: *'P'ra pentear?* [To comb (someone's hair)?].

Comparing Episodes 3 and 4, it can be pointed out how, with development, verbal language more effectively mediates the older children's coordination of roles. The girl (Vivi) in Episode 3 uses the term *tebelo* (childish form for the Portuguese word *cabelo* [hair]), derived from the activities of washing and combing the hair, to refer to the comb she is looking for ('Where is the hair?') and also to the combing activity ('Want hair!'), indicating that the syncretic way of apprehending the situation, already noticed in the previous episodes, is still frequent at that developmental period. However, in Episode 4, the comb and the combing activity have already been distinguished in linguistic terms, although the child (John) still makes the combing gesture while he verbally identifies the comb's functions in his culture.

Peer Interactions and Cultural learning

From this analysis, one can conclude that while playing roles in specific situations, the child has to follow, though not necessarily consciously, a way of acting that involves complex abilities, dealing with postures, gestures, and emerging representations. This way of acting requires the overcoming of some moments when the partners are seen in a more fusional state, where less role differentiation is experienced, and other moments when more differentiation between the partners' roles can be seen. By means of a dialectic imitation/opposition process between actions' contexts and their historical meanings, the children's gestures become linked with increasingly broader semiotic systems (and, therefore, with more complex roles), while they make the rules structuring their roles more explicit, renewing and sometimes updating them.

A child's development is thus created through a dialectical movement of alternation, confrontation and overcoming of social positions. As the child's abilities to contrast different situations and to assume different roles increases, he or she has more opportunities to analyse meanings, values, and attitudes related to them. By playing roles in here-and-now contexts, the child can practice various reactions to diverse situations and apprehend different discursive positions in a context-based way.

As the children practice and master new complex forms of action, they become able to represent the situation in more abstract ways, using diverse cognitive-affective psychological instruments to deal with the socially antagonistic conceptions and personal senses structuring it.

The concept of role, as a transactional view of human interactions permeated and made concrete by specific cultures, is very different from a merely instrumental, external version of the role concept. The roles were not seen as pre-given, fixed harnesses that society superimposes upon persons, but as personally-constructed, dynamic entities made available by the social world as a necessary interpretation of it through challenging constraints for adaptation. Through role coordinations, the active persons, by their action, accept to be submitted to some scripts, but exactly by doing so they transform cultural aspects to fit to the exigencies of each singular situation.

The interactional field created by the children's role coordinations, the zone of proximal development defined by Vygotsky, mediates psychological development and provides the individual with new resources to elaborate personal, although socially-based, aspects and to construct new self-constrained, although historically constructed, human ways of feeling, gesturing, moving, memorising, and thinking.

Admitting chance and denying a fixed and timeless reality, my proposal tries to be provocative for new research agendas that explore the collective construction of the young child's cognitive-affective system by the interweaving of similar and distinct roles in emerging settings.

References

Baldwin, J.M. (1895). The origin of a "thing" and its nature. *Psychological Review*, 2, 551-72.

Berger, P., & Luckmann, T. (1966). *The social construction of reality: A treatise in the sociology of knowledge*. Harmondsworth, England: Penguin.

Bergson, H. (1948). *Essai sur les données immediates de la conscience*. Paris: Presses Universitaires de France. (Original work published 1889)

Bronckart, J.-P. (1992). El discurso como acción: Por un nuevo paradigma psicolingüístico. *Anuario de Psicología*, 54(3), 3-48.

Bruner, J. (1999). Infancy and culture: A story. In S. Chaiklin, M. Hedegaard, & U.J. Jensen (eds.), *Activity theory and social practice*. Aarhus, Denmark: Aarhus University Press, 225-34.

Cole, M. (1985). The zone of proximal development: Where culture and cognition create each other. In J.V. Wertsch (ed.), *Culture, communication and cognition: Vygotskian perspectives*. Cambridge: Cambridge University Press, 146-61.

Doise, W., & Mugny, G. (1984). *The social development of the intellect*. Oxford: Pergamon.

Du Preez, P. (1991). *A science of mind: The quest for psychological reality*. London: Academic Press.

Guillaume, P. (1925). *L'imitation chez l'enfant*. Paris: Felix Alcan.

Harré, R. (1979). *Social being: A theory for social psychology*. Oxford: Blackwell.

James, W. (1890). *Principles of psychology*. New York: Holt.

Janet, P. (1929). *L'evolution psychologique de la personalité*. Paris: A. Chachine.

Levine, J.M., & Resnick, L.B. (1993). Social foundations of cognition. *Annual Review of Psychology*, 44, 585-612.

Mead, G.H. (1934). *Mind, self and society*. Chicago: University of Chicago Press.

Moreno, J.L. (1953). *Who shall survive? Foundations of sociometry, group psychotherapy and sociodrama*. Beacon, N.Y.: Beacon House.

Newman, D., Griffin, P., & Cole, M. (1989). *The construction zone: Working for cognitive change in school*. Cambridge: Cambridge University Press.

Oliveira, Z.M.R. (1988). Jogo de papéis: Uma perspectiva para análise do desenvolvimento humano. Unpublished doctoral dissertation, IPU São Paulo, Brazil.

Oliveira, Z.M.R. (1998). Peer interaction and the appropriation of gender representation by young children. In M.C.D.P. Lyra & J. Valsiner (eds.), *Construction of psychological processes in interpersonal communication*. Stamford, Conn.: Ablex, 103-15.

Oliveira, Z.M.R., & Rossetti-Ferreira, M.C. (1996). Understanding the co-constructive nature of human development: Role coordination in early peer interaction. In J. Valsiner & H. Voss (eds.), *The structure of learning processes*. Norwood, N.J.: Ablex, 117-204.

Oliveira, Z.M.R., & Valsiner, J. (1997). Play and imagination: The psychological construction of novelty. In A. Fogel, M.C.D.P. Lyra, & J. Valsiner (eds.), *Dynamics and indeterminism in developmental and social processes*. Mahwah, N.J.: Erlbaum, 119-34.

Río, P. del, & Álvarez, A. (1994). Ulises vuelve a su casa: Retornando al espacio del problema en el estudio del desarrollo. *Infancia y Aprendizaje*, 66, 21-45.

Rogoff, B. (1990). *Apprenticeship in thinking*. New York: Oxford University Press.

Royce, J. (1988). The world and the individual. In J.E. Smith & W. Kluback (eds.), *Josiah Royce: Selected writings*. New York: Paulist Press, 101-50. (Original work published 1901)

Shotter, J. (1989). Vygotsky's psychology: Joint activity in a developmental zone. *New Ideas in Psychology*, 7, 185-204.

Shotter, J. (1993). Vygotsky: The social negotiation of semiotic mediation. *New Ideas in Psychology*, 11, 61-75.

Smolka, A.L.B., Goes, M.C.R., & Pino, A. (1997). (In)determinacy and the semiotic constitution of subjectivity. In A. Fogel, M.C.D.P. Lyra, & J. Valsiner (eds.), *Dynamics and indeterminism in developmental and social processes*. Mahwah, N.J.: Erlbaum, 153-64.

Tudge, J. (1990). Vygotsky, the zone of proximal development, and peer collaboration: Implications for classroom practice. In L.C. Moll (ed.), *Vygotsky and education: Instructional implications and applications of sociohistorical psychology*. Cambridge: Cambridge University Press, 155-72.

Valsiner, J. (1987). *Culture and the development of children's action: A cultural historical theory of developmental psychology*. New York: Wiley.

Vygotsky, L.S. (1986). *Thought and language* (A. Kozulin, trans.). Cambridge, Mass.: MIT Press. (Original work published 1934)

Vygotsky, L.S. (1989). Concrete human psychology. *Soviet Psychology*, 27(2), 53-77.

Wallon, H. (1942). *De l'acte à la pensée: Essai de psychologie comparée*. Paris: Flammarion.

Wallon, H. (1959). Le role de 'l'autre' dans la conscience du 'moi'. *Enfance*, 3-4, 279-85.

Wallon, H. (1973). The emotions. *International Journal of Mental Health*, 1(4), 40-52.

Wertsch, J.V. (ed.) (1985). *Culture, communication and cognition: Vygotskian perspectives*. Cambridge: Cambridge University Press.

8   External and Internal: Another Comment on the Issue

Vladimir P. Zinchenko

> *Müsset im Naturbetrachten*
> *Immer Eins wie Alles achten*
> *Nichts ist drinnen, nichts ist draußen*
> *Denn was innen, das ist außen*
> *So ergreifet ohne Säumniß*
> *Heilig öffentlich Geheimnis*

J.W. Goethe (1973, 175)

The issue of internal and external seems to be an everlasting problem inherent in all domains of humanitarian knowledge. The issue takes various forms and faces. Many known phenomena have visible and invisible aspects: some tears are visible to the world and some are not; the moon has its visible and its dark side; words, symbols, myths, and works of art — all have a twofold nature. Human beings also possess visible and invisible organs: human soul, reason, will, honesty, conscience, memories, imaginations, and so forth are all invisible. Yet these entities, in some of their properties and the ways they function in human life, seem to be similar to anatomical or morphological human organs.

Some philologists relate this naive anatomy of human psyche to the archaic ideas that exist in, for example, Russian and possibly many other language-rooted representations of the world (see, e.g., Urysson 1997). Ukhtomskii's (1978) theory that focuses on the individual's functional organs (which, in contrast to morphological ones, are also invisible) makes such ideas not archaic, but quite up-to-date.

---

*   All quotations from Russian sources are in my translation.

Some Difficulties with the External and Internal

For a long time, scholars who concentrated their efforts on developing psychological activity theory considered their major task to be the explanation of how mind takes its origin in external object-related activity. It has been hypothesised that when such activity is performed repeatedly its external pattern (motoric or vocal) becomes reduced, and then internalisation of the activity occurs; that is, the activity undergoes the transition from its external, visible form into some internal and invisible one. Here we meet the first difficulty. Internal and invisible may not be congruent to each other. A person's image of the world is invisible to the outer observer, yet it is found outwardly. One can unexpectedly find one's image of something or such an image sometimes comes to a person (like, for example, as happens to artists or poets). But where are such entities like soul, reason, or notion situated? Indeed, we speak of things like projection, extrajection, transcendentalisation, externalisation, and the like. As language shows, one can 'take off the mysterious veil that covers human soul.' And Shpet (1989) wrote that 'human soul envelops a person with a soft, gentle veil' (p. 363). But all blows strike the person's outer look, not the veil itself. As Mandelshtam noted, even a very subtle mind is situated entirely outward.

Similarly, it is hard to say where the body of our wishes is situated. Passions can storm inside a person's soul, or a person may live surrounded by passions. Such situations are typical in artistic literature and poetry, when characters find themselves amidst their own feelings which attack them as if from the outside: 'Love sprung before us just as a murderer could leap out in the alley to strike both of us' (Bulgakov 1973, 556).

The second difficulty is related to internalisation when it is interpreted as 'a transition from outside to inside'. This is found in an old conceptual conflict that still exists in psychologies that take a too materialist understanding of object-related action (and the human mind in general). Such psychologies view external, object-related human action as being purely external and non-psychic. Therefore, through internalisation (if understood as a transition from outside to inside) external, object-related, non-psychic action becomes, as it were, a psychic action or operation. Such internalised action preserves the object-related features that were previously inherent to the action performed as external.

The difficulty does not arise, however, if internalisation is understood as a transition from intersubjective to intrasubjective, which is performed by mental functions. True, in the latter case, the prefix *intra* may seem somewhat provocative, because it can be understood as denoting internal subjectivity. This prefix, however, can also be understood as pointing to some entity that becomes inherent to a person, becomes his or her own, that is, a subjective function. Such an explanation eliminates the opposition between internal and external. An internalised function can be both external and internal and, consequently, both visible and invisible at the same time.

I think most researchers agree today that both external (visible) and internal (invisible) object-related actions possess some mind-related aspects. Tying a string around one's finger, the explorational tour of a new object, perceptional action performed by means of touch or eye movements — all these are mental actions in a complete sense. The functional structure of object-related action involves a rich content of cognitive and emotional-evaluational components (Gordeeva 1995, 285-88). In the model of object-related action, properly motoric, executive components take a decreasingly small place. In fact, to construct an object-related action is nothing else than filling movement with cognitive and emotional-evaluational components. For example, to construct artistic movement in ballet dance is to animate, to spiritualise the motion. As Hegel (1807/1959) wrote, 'man's true being is man's action in which individuality becomes actual' (p. 172). True being either possesses the modus of mental, or it is not being at all. Therefore, constructing the very object-related action presupposes that internal should be externalised, differentiated, and, finally, internalised, with its further playing-over in the internal plane being provided by the internalisation.

These preceding remarks are not meant to devalue the numerous research works that have dealt with the act of internalisation. These researches have yielded one very instructive conclusion. As resolution of research techniques grew, many mental functions, which were previously considered purely internal and unmeasurable, turned out to be external and quite observable. Examples of these techniques include the methods of microstructural and microdynamic analysis that are applied to executive and perceptual actions, as well as microstructal methods applied to analyse short-term memory and attention, which have been developed in cognitive psychology and related fields. Therefore, the border between external and internal, observable and non-observable tends to be rather flexible, if not to say relative. The relativity of the border between external and internal is evidenced by externalisational acts (i.e., by the processes in which internal transforms into external). One could hardly assume that internal mental acts that are being expressed externally lose all their mental modus.[1]

An Alternative Proposal

Now to return again to internalisation. There is an ambiguous moment in explaining internalisation as a transition from 'inter' to 'intra'. This moment is not related to external and internal, but rather to subjective and objective. Terms like *internal, mental, subjective*, and *ideal* are commonly listed in a row divided by commas, which reflects the view that external object-related action does not possess any mind- or psyche-related aspects. Such action — as the usual argumentation goes — is not only object-related, but also external and, consequently, objective. Thus, externalisation, or bringing the internal outward, often is viewed as something identical to the process in which the internal, subjective, or mental is objectified. There is something strange in this. Does the flexibility or the borders between external and internal correspond to flexibility of the borders between objective and subjective? If so, then in conducting experiments, the researcher plays the role of a magician who — by using complicated research techniques as some magic wand — tends not only to expand the limits of the external, but also turns subjective into objective. All this seems rather like mysticism or a scandal in the psychological community.

Maybe it would be more simple and more correct to assume that what is considered as mental, or subjective, is objective at the same time — without regard to whether it appears in its external or internal form, whether it is observable or not. Of course, in such a view, mental entities maintain their subjectivity, because they belong to a particular person only and not to any other (i.e., they keep their being as subjective and subject-related). In other words, I speak of the ontology of the mental in all its appearances.

As the first step, so to say, in ontologising mental entities I would suggest

---

1. Although there is a relativity of the border between external and internal and between observable and non-observable, this does not mean that all internal has good prospects to become external. Many domains of internal will long remain *terra incognita*, so psychological professions are not likely to perish.

a new cultural understanding of internalisation. One culturologically-oriented philosopher (Mikhailov 1997) focuses on such processes in the context of myth-semiotic accomplishment, or, as some scholars call it, myth-semiotic human activity. He distinguishes two different processes in such activity. The first process consists in:

All that is, as it were, immediately given irreversibly swept out — so that in the course of time more and more beliefs, opinions, judgements, and given things become questioned, criticised and do not exist anymore as simply given things. [In terms of psychology, such situations can be described as a mediated relation between nature and people that is formed, and the direct relation is respectively overcome — V.Z.] Second, such a process is directly linked to a basic human inter-relation with the world (i.e., with all existence, with everything that a person meets in life, including 'individual', as a phenomenon). This is a steady process of inter-nalisation, in which various contents of the world manifest themselves so that they belong to humans, to human personality, depend on personality and are directed by it, take origin in it, manifest themselves as an internal human property. Of course, the process of internalisation of the world can be interpreted in various terms; we would like to note that this process is also closely linked to dramatic interrelations between the individual and nature, so that when nature is objectified and, in doing so, is put into opposition to the individual as if it would be something alien to the individual in his or her essence, this means at the same time that nature is assimilated — it is something similar to appropriating nature as, so to say, a peripheral property situated at the border between one's own and not-own. (p. 181)

So the keywords found here are *own* and *not-own* instead of external-internal or visible-invisible. The border between own and not-own is as flexible as the border between external and internal, but has no regard to objectivity. For example, 'not-own not-own word', after having been appropriated becomes 'own not-own word', and only after then, if the situation is favourable, does it become a proper 'own word'. Here we recognise well-known motives of Bakhtin (1986), who compared individuality to man's own word in the culture, and Hegel — to the individual's own action.

The own, subjective, internalised, or converted word (or cosmos, or universe) does not lose its objectivity. On the other hand, such words can be true or false, senseful or senseless. The latter evaluating characteristics cannot be applied to what has not passed through the 'furnace' of internalisation. Following Bakhtin, let us make another step. Suppose that mind, just like culture, does not have its own enclosed territory, but is situated instead at the borders between own and not-own, between internalised and not-yet-internalised, or not-completely internalised. A vision of the world is constructed of the world's objectivity and personal interpretation or understanding; but already these two components cannot be separated; one cannot divide 'objectivity' out of a person's flow of perceptions, interpretations, and understanding. Similarly, 'pure subjectivity' cannot be divided from such a flow.

These ideas are not new. Ukhtomskii (1978), when describing his ideas about an individual's functional organs (as distinguished from morphological ones) and a person's functional states, wrote that the subjective is as objective as the so-called 'objective'. Later, Gibson (1979/1988) suggested a similar idea:

The domain of the objective and the domain of the subjective, which are supposed to exist independently, are in fact the only two poles for attention. There is no need to hypothesise a dualism of the observer and the surrounding world. (p. 174)

When discussing, from a culturological position, the issue of what constitutes an image of a particular era, Mikhailov (1997) expressed similar views, introducing the term *underinternalisation*:

And all that was 'underinternalised' is not, in fact, far off from us, but is situated quite near, close to our culture. Thus, for example, deep feeling or a passion, until it seizes a person, does not belong to him/her completely, but rather exists as a given thing, which comes to the person from outside and exists 'in general', in the world. Human life is surrounded by such outer forces; a person has to stand against such forces or become their victim. (p. 182)

Therefore, the notion of internalisation involves rather an active voice — not that external object-related activity drowns in some mental depth, nor immerses from outside to inside. Instead the person appropriates some quite real forces of nature and society (including his/her own forces), which stand in opposition and sometimes are quite alien.

Here we come close to the issue: What actually is internalised? What is the thing that is really appropriated? At the abstract level, answering this question may not be difficult. One could say that the human being is a micro-universe, which contains the whole universe in him- or herself and, therefore, is even more mysterious than the universe. Of course, the universe itself is not internalised, but rather its contents, which are expressed in some myth-semiotic 'text' (whether sensual, perceptual, imaginary, emotional, verbal, sign-symbolic, conceptual, or something else). Thus, an elementary external form of a symbol is not internalised; rather the symbol's unlimited internal content is internalised, which often 'grows into' a person without permission, independently from the person's wish and will. This 'growing into' occurs not in the physical, but in the symbolical 'body' of a person, into his/her spiritual organism, into the phenomenal 'body' of his/her wishes, motives, values, and consciousness. This may seem clear and simple at first glance. But such a spiritual organism, a symbolical or phenomenal body, which represents some space in which specific contents can be 'placed' or 'grown into' must first be constructed itself. In addition, this symbolical body should be constructed of the same symbols, whose contents are to be internalised subsequently. Therefore, internalisation must be preceded by some 'world creation' act (a person's own proper world, of course). Such an own world could hardly be generated out of one's own spirit, for the spirit still does not exist. All this is to say that internalisation still cannot be considered as a gnosiological act. Rather it is an ontological, viable, real act. In my opinion, Florenskii (1914/1990) suggested a characterisation of cognition, which also helps to characterise what is really internalisation and externalisation at the same time:

Cognition really occurs when the cognising person *comes outside* him/herself, or, which is, in fact, the same thing, when what is cognised *comes inside* the cognising person — a real merger of what is cognised with the cognising person. (p. 73)

In psychological terms, 'coming out' of oneself is called projection, transcendentalisation, or externalisation and 'coming into' is introjection, or internalisation. Now we can address the issue of external and internal again. The external world is situated outside and has to, in some or other (miraculous) way, become an internal one, or, more exactly, one's 'own'. There is little use in this process if during such a transition the world loses its objective properties, or becomes distorted, or drowns inside (which happens frequently). This means that the internal world (for the time being, let us consider it as subjective), in its turn, must have the opportunity to come outside, that is, in some or other (no less miraculous) way, to become an external one. (By the way, such transitions appear to be the tool for making comparisons between internal and external worlds.) An internal world, when it comes to be outside, does not become objectified, but, as it were, also comes to convince the internal of its proper objectiveness. If we assume such a position, then externalisation always accompanies and sometimes precedes internalisation. A genetic consequence of these two processes is a special issue that requires separate discussion.

Some Conclusions from the Alternative Proposal

The external world is constructed inside, that is, in a phenomenal, symbolical field-space, however narrow, flat, or limited it may be. The internal world is constructed outside. Of course, these two processes of world construction do not go separately. They are synergic, if we use the newly-fashioned old term. Such synergy, as it were, provides for two oppositely directed processes: subjective becomes objective and objective becomes subjective. To explain how the world is reflected in the human person, Leontiev (1983) has put forward his 'likening hypothesis', which assumes that a person's actions become adapted to (or try to follow) an object's properties. Zaporozhets and Zinchenko (1982) added to the hypothesis another, opposite process, in which the object becomes alike with those attitudes, settings, perceptual models, etc., that exist in the human person. The living creature not merely turns to this world, but, as it were, turns all its inside outward to meet the world (e.g., dedicates itself completely to hearing). A living creature can do this to such a great extent that sometimes it even becomes a screen between itself and the world and sees only itself, its own expectations, wishes, or fears. Of course, in everyday perceptual tasks, the observer sees not two, but only one world, which is situated on the border between external and internal, is objective and subjective at the same time, and appears as a result of extrajection and intrajection.

In my view, internalisation and externalisation should be distinguished from the acts of perceiving the world that involve extrajection and intrajection. The observed world is much vaster than the world that is internalised, appropriated, becomes own. The underinternalised world is a 'horizon of understanding' (Husserl), or 'zone of proximal development'. I would like to emphasise that not only the external world, but also a person's own symbolic, phenomenal, and even bodily world can be 'underinternalised'. This is really a difficult moment to understand. To make it clearer, I would like to mention the 'mirror stage' in human development, which has been hypothesised by Lacan (1949/1997). To see oneself and even to identify oneself still does not mean to know oneself, or to possess oneself.

Three Open Problems Concerning External and Internal

Finally, I note briefly three more problems that are directly related to the problem of external and internal, and which merit further study and reflections.

The first problem is related to time. When does the act of meeting between external and internal occur? Also, when does their knitting together occur, resulting in the construction of special, integrated, subjective-objective forms like images, personal experiences, intentions, value-relations, etc.? When does the 'myth-semiotic accomplishment' occur? Answering this question may seem very simple: always, during all human life. However, another sense of the question is interesting, namely, in which moments of life does this occur? As is known from Köhler's works, insight does not occur during violent, strained action. It happens instead during some pauses, intervals, or breaks in activity and actions, which have received various names. Bakhtin (1986) referred to them as 'the out-of-time gappings that are formed between two moments of real time'. These breaks sometimes are also named with terms like 'suspension', 'breaking', 'shift', 'reflectional space', 'gap in continual experience' (Mamardashvili 1993), and 'fixed point of intensity' (Descartes). Winnicott (1971) writes about space 'in between', or 'resting place'. Whatever it is called, this is some new space and new time constructed by a person (Ukhtomskii, 1978, called this *chronotope*, from Greek *chronos* and *topos*). This is a space where the active internal is developing. The most simple example is movement learning. As Bernshtein (1990) wrote, it is not enough to know how movement looks from 'outside', we must also know how it looks 'from within', which cannot be explained by any demonstration. Therefore, even to construct movement, one additional mirror is needed. Here, whether I wish it or not, association with Lewis Carroll's *Through the Looking Glass* comes to mind, which he described so wonderfully. This is a serious challenge to psychology in general and to psychological activity theory, in particular. Indeed, to create one mirror for outer reality and another mirror for inner reality is not enough. This is only the start of an infinite human task: to keep internal and external realities separated and, at the same time, maintain their interconnection and interaction (similar motives are found in Winnicott's works). At the same time this prepares a person for the possibility that external (and sometimes even internal) reality may appear as either an 'own', desirable, or 'not-own', alien one.

A second problem that merits further reflection and study was already mentioned: the genetical succession of internalisation and externalisation. Who is the subject of inner space 'creation'? Winnicott suggested an interesting hypothesis, which could equally be called a fantasy. It rests upon ideas about good and bad breast, good and bad mother, which were originally put forward by Melanie Klein (1957/1997). She related feelings of envy and gratitude in infants to feeding acts. Erikson (1968/1996) also related feeding to such basic infant attitudes like trusting or distrusting the world. Winnicott seems to make the next step, suggesting a more advanced version of what happens in infancy. When experiencing the need for food the infant shows this in one or other way. The mother, noticing this, gives her breast to the infant at a specific time and in a specific spot. Because of this, the infant comes to a clear illusory feeling of being able to generate the breast him- or herself. According to Winnicott, this is the infant's illusion of his or her own magic power and almightiness. Clearly, such an illusion arises as a consequence of a loving mother's careful attention to the signs shown by her infant. A. Zinchenko and I (personal communication, 1998) have elaborated Winnicott's hypothesis with the further hypothesis that due to the loving mother's 'right guessing', her infant creates a small Eden. As if by his or her own will, the infant evokes feeding, lulling, lullaby singing, communication, etc. The infant 'creates' all this by him- or herself and then switches onto other transitive objects delivered by adults, who fill, expand, and enrich the world created by the infant. In real life, however, not all is so sunny, as is described in Winnicott's conceptualisation. If the infant fails to discover a small Eden, then the infant can generate instead its own small Hell, which in subsequent life can become a Big Hell to others.

Even if there is no proof for Winnicott's idea, we still think it is pretty good. The infant generates not only signs that are clear to adults, but generates his or her own world as well. As the Russian poet Voloshin (1989, 24) wrote:

> Child is unacknowledged genius
> Admidst ordinary humdrum people.

Of course, an active, sympathising adult participates in the child's generation. The events here follow Vygotsky's reasoning: from intersubjective, dialogical, to intrasubjective which, after it becomes autonomous, maintains its dialogical nature. Of special interest in Winnicott's conceptualisation is the fact that from the very beginning the child appears not only as a partner in joint activity, but as a full-fledged individual. The child creates what no other person — even the most loving and careful person — can create for him or her. The child creates his or her own internal world. And this is a creation 'out of self' or coming out of self, when the child projects and externalises the world outwards. Another question is how the child manages subsequently to overcome the illusion of almightiness (or of despair), to extend the constructed world, and to internalise, that is, to appropriate it.

Finally, the last problem is related to the ontology of mental. Let us turn to the individual's so-called functional organs. As Ukhtomskii (1978) emphasised, such organs bear active functions. In his conceptualisations he described a functional organ as a 'mobile agent', 'Cartesian whirling motion', or 'temporal combination of forces capable of accomplishing certain achievements' and the like. In other words, he repeatedly emphasised that the individual's functional organs possess energetic properties. Ukhtomskii's conceptualisations were based on ideas about an 'individual's energetical projection', which have been developed in orthodox patristics and in hesychastic anthropology (in Eastern Christianity). For example, the Byzantine theologian Saint Gregory Palamas (1296-1359) systematised tendencies in Hesychast spirituality, which strove to bridge the gulf between human and divine existence by postulating the necessity of an intermediary relationship between man's world (immanence) and God's eternity (transcendence). If one translates some of his ideas into contemporary psychological language, then mental functions can be represented as *combinations of energies*. In my opinion, such ideas are much more interesting than conceptions like Penfield's 'brain man'. S.S. Khoruzhy and I, on the basis of theological works, have made explicit conclusions about the true sources of the individual's energetical and actional projections.[2]

Conclusion

The arguments presented in this chapter have aimed to show that it is inadequate for modern psychology to use such vague notions like

---

2. As part of our work, we have shown how the study of psychological activity in the Soviet Union also drew on pre-Marxist sources (e.g., J.G. Fichte, John Dewey, and Henri Bergson), as well as fine arts and literature (e.g., analyses of stage actions for actors).

'external' and 'internal'. Starting from von Humboldt, the human sciences have utilised conceptions of external and internal form. They are as real as explicit and implicit text. Maybe the latter is even more real than the former. Explicit text goes and implicit text remains. The ability of external and internal forms to convert into one another is additional evidence for their reality. This issue requires special discussion and argumentation. Real examples of convertible forms exist. Such convertibility would be impossible if external form did not contain an internal one. The latter is as self-standing as the former. In more traditional terms, internal forms determine behaviours no less than external ones. Internal is, in fact, not a concomitant condition that participates in determination of behaviour, but rather a source of free behaviour, free action.

References

Bakhtin, M.M. (1986). *Literaturno-kriticheskie stat'i* [Articles on literary criticism]. Moscow: Khudozhestvennaia literatura.

Bernshtein, N.A. (1990). *Fiziologiia dvizhenii i aktivnost'* [Physiology of movements and activity] (O.G. Gazenko, ed.). Moscow: Nauka.

Bulgakov, M.A. (1973). Master i Margarita [Master and Marguerite]. In *Romany*. Leningrad: Khudozhestvennaia literatura.

Erikson, E.H. (1996). *Identichnost': Yunost' i krizis* [Identity, youth, and crisis]. Moscow: Progress. (Original work published 1968)

Florenskii, P.A. (1990). *Stolp i utverzhdenie istiny: Opyt pravoslavnoi feoditsei v dvenadtsati pis'makh* [The pillar and ground of truth: An attempt at an orthodox theodicy in twelve letters]. Moscow: Pravda. (Original work published 1914)

Gibson, J.J. (1988). *Ecologicheskii podhod k zritel'nomu vospriyatiyu* [The ecological approach to visual perception]. Moscow: Progress. (Original work published 1979)

Goethe, J.W. (1973). Epiremma [Epigrams]. In *J.W. Goethe ob iskusstve*. Moscow: Iskusstvo.

Gordeeva, N.D. (1995). *Eksperimental'naia psikhologiia ispolnitel'nogo deistviia* [The experimental psychology of executive action]. Moscow: Trivola.

Hegel, G.W.F. (1959). Fenomenologiia dukha [Phenomenology of spirit]. In *Sochineniia*: Vol. 4. Moscow: Politizdat. (Original work published 1807)

Klein, M. (1997). *Zavist' i blagodarnost': Issledovaniye bessoznatel'nyh istochnikov* [Envy and gratitude: A study of unconscious sources]. St. Petersburg: B.S.K. (Original work published 1957)

Lacan, J. (1997). [La stadie du mirroir comme formateur de la fonction du Je]. In *Instantsiia bukvy ili sud'ba razuma posle Freida*. Moscow: Russkoi Fenomeno-logicheskoye Obschestvo. (Original work published 1949)

Leontiev, A.N. (1983). *Izbrannye psikhologicheskie proizvedeniia v dvukh tomakh* [Selected psychological works in two volumes] (V.V. Davydov, ed.). Moscow: Pedagogika.

Mamardashvili, M.K. (1993). *Kartezianskie razmyshleniia* [Cartesian reflections] (IU.P. Senokosova, ed.). Moscow: Progress.

Mikhailov, A.V. (1997). *IAzyki kul'tury: Uchebnoe posobie po kul'turologii* [Languages of culture: Textbook for culturology]. Moscow: IAzyki Russkoi Kul'tury.

Shpet, G.G. (1989). *Sochineniia* [Works] (E.V. Pasternak, ed.). Moscow: Pravda.

Ukhtomskii, A.A. (1978). *Izbrannye trudy* [Selected works] (E.M. Krepsa, ed.). Leningrad: Nauka.

Urysson, E.V. (1997). Arkhaichnye predstavleniya v russkoi yazykovoi kartine mira [Archaic conceptions in Russian language-rooted representations of the world]. Doctoral thesis resume.

Voloshin, M.A. (1989). *"Sredotoch'e vsekh putei–": Izbrannye stikhotvoreniia i poemy, proza, kritika, dnevniki* ["Focus of all ways–": Selected verses and poems, prose, criticism, diaries]. Moscow: Moskovskii rabochii.

Winnicott, D.W. (1971). *Playing and reality*. London: Tavistock.

Zaporozhets, A.V., & Zinchenko, V.P. (1982). *Vospriyatie, dvizhenie, deistvie: Poznavatel'nye protsessy, oschuschenie, vospriyatie* [Perception, movement, action: Cognition, sensation, perception]. Moscow: Pedagogika.

9 Semiotic Mediation and Internalisation: The Role of Referential Perspective in Instructional Actions

Andrés Santamaría

The aim of this chapter is to analyse instructional interactions in which one participant structures the overall solving of the task so that the other participant internalises the skills and abilities that were accomplished jointly. This kind of instructional interaction has also been termed *guided participation* (Rogoff 1990) or *mastery* (Wertsch 1991).

The work reported here aims to contribute to a better understanding of instruction from the perspective of *internalisation*. A primary interest in this chapter is to examine the semiotic mechanisms involved in the instructor-learner interaction, as a way to understand the sociogenesis of mental processes. Additionally, it is important to examine how the instructor's actions may influence both the way in which learners solve a task, and the level of responsibility that the learners adopt while solving it.

The relationship between social interaction and cognitive development has been an important research focus, and analysed from a wide range of perspectives. The way in which research is conducted in this area has been changing continually from the initial field studies in the beginning of the 1980s to the present day, where there is a renaissance of interest in the questions that arise when investigating the concept of internalisation.

Sociocultural psychology provides a useful approach for the study of internalisation, particularly the instruments necessary for the analysis of the factors and mechanisms involved in the acquisition and development of instructional actions. For example, the Vygotskian conception of semiotic mediation is crucial and essentially different from other approaches that also emphasise the importance of signs (like Peirce, Saussure, the Prague school, Piaget, and so forth). Vygotsky, like Bakhtin (1979/1986) and other Marxian researchers, did not just defend the social genesis of semiotic mediation but, inspired by his Marxist perspective, also situated its emergence in the practical activity of individuals (see Tolman, this volume). In Vygotsky's view, the notion of development is important for explaining psychological functioning, and he used a genetic method to analyse it. In this chapter, I shall analyse changes of actions from two genetic domains (Wertsch 1985): *sociocultural development*, that is, the changes associated with participation in activities of formal schooling, and the *microgenetic domain*, those changes in development that take place during the experimental task.

For that reason I think it is important to analyse the relationships between explanatory variables, associated with genetic domains (Wertsch 1985) (what can be called *genetic variables*), and the actions performed by instructors and learners. In the experiment reported here, I consider three explanatory variables. For the genetic domain of sociocultural development, which in this case is experience in formal education activities, the explanatory variable is the educational level of the instructor (nonliterate, literate and teacher). For the microgenetic domain, it is the task and period in the task. Some studies have shown that the microgenetic domain is crucial in the analysis of changes in psychological processes (Wertsch & Hickman 1987; Wertsch & Stone 1978).

The concept of activity (Leontiev 1981) is central to these kinds of studies about social interaction in problem solving. In the sociocultural version of activity theory, the concept of action is useful for integrating sociocultural and psychological levels of analysis. According to Wertsch (1985), action does not just refer to intra- or interpsychological functioning, instead both are an inherent part of the concept of action. Put another way, action simultaneously encapsulates individual and sociocultural aspects of human life. Action is individual because it is developed through the particular behaviour of a person. Action is social because it reflects forms of behaviour that are historically organised and defined, and it is acquired through participation and interaction in collective groups. So action allows us to observe simultaneously the functioning of psychological processes and the projection of culture on these processes (Ramírez, Cubero, & Santamaría 1990).

In the sociocultural approach, activity becomes an unit of analysis of institutional factors, while semiotically-mediated action constitutes the unit of analysis on a strictly psychological level (interpsychological and intrapsychological). This notion of mediated action (Zinchenko 1985) allows us to understand signs as tools of action and to explain the latter through activity.

In the sociocultural perspective, the instruction of a learner by a more expert member of the culture is one of the key situations in which learning and ontogenesis take place. In recent years, research on instruction has centred on communication and the instructor-learner dyadic interaction (e.g., Elbers 1987; Elbers, Maier, Hoekstra, & Hoogsteder 1992; González 1996). As will be discussed in more detail later, the sociocultural approach understands that this communication process and the subsequent progress of the learner takes place in the zone of proximal development constructed in joint activity.

In this chapter, instruction is viewed in terms of semiotically-mediated actions. Instruction, and thus internalisation, is considered to be the result of inter-actions that instructors and learners develop in joint problem-solving. Given the semiotic nature of these actions, instruction will be produced through signs that structure them. Semiotic mediation shapes instructional actions in line with the particular sociocultural activity in which these actions are employed (Vygotsky 1978). In my view, this consideration allows us to define both instruction and internalisation in a much more productive way than has previously been the case.

Therefore, *instructional actions* are not merely individual; instead they move from an interpsychological to an intrapsychological plane. This transition is linked to the establishment of an intersubjective agreement between instructor and learner which takes place in the zone of proximal development (e.g., Wertsch 1984), and is linked to changes in the situation definition of both participants (González & Palacios 1990).

Changes within the zone of proximal development have been characterised traditionally as individual changes that imply that the learner may do today what he/she could only do yesterday with help. This led to an understanding of internalisation as the transfer of skills that are in a social plane of functioning for the individual, where the learner is conceptualised as a passive receiver of this social material. However, I think the critical, developmental aspect in the zone of proximal development concerns the changes that result from the appropriation and mastering of new forms of mediation. This appropriation refers not only to individual learning after guided joint practice, but also to the capacity of the learner to participate in new collaborative activities (Newman, Griffin, & Cole 1989). As we shall see, the focus will not be on the transfer of skills from those who know more to those who know less, but instead on the shared use of new forms of communication for creating and communicating meaning (McLane 1987; McNamee 1987).

However, this general approach to the notion of internalisation is not sufficient theoretically, nor does it facilitate the development of methodologies for empirical research. To go beyond these generalities one has to specify more concrete aspects of internalisation. Perhaps the main attraction of the sociocultural theory lies in the importance given to the analysis of cognitive development in sociocultural activity. The basic unit of analysis is not the individual, but the sociocultural activity insofar as this activity implies the active participation of individuals in practices that are socially established and maintained (van der Veer, this volume; Vygotsky 1981).

I believe that semiotic aspects play a fundamental role in the instructional process that enables the learner to appropriate new skills and control during a task. This idea has to do with the Vygotskian view about internalisation. The human being, in his/her development, has to learn to master the tools, especially semiotic tools, involved in solving tasks.

Most instructional research from a sociocultural perspective usually concludes that efficient instruction is that which takes the initial level of the learner into account, and goes beyond this to the area where the learner is still not able to act alone (de la Mata 1993; Laboratory of Comparative Human Cognition 1983; Rogoff 1982; Wertsch 1984, 1985, 1989; Wertsch & Hickman 1987; Wertsch & Rogoff 1984). Notions such as the zone of proximal development, semiotic challenge, guided participation, and intersubjectivity play an important role in this discussion and have been crucial in this research.

However, these studies have not considered sufficiently the semiotic aspects involved in the instructional process. People learn to use semiotic tools in interaction with other members of their culture, and as they become more expert in using these tools, they appropriate them (Lawrence & Valsiner 1993; Rogoff 1990, 1993; Valsiner 1991; Wertsch 1985, 1989).

According to this line of argument, the use of different semiotic mechanisms, particularly reference, may have contributed to this appropriation. In order to function effectively in joint activity, interlocutors must be able to direct one another's attention to specific objects and events. The way to do that is by using utterances in which a speaker identifies a nonlinguistic referent in the speech situation.

An important fact about reference is that one and the same referent can be referred to or identified in different ways, by using different referring expressions (i.e., by using what is called *referential perspective*). Referential perspective is related to the point of view used by the speaker to identify a referent in communication (Wertsch 1985, 1989). It is a necessary part of any act of referring. But this fact is only the starting point of my argument. The main question I want to study is how and why a speaker (instructor or learner) introduces a particular perspective. As Wertsch (1989) says, an examination of the semiotic tools that can be used to introduce a referential perspective shows that there can be different semiotic options available to a speaker. I suggest that referential perspective is one of the most important semiotic mechanisms through which situation definition in joint activity is established and modified. Thus, instructional action (i.e., the process by which an instructor and learner structure their joint activity through the use of semiotic devices), and not the individual, constitutes my object of study.

One of the main themes of this chapter is to show how referential perspective serves as an important device for mediating the transition from interpsychological to intrapsychological functioning, and as a means for linking activities and actions (Santamaría 1997). In order to investigate changes of referential perspective in instructional interactions, a task was used in which two persons, with different levels of literacy competence, jointly constructed a story. In the present investigation, adult literacy students were instructed to construct a story employing a set of cards with pictures. The students were assisted by an 'instructor' who was either another literacy student (from the beginning or advanced course) or a teacher from the adult education school.

The task was chosen so that cognitive and interactive demands of the task would be suitable for the persons taking part in the experiment. Moreover, the demands of the task are similar to the demands of many activities that are found in formal schooling. In particular, the participants must develop a general, semantic representation of the cards that goes beyond what each one represents, and then bring them together into a whole story. They must also learn to solve problems and follow instructions.

One of the most interesting aspects of this task was the different forms of semiotic mediation embodied in the instructional actions employed by instructors from different educational levels. By using instructors with different levels of literacy competence, it was possible to observe differences in the modes of instruction, the ways that specific semiotic mechanisms were used to change referential perspectives, and the role that referential perspective played in the story-constructing task. The experiment also provides evidence for some of the semiotic mechanisms through which instructional action might facilitate the transfer of responsibility from the instructor to the learner in the control of the actions necessary to solve a task.

The acquisition of literacy, especially in adults, offers the possibility to study the influence of cultural activities on the development of the individual. The program of learning literacy, which is taking place in Andalusia (southern Spain), provides a natural laboratory for studying the process of learning literacy as well as the changes of the sociocognitive skills related to it. The educational practices in the literacy program try to adapt to the social and cultural reality of the students, reflecting the problems of the community, and at the same time giving them an active role in the teaching-learning process. So, in this experiment, adult education can be viewed as a set of social, cultural and discursive practices (Ramírez, Sánchez, & Santamaría 1996).

The choice of the instructional interaction between adults as the object of this empirical study stems from the consideration that it represents a privileged situation that allows one to consider the influence of participation in activities of formal schooling. It also gives the opportunity to observe the instructional actions performed by different instructors, both on an interpsychological and intrapsychological plane.

To study the mechanisms that allow relating activities of formal education and instructional actions, I use descriptive and observational procedures more than strictly experimental ones. This enables me to analyse the elements and mechanisms that are operating in the joint story-construction task. In the long run, I would like to be able to give an exhaustive analysis of how the experiment participants act over the course of the task. For now, I pay particular attention to the semiotic mechanisms, especially referential mechanisms, present in the instructor-learner interaction. I also conduct a microgenetic analysis that shows the changes in which semiotic mediations are used over the course of performing the task. From these changes, I am able to infer how these mediations are used to facilitate the internalisation process.

Method

Participants

The sample consisted of 30 participants (25 students and 5 teachers) from two adult education schools (*Programa de Educación de Personas Adultas*) in the city of Seville, Spain, and one school from a nearby rural area. The program, developed by the Regional Government of Andalusia, is designed primarily for adults who have had either no previous schooling experience or brief, discontinuous school attendance. There is also a small number of students who, for different reasons, were not able to get their primary education diploma, and see the need to go back to school to finish. The majority of the students who attend literacy courses are women whose age varies between 30 and 60 years old, with most being 40 to 45 years old. All the students belong to the working class, they have poor socioeconomic backgrounds and high unemployment rates in their families.

In this experiment all the subjects were women, and they were all between 40 and 45 years old. Twenty of the students were in the basic literacy course; five were in the advanced literacy course.[1]

Materials

Two sets of cards were used. The first set had 22 cards; the second set had 24 cards. Each card had a black and white drawing that depicted a scene. For each set of cards, there were four subsets of drawings that could be placed in an ordered sequence that illustrated a story. For the first set, the four stories consisted of three, four, five or six cards respectively. The remaining four cards were the first card for each of the four stories in the second set, and did not correspond to any story in the first set. They were included as distractors. For the second set, the four stories consisted of three, five, six and six cards respectively, with the four remaining distractor cards being the first story card for each of the stories in the first set. For both sets of cards, there was only one correct way to complete the different stories.

Procedure

In the experimental task, participants worked in pairs. For each pair, one person was designated as the 'instructor', while the other person was responsible for constructing the stories. The task started with the instructor presenting the first card for all four stories. The other person had to place the cards so that all four stories were constructed, and then provide a narrative description of the four stories. This task was then repeated with the second set of cards. The entire task performance was video and audio recorded.

---

1. Students are placed in the basic or advanced course according to their performance on an entrance test. Advanced course students were able to read simple texts, and could write short narratives. Both courses meet 10 hours per week, and the students in the current experiment had been attending the course for 32 weeks.

The experimental design had three experimental groups, corresponding to the three educational levels of the instructors. There were five pairs in each group. For all 15 pairs, the person who was responsible for constructing the story was from the beginning literacy course. The instructor in five of the pairs was also from the beginning literacy course (*nonliterate-instructor* group). For another five pairs, the instructor was from the advanced literacy course (*literate-instructor* group), while the final five pairs had a teacher from the adult education school as the instructor (*teacher-instructor* group). For the teachers in the teacher-instructor group, their partner was also a student in the teacher's course at the adult education school.

Each pair of participants was tested separately. The experiment started with the researcher calling the instructor into the testing room which was a classroom in the school where the students normally attended. The researcher sat opposite the instructor and placed on the table the initial card for each of the four stories from one of the card sets to be used in the experiment. The researcher gave the following instructions:

Here you've got the start of four stories that later on, with your partner, you are going to have to construct (the researcher points out the start of each of the four stories). And here you've got a pile of cards with which you can make the stories (while he shows the rest of the cards).

The researcher then pointed to the drawing on the first card for each story and summarised their respective content in the following way:

This is the beginning of a story about a bird and its nest; and this is one about a thief; this is about a man driving in his car; and this last one is the start of a story about two children who want the same comic book.

The researcher told the instructor about the four distractor cards, and then explained each of the stories, showing the drawings on the cards, and explained that there was only one correct sequence for each story. Then the instructor was given the following instructions:

Now that you know the stories and how they are built, we're going to call your partner in and she is going to sit down with you and she is going to have to construct the stories with the cards. She must try and do it on her own, but if you feel she needs help or if she asks you to help her, you may do so.

Action Plane

Type of action. The way the instructor and learner acted during the course of the task.

Orientation. Actions aimed at the identification, search for and/or selection of the elements necessary to perform the task.

Placing. Actions aimed at placing a card in a story.

Evaluation. Actions aimed at assessing, reviewing, or confirming aspects to do with the development of the task.

Planning. Actions in which the instructor established the procedures or steps necessary to perform the task.

Regulation of the action. Distribution of responsibility when directing and carrying out the actions.

Regulation by the learner. The responsibility and initiative of the action fell on the learner.

Joint regulation. Action in which both members of the pair had some responsibility in the control and development of the action.

Regulation by the instructor. The responsibility and initiative for the action fell on the instructor.

Type of instruction. Nature of the instruction. Amount of autonomy and responsibility given by the instructor to the learner during the task.

Guide. Suggestions that attempt to direct attention to something that could facilitate the task solving.

Indication. Suggestions that indicate which card has to be placed (e.g., pointing).

Demonstration. The instructor places the card with or without emitting some type of verbalisation.

Strategical level. Level of planning of the action (i.e., the goal behind the action).

Nonstrategical. The goal is the card.

Strategical. The goal directing the action is that of completing the stories. A plan exists.

Effectiveness. Performance of the participants (i.e., whether or not they place the cards correctly.

Correct placing. Inclusion of the card in its story, and in the correct order.

Partially correct placing. Inclusion of the card in its story, but not in the right order.

Incorrect placing. Inclusion of the card in a story to which it does not belong.

Mediation-of-Action Plane

Type of utterance. Nature of the utterance within the continuum directivity — non-directivity

     Imperative. Utterances that involve the maximum amount of directivity.

     Direct suggestions. Utterances that involve less directivity and allow greater responsibility for the listener in the solving of the task.

     Indirect suggestions. Utterances that do not express any directivity but instead attempt to establish guides or support.

     Descriptive. Utterances that involve an orientation in the constructing of the story.

Referential perspective. The way in which speakers refer to the different objects or procedures involved in the task.

     Deictic and extralinguistic indexes. Expressions that include indexical signs that provide minimal information about the speaker's perspective.

     Common referential expressions. Expressions that identify a card by using the common name of object represented in the drawing, providing little information about the speaker's perspective.

     Referential expressions informing about the context. Expressions that imply a certain level of categorisation of the different cards and the inclusion of these in the overall sequence of the story to be built.

Figure 9.1. Category system used to code performance in the interactive story-constructing task.

Once the story constructor is seated next to the instructor, the researcher gave the constructor the following instructions:

You've got four cards here that represent the beginning of four stories (pointing them out and naming each one). With these other cards (showing the pile of cards) you can complete each of the stories. But you should be aware of the fact that there are some cards that are of no use, that do not fit with these stories, and you should leave these out. You must try and do it on your own, but if you have difficulties or do not know what to do, your partner who has already done it, may help you, OK?

Once they started to work, the researcher withdrew to the other side of the classroom. All cards had to be placed in a narrative sequence. Once they had finished the task of constructing the stories, the learner was asked to narrate the content of each of the stories.

Data Analysis

The analyses are, in general terms, inspired by those used by Wertsch, Minick, and Arns (1984), as well as work carried out at the Laboratorio de Actividad Humana (1988, 1993) and some of its members (de la Mata 1993; Ramírez 1995; Sánchez 1995).

The video recordings were coded according to individual episodes of action. (The audio recordings were transcribed and used when the video recording was inaudible.) An episode was related to everything that a pair did or said with a single card. When the interaction changed to another card, this was counted as a new episode. Each episode was categorised according to two different analytical perspectives: the action plane and the mediation-of-action plane (see Figure 9.1). For each analytic plane, each episode was categorised according to all the categories, with each category receiving only one of the possibilities shown under each category. On the action plane, the category system considered the way that the task was carried out. That is, if the pairs could orient, evaluate, place a card, or make a plan. This action could be done in a strategical or nonstrategical way, with a particular effectiveness. Similarly, the action could be regulated and instructed in different ways. On the mediation-of-action plane, the focus was on the type of expressions that were made and the referential perspective that was used.

Note that individual performance is not being coded here. Rather it is the joint performance of the pair in a given episode. The main focus of the data analysis was to compare differences in the distribution of coded performance within categories among the three experimental groups.

The microgenetic development of the actions was analysed in two different ways. For each experimental couple, the total number of episodes across the two task performances were combined and divided into three equal parts, such that the first part contained the episodes performed in the first third of the total experimental session, the second third from the middle, and the final third from the end of the experimental session. The respective parts for each pair were then combined across the three experimental groups.

The microgenetic development of the actions was analysed in two different ways. For each experimental couple, the total number of episodes across the two task performances were combined and divided into three equal parts, such that the first part contained the episodes performed in the first third of the total experimental session, the second third from the middle, and the final third from the end of the experimental session. The respective parts for each pair were then combined across the three experimental groups.

Given the qualitative nature of the data, hierarchical log-linear models were used to analyse the results (Kennedy 1983). This statistical technique is particularly suitable for showing relationships between factors in multiple-entry tables. See Santamaría (1997) for more detailed information on the results and the statistical tests.

Results and Discussion

This section presents a selection of results that are most relevant to my conception of instruction as semiotically-mediated actions between instructors and learners. In particular, I am going to present and discuss results about (a) the extent to which placing actions were strategical and effective; (b) the types of regulation of the instructional actions used in placing; and (c) the use of referential perspective as a mediating mechanism of these actions.

Strategic and Effective Placing of Cards

There was a clear and progressive increase in the extent to which strategic placing actions were used as the educational level of the instructor increased (see Table 9.1). The teacher-instructor group was more strategical than the nonliterate-instructor and literate-instructor groups. In other words, higher educational levels were related to greater planning in guiding placing actions by using a specific and overall objective (the story) and not just by placing one card followed by another.

The analysis of the microgenetic development of the placing actions showed a statistically significant increase in the use of strategical actions over the course of the task (see Table 9.2). An additional microgenetic analysis looked at the development of strategical actions in relation to the educational level of instructor (see Table 9.3). All three groups used relatively greater numbers of strategical actions across the different task periods. The literate and teacher groups had their greatest increase from the first to the second

Instructor's educational level	Strategical level					
	Nonstrategical			Strategical		
	n	%	λ	n	%	λ
Nonliterate	142	70	0.77**	60	30	-0.77**
Literate	98	48	0.18*	105	52	-0.18*
Teacher	27	14	-0.95**	172	86	0.95**

$L^2 = 170.31$; $df = 2$; $p < .0001$ *$\alpha < .05$ **$\alpha < .01$

Table 9.1. Frequency of nonstrategical and strategical actions by instructor's educational level.

Task period	Strategical level					
	Nonstrategical			Strategical		
	n	%	λ	n	%	λ
First period	129	58	0.55*	92	42	-0.55*
Second period	82	41	0	116	59	0
Third period	56	30	-0.54*	129	70	0.54*

$L^2 = 53.14$; $df = 2$; $p <. 0001$ *$\alpha <. 01$

Table 9.2. Frequency of nonstrategical and strategical actions for three task periods for all instructors.

Instructor's educational level	Task period					
	First		Second		Third	
	%	λ	%	λ	%	λ
Nonliterate	14	0.01	26	-0.06	52	0.20*
Literate	37	-0.21*	59	0.13	60	0.28
Teacher	82	0.07	92	-0.21	100	0.33*

$L^2 = 13.51$; $df = 4$; $p < .0001$ $*\alpha < .05$

Table 9.3. Percentage of strategical actions used for each task period.

period. This shows that these two groups learned to use strategical actions to solve the task, arriving at the 'top' of their performance, while the non-literate group continued to learn to use strategical actions across all three periods.

The teacher-instructor group showed greater effectiveness in placing cards compared to the other two groups, and they did not place any cards incorrectly (see Table 9.4).

This result about effectiveness is more interesting when considered together with the results on strategic placing. Together they provide an impression about the general pattern of action exhibited by the different pairs. The lower effectiveness of the nonliterate-instructor group coincided with a higher percentage of nonstrategical actions during the performance of the task (see Tables 9.1 and 9.4). For the teacher-instructor group, the situation was the reverse: greater use of strategical placing actions was accompanied by a greater effectiveness in story constructing. In short, the teacher-instructor pairs carried out more strategical and effective actions, while the other two experimental groups were less strategical and less effective.

	Effectiveness								
	Correct			Partially correct			Incorrect		
Instructor's educational level	n	%	λ	n	%	λ	n	%	λ
Nonliterate	118	58	-0.30*	68	34	-0.1	16	8	0.4
Literate	129	64	-0.10	66	33	0	8	4	0.1
Teacher	145	73	0.38*	54	27	0.11	0	0	-0.4

$L^2 = 29.01$; $df = 4$; $p < .0001$ *$\alpha < .05$

Table 9.4. Frequency of effective placing of cards by the instructor's educational level.

Instructional Actions and Type of Regulation

A crucial aspect that might explain the differences in placing actions is the type of instructional action used throughout the story-constructing tasks. An analysis of types of instructional actions showed that as the educational level of the instructors increased they used less directive guidance in their participation, leaving more room for the initiative and responsibility of the learners (see Table 9.5). The nonliterate-instructor group preferred to use instructional actions that involved either a direct indication of the card to be placed or where it was to be placed (53%), or an explicit physical demonstration (43%). Only 3% of their instructional actions involved a more indirect form of guidance. The literate-instructor group showed a different tendency. Most of their instructional behaviour consisted of signalling, with gestures or words, the card to be placed or where to place it (76%). Compared to the nonliterate-instructors, they used less explicit demonstration and more non-directive instruction. Finally, the performance of the teacher-instructors group was notably different from the other two groups. Their instructional actions involved giving support and clues to help the learner perform the task, while those that involved the greatest possible level of directivity, physical demonstration, were almost absent.

	Instructional action								
	Guide			Indication			Demonstration		
Instructor's educational level	*n*	*%*	λ	*n*	*%*	λ	*n*	*%*	λ
Nonliterate	4	3	-1.09**	65	53	0	53	43	1.09**
Literate	12	11	-0.34	86	76	0.33*	15	13	0.01
Teacher	42	53	1.43**	37	46	-0.3	1	1	-1.10**

$L^2 = 122.35$; $df = 4$; $p < .0001$ $*\alpha < .05$ $**\alpha < .01$

Table 9.5. Frequency of instructional action type by instructor's educational level.

These findings show that the story constructors in the nonliterate-instructor group had a lower level of participation and autonomy in the development of the task, primarily because the instructors placed the cards, or at least indicated where they should be placed.

These results gain even more interest when they are considered together with the results about the regulation of placing actions (see Table 9.6). The instructors in the nonliterate-instructor group regulated the actions more frequently than the other two groups. This might seem slightly strange, if one expects that professional teachers are more likely to regulate student actions because it corresponds to their normal practice. However, when considering the type of instruction variable (see Table 9.5), we see that the nonliterate instructors used a very direct form of control, leaving little initiative to the learner. It was almost a case of the nonliterate instructors performing the task themselves. Thus, this greater control on the part of the nonliterate instructor corresponded to the development of a greater number of less complex and more directive instructional actions: most of their actions corresponded to physical indications and demonstrations and with little suggestive guidance (see Table 9.5).

In contrast, the literate-instructor group left an increasingly wider responsibility for the learners, although this was still not all that accentuated.

	Regulation of actions								
	Learner			Joint			Instructor		
Instructor's educational level	n	%	λ	n	%	λ	n	%	λ
Nonliterate	74	31	-0.25**	104	43	-0.11	62	26	0.36**
Literate	105	37	0.05	142	50	0.11*	36	13	-0.16
Teacher	142	43	0.20**	145	44	-0.01	44	13	-0.19*

$L^2 = 23.13$; $df = 4$; $p < .0001$ $*\alpha < .05$ $**\alpha < .01$

Table 9.6. Frequency of different types of action regulation by instructor's educational level.

Finally, the least amount of regulation on the part of the instructor in the teacher-instructor group (13%) corresponded to a greater percentage of non-directive instructional actions (53%). I believe this result reflects the fact that greater experience in school contexts provides the instructors with more resources that they can use to regulate the learner's actions, and more experience about when to use these regulations.

These results about the regulation of actions, together with the results about strategic and effective placing, show that the actions of the story constructors in the teacher-instructor group improve over the course of the task. That is, these pairs placed more cards correctly, in a strategic way, with fewer placing actions.

These findings support a hypothesis that different types of instructional actions can have important consequences for the subsequent internalisation of the skills necessary to construct the stories. They are also consistent with the findings obtained by studies that have investigated the relationship between instruction and experience in school contexts (Rogoff 1990; Wertsch et al. 1984). These studies show how the type of instructional action changes in relation to the level of competence of the instructor. Instruction by a more expert member of a cultural practice (e.g., a teacher in activities of formal schooling) constitutes a basic condition for this internalisation.

Instructor's educational level	Referential perspective								
	Deictic and extralinguistic indexes			Common			Informing about context		
	n	%	λ	*n*	%	λ	*n*	%	λ
Nonliterate	211	71	0.55**	86	29	0.1	0	0	-0.60*
Literate	262	61	0	153	36	0	13	3	0.03
Teacher	327	44	-0.55**	357	49	0	54	7	0.56**

$L^2 = 91.41$; $df = 4$; $p < .0001$ *$\alpha < .05$ **$\alpha < .01$

Table 9.7. Frequency of referential perspectives used by instructor's educational level.

Semiotic Mediation of Instructional Actions: The Role of Referential Perspective

Some researchers, such as Rommetveit (1979), claim that speech imposes a certain perspective on the situations to which it refers. Therefore, the use of different referential expressions imposes a perspective on the situation. In this experiment, referential expressions are used to inform about the context (see Figure 9.1), which means that the different cards are not to be considered as independent, unrelated elements. Rather they are units related to each other by a common, overall meaningful objective (i.e., constructing of the story), which may have permitted a more strategical structuring of the action.

What types of actions did the different pairs use? The answer to this question is crucial in my research because it involves the analysis of the semiotic procedures used in the mediation of instructional actions. The analyses presented here include: the level on which the utterances were produced, the type of utterance, who produced it and the referential perspective expressed in the utterance.

There were clear differences in the type of procedure used by the three experimental groups to refer to the objects present in the task (see Table 9.7). The teacher-instructor group used the most complex referential perspective compared with the other two groups. For example, teacher-instructors used the more complex referential expressions (common and informative about context) 56% of the time, compared to 29% for the nonliterate instructors. Conversely, the nonliterate-instructor and literate-instructor groups used deictic and extralinguistic indexes more frequently than the teacher-instructor group.

I hypothesise that the greater experience of the teachers in formal educational activities led them to use more informative referential expressions. This allowed them to characterise the elements involved in the task, emphasising mainly the aspects related to the narrative structure that orders and integrates the cards, rather than the content of the cards. In other words, the use of this type of referential expression allowed them to define the situation as a story-constructing task and not merely as a placing of a series of cards, thus making the referential expression a resource for facilitating change in the learner's situation definition.

The analysis of microgenetic development showed a decrease in the use of deictic and extralinguistic indexes from one task to another ($L^2 = 14.29$, $df = 2$, $p < .001$). They constituted 60% of total referential expressions during the first task descending to 47% in the second.

It seems, therefore, that as the instructors and learners became accustomed to the task situation, and what it consisted of, they began to replace deictic and and extralinguistic indexes with referential expressions that were more detached from the immediate context. This shift in expression use constituted a greater challenge for the participants to reach agreements about the situation definition.

Let us now consider the role of referential perspective as a mechanism for mediating actions. Table 9.8 shows the results of the analyses about the use of referential perspective in relation to the strategical level of the actions of placing. Taken as a whole, the total number of nonstrategical actions occurred less frequently compared to the strategical ones when referential expressions were used (37% vs. 63%). For the nonstrategical actions, most of the referential expressions were deictic and extralinguistic indexes. This shows that the differences were found in the semiotic mediation of the actions (strategical or nonstrategical), and not in the actions themselves. It seems that for nonstrategical actions, when the speakers referred to the elements necessary for the story-constructing, they categorised them minimal-

Strategical level	Referential perspective								
	Deictic and extra-linguistic indexes			Common			Informing about context		
	n	%	λ	n	%	λ	n	%	λ
Nonstrategical	247	78	0.12	66	21	0.01	3	1	0.13
Strategical	264	49	-0.13	260	48	-0.12	20	4	-0.01

$L^2 = 40.18$; $df = 2$; $p < .0001$

Table 9.8. Frequency of nonstrategical and strategical actions for different referential perspectives for all three instructor levels.

ly; that is, they hardly introduced any new information about the situation definition (Wertsch 1989).

Instructional Actions and Referential Perspective: Some Conclusions

Theoretically, formal education is viewed as a set of sociocultural practices and activities that do not belong strictly to a psychological level of analysis (Wertsch 1985). One of the most important problems for the study of the instructional process is the separation from sociocultural activities within which this process gains meaning. Together with this institutional level of analysis, I have adopted a unit of analysis that is strictly psycholog-ical, namely, semiotically-mediated action. Instruction has been considered in terms of semiotically-mediated actions. With these two levels of analysis, I have attempted to open a path for integrating semiotic aspects as instru-ments for mediating the instructional actions that are generated within the framework of sociocultural activities (especially formal education) and that are privileged by them.

From this standpoint, instructional actions are not limited to the individ-ual plane, they move on both interpsychological and intrapsychological planes. The transition from an interpsychological to an intrapsychological plane is tied to the participants' establishing a shared situation definition. In a situation where there is an asymmetry in the participants' competence, such as in this experiment, it is likely that the instructor's situation definition, as the most expert member of the pair, will be different from the learner's situation definition. This difference presents opportunities for trying to reach agreements about the situation definition. Changes to the situation definition would be linked to transfers of action in the zone of proximal development (Wertsch 1984).

The experimental results presented in this chapter provide support for the idea that instructor-learner interaction should be analysed in depth in order to discover the processes that relate the activities of formal education and instructional actions, as well as their influence on learner development. The most advanced way to instruct in this experiment was characterised by a progressive decrease of the instructor's control and regulation of how the learner constructed and subsequently narrated the stories. This may not constitute the 'best' form of instruction, but it represents modes of instruction that are characteristic of the activities of formal education (Wertsch 1991). The fact that they are often considered, either implicitly or explicitly, better than others should not lead one to deny their cultural specificity. On the contrary, it highlights the importance attributed to these activities in our culture.

In this experiment, the use of different referential procedures was essential for changing the participants' situation definition. From this perspective, it is possible to consider questions about the role of referential perspective in instructional action. The analysis of referential perspective also examined microgenetic changes in both tasks and in different periods of each task. This analysis showed an increased use of referential expressions over the course of the task, and an increased use in the complexity of the referential expressions. These referential expressions lead to the introduction of new information which provides a clearer view of the speaker's situation definition. This new information implies an important change in the hearer's task-situation representation. This development is consistent with the theoretical and methodological analyses about the relation between the instructor's educational level and learning described in studies on adult-child interactions by James Wertsch (Wertsch 1979, 1989; Wertsch & Hickman 1987; Wertsch et al. 1984).

From a theoretical point of view it is important to highlight the effect of different types of instructional actions for the learner's subsequent internalisation (appropriation) of the skills necessary for solving the task, and especially for acquiring greater responsibility and control in the task (Rogoff 1990). In Rogoff's terms, guided participation in activities of formal schooling may constitute a basic condition for this internalisation.

The experiment reported here provides evidence for some semiotic mechanisms through which this interaction might facilitate the transfer of responsibility from the instructor to the learner in the control of the actions necessary for solving the task. In concluding, I would like to discuss two points that are relevant to this issue. First, one of the most interesting results was the different kinds of instructional actions employed by instructors from different educational levels. Second, the role that semiotic mediational tools, such as referential perspective, played in the development of instructional actions is an important mechanism for moving interpsychological actions to the intrapsychological plane.

The teacher-instructor group used more indirect instructional actions than the nonliterate-instructor and literate-instructor groups, which I attribute to the greater level of schoolteaching experience among the teachers in the teacher-instructor group. At the same time, the teacher-instructor group also had a greater effectiveness in task solving. This greater effectiveness was also associated with a progressive increase in responsibility assumed by learners in the performance of the task.

These instructional actions (particularly indirect guidance) were characterised by the use of referential procedures with strong narrative elements: aspects such as sequentiality, the existence of a series of characters, actions, and instruments. The teacher-instructor group used a greater number of these referential procedures (informative and common references) than literate-instructor group and the nonliterate-instructor group.

Concerning referential perspective, as I stated before, this semiotic mechanism is considered crucial for explaining the transition from the interpsychological plane of development to the intrapsychological plane. At the same time, referential perspective offers a path for analysing the relationship between activities and actions, insofar as referential perspective is tied to the sociocultural activities in which it arises and where its use is privileged (Wertsch 1991). This path is similar to the referential perspective and works as an instrument for mediating actions.

In the study reported here, important results were obtained about the relationship between referential perspective and the genetic variables, which helps formulate the role that referential perspective might play in the mediation of the different actions in constructing stories. For example, we saw occasions in which the teacher-instructors used deictic and extralinguistic indexes in their utterances as a resource to help establish a minimum level of agreement over the object being referred to. This agreement allowed the establishment of a minimum level of intersubjectivity between the participants in the interaction, thereby assuring communication between them. To illustrate this point, consider the following transcript of an interaction episode between a teacher-instructor and a nonliterate learner jointly constructing a story.

Instructor: *What does he have here?* (pointing at the card).
Learner: *A gun ... Isn't it?* (looking for teacher approbation).
Instructor: (while learner has the card in her hands) *A gun. This looks like a gun. Here you have this, another one ...* (pointing).
Learner: *Oh, yes. Look, here I can see the policeman* (pointing).
Instructor: *Come on! What happens now?*
Learner: *Then ...* (she hesitates) *then the police catch this man* (pointing to the card that she had placed before).
Learner: *... and here, here he is in the jail.*

This episode illustrates some important aspects about the degree of intersubjectivity achieved during the joint construction of a story, and about the importance of the instructor and learner using different referential perspectives during joint activity.

In this episode, the instructor, a more experienced member of the culture, tries to 'lure' the learner toward a more appropriate situation definition for carrying out the task. In an attempt to create a shared situation definition, the instructor adjusted her utterances and expressions so that the learner could interpret them. These adjustments involved the use of semiotic tools, especially referential perspective. Five different referring expressions were used: *here, gun, this,* pointing to a card, and *what happens now?* By using these different referential perspectives she tries to get the learner to assume increasing responsibility in the task. Only at the end does she use an informative referential perspective ('what happens now?') to retest the learner's situation definition to determine whether she was capable of redefining the objects (cards) in the communicative setting in an appropriate way. This referential perspective implies a more explicit, clearer situation definition of the instructor, which helps modify the learner's situation definition (Wertsch 1989).

However, by using referential perspectives that imply a lower 'semiotic challenge' for the learner to understand a more appropriate situation definition (common referring expressions or deictic and extralinguistic indexes: here, this, pointing or gun), the instructor tries to see if the learner can get a new autoregulation level in the solving task (Wertsch 1985).

Given the potential importance of referential procedures, it is necessary to develop a more complete microgenetic analysis of the instructional process. One worthy starting point would be the further examination of referential procedures, because of their apparent importance in changing a learner's situation definition. A second place would be to separate the contribution of the instructor from that of the learner in the use of referential procedures, as well as the learner's contribution to the instructional process or the influence of the nature of the task. In my view, this kind of research can contribute to understanding how instructional interactions take place and, in particular, which semiotic mechanisms are involved in these interactions.

References

Bakhtin, M.M. (1986). *Speech genres and other late essays* (C. Emerson & M. Holquist, eds.; V.W. McGee, trans.). Austin, Tex.: University of Texas Press. (Original work published 1979)

de la Mata, M.L. (1993). Mediación semiótica y acciones de memoria: Un estudio sobre la interacción profesor-alumno en educación formal de adultos. Unpublished doctoral dissertation, University of Seville, Spain.

Elbers, E. (1987). Interaction and instruction in the conservation experiment. *European Journal of Psychology of Education*, 1, 77-89.

Elbers, E., Maier, R., Hoekstra, T., & Hoogsteder, M. (1992). Internalization and adult-child interaction. *Learning and Instruction*, 2, 101-18.

González, M.M. (1996). Tasks and activities: A parent-child interaction analysis. *Learning and Instruction*, 6, 287-306.

González, M.M., & Palacios, J. (1990). La zona de desarrollo próximo como tarea de construcción. *Infancia y Aprendizaje*, 51-52, 99-122.

Kennedy, J.J. (1983). *Analyzing qualitative data: Introductory log-linear analysis for behavioral research*. New York: Praeger.

Laboratorio de Actividad Humana (1988). *Educación y procesos cognitivos: Una aproximación sociocultural* (Monografía No. 5 de Educación de Adultos). Sevilla: Junta de Andalucía

Laboratorio de Actividad Humana (1993). *La educación de adultos y el cambio de va-*

lores, actitudes y modos de pensamiento de la mujer: Un estudio etnográfico del discurso (Memoria de Investigación). Sevilla: Universidad de Sevilla, Departmento Psicología Experimental.

Laboratory of Comparative Human Cognition (1983). Culture and cognitive development. In P.H. Mussen (series ed.) & W. Kessen (vol. ed.), *Handbook of child psychology: Vol. 1. History, theory and methods* (4th ed.). New York: Wiley, 295-356.

Lawrence, J.A., & Valsiner, J. (1993). Conceptual roots of internalization: From transmission to transformation. *Human Development, 36,* 150-67.

Leontiev, A.N. (1981). The problem of activity in psychology. In J.V. Wertsch (ed. and trans.), *The concept of activity in soviet psychology.* Armonk, N.Y.: Sharpe, 37-71.

McLane, B. (1987). Interaction, context and the zone of proximal development. In M. Hickman (ed.), *Social and functional approaches to language and thought.* Orlando, Fla.: Academic Press, 267-85.

McNamee, G.D. (1987). The social origins of narrative skills. In M. Hickman (ed.), *Social and functional approaches to language and thought.* Orlando, Fla.: Academic Press, 287-303.

Newman, D., Griffin, P., & Cole, M. (1989). *The construction zone: Working for cognitive change in school.* Cambridge: Cambridge University Press.

Ramírez, J.D. (1995). *Usos de la palabra y sus tecnologías. Una aproximación dialógica al estudio de la alfabetización.* Buenos Aires: Miño y Dávila.

Ramírez, J.D., Cubero, M., & Santamaría, A. (1990). Cambio sociocognitivo y organización de las acciones: Una perspectiva sociocultural para el estudio de la educación de adultos. *Infancia y Aprendizaje, 51-52,* 169-90.

Ramírez, J.D., Sánchez, J.A., & Santamaría, A. (1996). Making literacy: A dialogical perspective on discourse in adult education. In J. Valsiner & H.G. Voss (eds.), *The structure of learning processes.* Norwood, N.J.: Ablex, 229-45.

Rogoff, B. (1982). Integrating context and cognitive development. In M.E. Lamb & A.L. Brown (eds.), *Advances in developmental psychology* (vol. 2). Hillsdale, N.J.: Erlbaum, 125-70.

Rogoff, B. (1990). *Apprenticeship in thinking: Cognitive development in social context.* New York: Oxford University Press.

Rogoff, B. (1993). Children's guided participation and participatory appropriation in sociocultural activity. In R.H. Wozniak & K.W. Fisher (eds.), *Development in context.* Hillsdale, N.J.: Erlbaum, 121-53.

Rommetveit, R. (1979). On the architecture of intersubjectivity. In R. Rommetveit & R.M. Blakar (eds.), *Studies of language, thought and verbal communication.* London: Academic Press, 93-107.

Sánchez, J.A. (1995). Habla egocéntrica y acción mediada. Un análisis conceptual y metodológico. Unpublished doctoral dissertation, University of Seville, Spain.

Santamaría, A. (1997). Mediación semiótica, acciones instruccionales e interiorización: Un estudio de interacciones en educación de personas adultas. Unpublished doctoral dissertation, University of Seville, Spain.

Valsiner, J. (1991). Building theoretical bridges over a lagoon of everyday events: A review of *Apprenticeship in thinking: Cognitive development in social context* by Barbara Rogoff, *Human Development*, 34, 307-15.

Vygotsky, L.S. (1978). *Mind in society: The development of higher psychological processes* (M. Cole, V. John-Steiner, S. Scribner, & E. Souberman, eds.; M. Cole & M. Lopez-Morillas, trans.). Cambridge, Mass.: Harvard University Press.

Vygotsky, L.S. (1981). The genesis of higher mental functions. In J.V. Wertsch (ed. and trans.), *The concept of activity in Soviet psychology*. Armonk, N.Y.: Sharpe, 144-88.

Wertsch, J.V. (1979). From social interaction to higher psychological processes: A clarification and application of Vygotsky's theory. *Human Development*, 22, 1-22.

Wertsch, J.V. (1984). The zone of proximal development: Some conceptual issues. In B. Rogoff & J.V. Wertsch (eds.), *Children's learning in the zone of proximal development*. San Francisco: Jossey-Bass, 7-17.

Wertsch, J.V. (1985). *Vygotsky and the social formation of mind*. Cambridge, Mass.: Harvard University Press.

Wertsch, J.V. (1989). Semiotic mechanisms in joint cognitive activity. *Infancia y Aprendizaje*, 47, 3-36.

Wertsch, J.V. (1991). *Voices of the mind: A sociocultural approach to mediated action*. Cambridge, Mass.: Harvard University Press.

Wertsch, J.V., & Hickman, M. (1987). Problem solving in social interaction: A microgenetic analysis. In M. Hickman (ed.), *Social and functional approaches to language and thought*. Orlando, Fla.: Academic Press, 251-66.

Wertsch, J.V., Minick, N., & Arns, F.J. (1984). The creation of context in joint problem solving. In B. Rogoff & J. Lave (eds.), *Everyday cognition: Its development in social context*. Cambridge, Mass.: Harvard University Press, 151-72.

Wertsch, J.V., & Rogoff, B. (eds.) (1984). *Children's learning in the zone of proximal development*. San Francisco: Jossey-Bass.

Wertsch, J.V., & Stone, C.A. (1978). Microgenesis as a tool for developmental analysis. *Quarterly Newsletter of the Laboratory of Comparative Cognition*, 1, 8-9.

Zinchenko, V.P. (1985). Vygotsky's ideas about units for the analysis of mind. In J.V. Wertsch (ed.), *Culture, communication and cognition: Vygotskian perspectives*. Cambridge: Cambridge University Press, 94-118.

10 Intersubjectivity in Models of Learning and Teaching: Reflections from a Study of Teaching and Learning in a Mexican Mazahua Community

Mariëtte de Haan

Introduction

It is commonly believed that cultures and communities differ in how they socialise and teach their youngsters. These beliefs can be justified with many research findings on cultural differences mainly from anthropology (e.g., Paradise 1996; Stairs 1991), sociolinguistics (e.g., Ochs & Schieffelin 1984) as well as developmental psychology (e.g., Hwang, Lamb, & Sigel 1996). In this chapter it is shown how these cultural differences have consequences for theorising on learning and instruction. In particular the focus will be on the concept of intersubjectivity and how this concept is applied in models of learning and instruction. It will be argued that intersubjectivity is not a culturally neutral concept that can be used in theorising without considering the particular ways in which intersubjectivity is established in specific social practices. In other words, attention is drawn to the communicative presumptions that are relevant for establishing meaning and knowledge and the consequences for thinking about learning and instruction.

First, it will be shown how the concept of intersubjectivity is used in studies on learning and instruction in sociocultural theory. It will become clear that intersubjectivity is an important underlying notion in descriptions of interactional learning situations. Then, it will be argued that these studies, particularly one group of studies, hold specific assumptions about the nature of intersubjectivity. Through presenting data about interactions in a learning situation in a Mexican Mazahua community I hope to demonstrate that these assumptions do not apply to all learning practices, and point out that other assumptions can be formulated from a different set of practices than those on which most sociocultural studies rely. Finally, implications of these findings for the use of intersubjectivity in theories of learning and instruction will be discussed.

How is Intersubjectivity Used in Sociocultural Studies of Learning and Instruction?

Different Usages of the Concept of Intersubjectivity

The concept of *intersubjectivity* points to the idea that different inter-locutors may have different representations of the same object, activity or event and in order to (start to) communicate they should be able to find a way to share perspectives or coordinate their actions. Before the concept of intersubjectivity entered sociocultural thinking, via such researchers as Rommetveit (1985) and Trevarthen (1986), the term was used in philosophy of language (see e.g., Bruner 1996, 175; Rommetveit 1985, 184-193), mainly to argue against traditional, objectivistic linguistic viewpoints and to advance perspectives in which language is seen as inextricably linked to the social situations in which it is used.

The concept of intersubjectivity has been used in the sociocultural tradition in a number of different ways. Wertsch (1985) adopted the concept to point to the semiotic aspects of adult-child interaction in instructive contexts, and to explain how adults and children reach a common understanding or a common situation definition in adult-child interaction in the zone of proximal development. He argued that children often do not understand the definition of objects or the significance of behaviours that are assumed by the adult. Building upon the work of Rommetveit (1974, 1985), he introduced the idea of levels of intersubjectivity and claimed that through an adult-child dialogue increasing levels of intersubjectivity can be created through which the adult and the child are able to transcend their private worlds. In Wertsch's view, the challenge is for the adult to find a way to communicate with the child so that the child is able to participate and can eventually come to define the task setting in a new, culturally appropriate way. Through concrete examples in which adults and children are involved in a construction task Wertsch shows how the child gradually takes over responsibility for carrying out the task and how this transformation is equivalent to a semiotic change in the communication of the dyad. By describing these different steps or levels, Wertsch shows how the child is finally capable of mastering the situation definition with which the adult originally approached the task. In this last stage there is almost complete intersubjectivity between the child and the adult (though Wertsch does not claim that their situation definitions are fused). Wertsch's analysis uses the concept of intersubjectivity to under-pin, in semiotic terms, the outcomes of studies on how children learn from social interactions and how this helps them build their interpsychological functions.

Another slightly different domain in sociocultural studies in which the concept of intersubjectivity is applied is the study of the origin and develop-ment of adult-child communication (e.g., Bruner 1996; Rogoff 1990; Scaife & Bruner 1975). The problem addressed here is how we understand the men-tal life of others and how this capacity originates, develops and matures (Bruner 1996, 174). This research originated in efforts to explain the extraor-dinary synchrony in nonverbal and verbal communication patterns between infants and caregivers (Trevarthen 1986). Questions about the extent to which intersubjectivity is given at birth or constructed at later ages, and how it develops during childhood are the main problems in this field of study. Rogoff (1990), for instance, describes changes in the asymmetric relationship between adults and children in processes of the development of intersubjec-tivity (pp. 78-85).

Furthermore, the concept of intersubjectivity is used in sociocultural the-ory by researchers such as Rogoff (1990), Bruner (1996), Matusov (1996) and Wertsch (1998) to reflect critically on the concepts of learning and teaching that have been developed from a communication perspective. Rogoff, for instance, claims that the prototype of intersubjectivity in the literature is a symmetrical dialogue. She states that there are other arrangements of inter-subjectivity to consider, which vary in the degree of responsibility given to each participant according to the social partners of the child and the cultural variation in models of child rearing (pp. 204-10). Bruner states that our West-ern pedagogical tradition hardly does justice to the importance of intersub-jectivity, defined here as the human ability to understand the minds of others. Teaching is too often depicted as the actions of 'a single, presumably omni-scient teacher who explicitly tells or shows unknowing learners something they presumably know nothing about' (p. 20). According to Bruner, an inter-subjective pedagogy should depict learning as an interactive process in which people learn from each other, thus recognising the mutuality which is implied in the concept of intersubjectivity. Matusov criticises the concept of intersubjectivity itself (how it is defined and used in sociocultural studies and elsewhere) and shows what consequences these definitions and uses have for research on learning and communication. He criticises a definition of intersubjectivity in which intersubjectivity is defined as 'having in common' or 'overlapping subjectivities' and pleas for a concept of intersubjectivity in which it is seen as a process of coordination of individual participations in joint activities. In particular he shows how disagreement, instead of agreement alone, can be part of this process of reaching common understandings and coordination of activities. He advances a concept of intersubjectivity that acknowledges different ways to create mutual understanding. Wertsch considers intersubjectivity and Bakhtin's notion of 'alterity' as two opposing processes that characterise social interaction. He states that both processes of creating shared meanings and processes of conflict and 'multivoicedness' play an important part in development.

In sum, the concept of intersubjectivity has been used in the sociocultural tradition to underpin, develop and criticise pedagogical models from a semiotic perspective (i.e., from the perspective of how children and adults create joint meaning in their interactions). These semiotic processes are considered to be essential for understanding learning and instruction and viewed as highly interwoven with them. Especially from the last mentioned set of studies it has become clear that the concept of intersubjectivity has important consequences for how pedagogical models are viewed and described. In the next section this idea is elaborated further, mainly through pointing out the characteristics of the intersubjectivity model held in most interactional studies inspired by the Vygotskian concept of zone of proximal development.[1]

Assumptions About Intersubjectivity in Sociocultural Studies on Learning

The Vygotskian concept of zone of proximal development (ZPD) inspired a research agenda that focused on the interactional mechanisms through which a child under the guidance of an adult appropriates new skills. A general interest in these studies is how shifts of responsibilities take

---

1. Of course these characteristics do not necessarily match with what actually happens in those interactional situations. Hoogsteder (1995), for instance, showed that certain aspects of learning — particularly the child's own reconstruction of the context in which the interaction takes place — are systematically disregarded in sociocultural studies in which the concept of the zone of proximal development is elaborated.

place from the adult to the child in performing activities. The attention for shifts in responsibilities stems from an interest in how social interactions become internalised or become a part of the child's psychological organisation. In some of these studies the focus is more on how adults succeed in establishing a common ground for communication and reach a shared world (Wertsch 1978; Wertsch, McNamee, McLane, & Budwig 1980). In other studies, the focus is on how levels of instruction can be established so that the right balance between intervening and withdrawing is reached, also referred to as the contingency rule or the scaffolding principle (Wood, Bruner, & Ross 1976; Wood & Middleton 1975). A common point in these studies is a focus on the interactional mechanisms with which the adult succeeds in transferring knowledge, skills and responsibilities to the child. These studies have functioned in sociocultural research as the main metaphor or the prototype of a learning situation.[2]

If we now look at the communicative aspects of these prototypical teaching-learning situations, several aspects can be mentioned that are related to a conception of intersubjectivity. Here I distinguish three different dimensions of intersubjectivity: context creation, identity of the interlocutors, and semiotic devices used to reach intersubjectivity. These dimensions are used to describe the typical character of these prototypical models of learning and instruction and will be used later in the discussion section to describe other models that differ from the prototypical models.

Context creation refers to the method by and extent to which interlocutors assume communality, and how a balance is created between assuming communality as given and as something that needs to be established. In ZPD-related studies, and particularly those in which the notion of creating a common situation definition is a central metaphor, the focus is on the individual interpretations of the interlocutors and on the explicit efforts needed to reach higher levels of communality or intersubjectivity. Wertsch (1985), for instance, indicates that he borrows his intersubjectivity concept from Rommetveit (e.g., 1985) according to which communication aims at transcending private worlds. Rommetveit stresses that we can only transcend private worlds up to a certain level and that we constantly need to agree upon what we consider common background knowledge, called a 'draft of a contract'

---

2. These studies have also received serious critiques (e.g., Brown & Palincsar 1982; Rogoff 1990; Tharp & Gallimore 1988), which have cast doubts on some of the fundamental characteristics of these prototypes, and pointed to alternative models of learning.

upon which the communication can be based. Through this view, attention becomes drawn to the subsequent and accumulating communicative efforts of a particular speech context rather than on previously shared perspectives and common knowledge resulting from, for instance, having been involved in similar situations or contexts or through sharing basic social meanings. In the examples Wertsch (1985) uses to illustrate his intersubjectivity concept (pp. 162-66) he stresses the differences between the adult and child in perceiving the goal of the task and the procedure (to be) followed to overcome those differences. He describes the communication between adults and children as initially 'extremely difficult' (p. 162) as a consequence of their different situation definitions. In sum, the emphasis is on the immediate context and the ability to negotiate or transfer meanings by explicit communicative efforts.

Identity of the interlocutors refers to the kind of roles or identities that are assumed or created for the child compared to the adult. In ZPD-related studies an asymmetrical responsibility is assumed between the child and the adult. The adult has the main responsibility to convince the child to adopt the situation definition of the adult and to make sure that the instruction level is adapted to the child's needs and capacities as a learner. Also, in these studies the child is given the role of the main performer of the activity whereas the adult takes on the role of supervisor (the so-called 'child as a performer' principle, see Wertsch, Minick, & Arns 1984). However, the adult is in control of the child's performance and observes and registers the child's behaviour in order to adjust his pedagogical strategy if necessary. Wertsch (1998, 122) also points to the asymmetric relationship between teachers and pupils and their differential responsibilities in instructional discourse in general: teachers have the responsibility to ask instructional questions and pupils to answer them, but not vice versa. He links this with a particular organisation of power and authority, which is reflected in the fact that pupils are not allowed to fulfil 'significant and serious epistemic roles' (p. 122). In sum, in the intersubjectivity concept that lies behind ZPD-related studies and most school-oriented pedagogical situations, adults take the overall responsibility for establishing intersubjectivity (which in a certain sense is mutually disregarded) whereas at the same time they require that the child actually performs or takes the necessary steps to 'give proof' of intersubjectivity.

Semiotic devices used to reach intersubjectivity refers to the kind of communicative structures and means that are created to organise coordination and

common understanding. In most ZPD-related studies, communality or trans-
ference of perspectives is described as being reached through a process of
successive turn-taking. It is assumed that the main means by which intersubjectivity is reached is the shifting of verbal exchanges between the adult and
the child. Mostly, the activity or task is divided into subunits that are supposed to be connected in a linear way to establishing intersubjectivity. That
is, they are seen as additive, molar units that, taken together, will finally
result in communality. For instance, Wertsch (1985, 163) writes about subsequent steps that need to be taken and, to some degree, that need to be specified by the adult (depending on how well the child is doing). From the
responsibilities described above, it is clear that all interlocutors (are expected
to) focus on the same aspect or step to be taken. This means that only one
strategy to reach intersubjectivity (based on verbal exchanges) is followed at
a time and that all interlocutors are expected to be involved in it.

The just-described assumptions about intersubjectivity only reflect the
(presupposed) underlying communicative patterns of typical, school-oriented Western teaching-learning situations. Other assumptions, associated
with other cultural traditions and other communicative patterns, can be
reflected in other teaching-learning situations.

The perspective that communication patterns between adults and children differ for particular cultures and communities and that these differences
have consequences for children's learning is not new. Paradise (1996, 1998),
for instance, has shown how Mazahua children are socialised in a non-inter-
ventionist communicative role pattern in which participants follow their
own course of action relatively autonomously and which influences children's learning patterns. Other empirical studies have also argued that different communicative arrangements exist for children across the world and
that these arrangements have consequences for pedagogical practices (e.g.,
Ochs 1988; Ochs & Schieffelin 1984; Philips 1983; Rogoff 1990; Rogoff, Mistry, Göncü, & Mosier 1993; Scollon & Scollon 1981). However, the consequences of these studies for conceptualisations of learning and instruction are
only taken up by sociocultural researchers to a limited degree (see de Haan
1999, 6-12, for a more extensive argument on this point). In this chapter the
implications of these differences in communicative arrangements for theorising about learning and instruction is shown through a detailed comparison
between the assumptions on intersubjectivity in prototypical pedagogical
models in socio-cultural theory and those that lay behind teaching-learning
situations in a Mexican Mazahua group.

A Study of Learning Practices in a Mexican Mazahua Community

In this section the results of a study of Mexican Mazahua teaching-learning practices are presented and contrasted to those of Mexican Mestizo teachers and their pupils.[3] The central aim of this study was to find out how Mexican Mazahua teaching and learning practices match with or differ from the prototypical models of teaching and learning found in sociocultural theory, thereby permitting an evaluation of the universal or culture-specific character of the prototypical models. To realise this goal, extensive fieldwork was set up in a traditional Mexican Mazahua village (two periods of four months) to study community life in general and in particular the question of how children became (or were expected to become) familiar with new tasks and responsibilities. In the second fieldwork period a research setting was designed in which both Mazahua parents from the community and teachers from the local school were invited to teach a child both a construction task and a math task. The teacher-pupil pairs were used to make a comparison between Mazahua teaching-learning patterns and patterns that were expected to correspond with Western, school-oriented practices.

Participants

All participants lived or worked in the Mazahua village where the study was conducted. The village clearly is traditionally Mazahua as recognised by, for instance, traditional clothing, maintenance of traditional maize growing practices, use of the Mazahua language and traditional religious celebrations. However, the villagers are also familiar with and oriented towards more 'external' or 'foreign' practices as indicated by links with the money economy in their commercial activities, migration labour, fluency in Spanish, and handling of complex machinery such as cars, tractors and electronic maize mills.

Thirty Mazahua children were selected from among the children who attended the second, third or fourth grade in the local primary school in the village. To be selected, the child's parent had to be involved in some commercial activity (to guarantee their knowledge of math). A selected child was

3. The experimental study presented here comes from a larger study in which interview data and ethnographic data are also presented (de Haan 1999). Only those analyses of the experimental study that are most relevant for the argument being made here are presented.

then formed into a pair with his or her parent.[4,5] Fifteen teachers (13 from the same local school and 2 who lived in the village but worked in another school in the same region) were also paired with a child from the local school. These children were selected so that their sex and school grade matched the children who were paired with their parents. In most cases, the child was the teacher's own pupil, or a child they knew. Most of the teachers identified themselves as Mestizo. About half of them lived in the village and half of them lived in bigger towns nearby in the Mazahua region. The average age of the children (23 girls and 22 boys) was 9 years ($SD = 1$), with a range from 7 years to 11 years old.

Task Setting

Two tasks were constructed that reflected everyday activities for both the parent-child and teacher-pupil pairs. The tasks, a construction task and a math task, were related to marketing which is recognised as a traditional Mazahua *oficio* (Paradise 1987). The tasks were also related to school activities, particularly through the measurement skills that were involved. The task sitution was set up in the schoolyard, a terrain that is familiar to both teachers and parents.

In the *construction* task the pair is asked to build a shelter to protect a market stall from the sun or rain. The pair is provided with a market stall without a protective shelter on which toy cassette recorders are stored, three sheets of nylon of different sizes, three sets of four sticks of different sizes, three sets of four strings of different sizes, and four stones.

In the *math* task the pair is asked to physically extend, using calculation, a half-built market stall in such a way that the product to be sold from the stall will cover the stall's entire surface space. The half-built stall consisted of two wooden crates and one board (25 × 25 cm) placed on top of the crates. The product is a toy drawing board in a cardboard box (25 cm × 25 cm). Four of these boxes were placed on top of the half-built stall. In addition to the

---

4. Both parents were invited. In practice, only the mother participated, except in one case in which the father also participated.
5. An early phase of the research provided indications that schooling of the parent was also a relevant factor in determining their teaching behaviour, so 15 parents had 0 to 1 years of schooling and 15 parents had 2 to 12 years. The results of an analysis of the relation between schooling of the parent and teaching patterns are not reported here. The results reported here apply to both schooled and non-schooled parents; when there were differences the non-schooled parents are taken as a point of reference.

half-built stall, there was one extra board of 25×25 cm, four extra boards of 50×100 cm, six extra crates, a tape measure, paper and a pencil, a piece of string and a piece of chalk. The pairs were asked to build at least three different stalls that could hold 8, 12 and 16 boxes respectively, but they could continue up to 40 boxes if they wished to do so (given the number of boards available). Because only four boxes were physically available, the pairs had to represent the additional boxes in order to calculate the amount of space that was needed.

The two tasks were explained to the parents and teachers without the presence of the child in their pair. The parents and teachers were asked to teach the tasks to their child in such a way that the child would learn to perform them. The tasks were conducted in Spanish, a language all participants were proficient in and would use in a similar situation. After the completion of both tasks, a small interview was held with each participant. The parents and teachers were asked about their strategies of teaching and their interpretations of the present activity. The children were asked about the adult's teaching method and what they had learned. The task activity was videotaped; the interview was audiotaped.

Data Analysis: Questions and Instruments

The analysis was aimed at identifying the pedagogical models and concepts of intersubjectivity used by the pairs. The assumption was that organisational patterns and communicative roles would reflect their pedagogical models and concepts of intersubjectivity. Therefore, the main questions that guided the analysis were (a) how the pairs organise their activities to create learning opportunities and (b) how their behaviour was translated into communicative patterns and roles. Two kinds of analyses were made. The first was a qualitative analysis of the organisational structure of the interactions and of the role divisions that were set up; the second looked at the specific pattern of participation structures and control strategies.

The two analyses are complementary in several ways. In the qualitative analysis, an image can be formed of the overall strategy of the participants and how their strategy develops over time. Also, the behaviours of the participants can be interpreted against specific situational contexts that develop during the interaction. In the pattern analysis a more precise, though in a certain sense static, image can be formed of the participants's strategies by examining specific aspects that were considered essential for understanding the kind of didactic model that was operating (e.g., how responsibility for subtasks was distributed, how the adult would control the child's behaviour). The results of the pattern analysis are also more easily quantified so that group and task comparisons become easier.

Qualitative analysis. A qualitative description of the structuring of the activity was made by using a checklist of questions (e.g., How did the pair structure the activity? How did the participants organise the activity so that learning could take place? Was the activity structure interrupted for the sake of learning? What responsibilities for the task were assumed or given to the participants? Who had the right to bring in knowledge?). All tapes were described with the help of this checklist. However, attention was paid to both the regularities and variety in the strategies chosen by the participants, and when relevant, specific contextual information was described as well (e.g., referring to earlier moments in the interaction so that the description contained information about the kind of process that took place).

Pattern analysis of the participation structures and control strategies. The question of how learning was organised and what communicative patterns and roles were set up for learning to take place was also addressed by a pattern analysis that focused on subtask level. In order to do this, a task analysis was done that identified subtasks within the overall task. For example, for the construction task, the subtasks were: replace an object, attach one object to another, put an object in place, and unfold an object. The math task analysis is more complex with 17 subtasks. The length of each subtask and their specific order of occurrence depended on how the pair dealt with the overall task. For each subtask the following questions were answered:

- Who took the initiative for this subtask (adult or child)?
- To whom was the initiative directed (adult or child)? Thus, initiatives can, for instance, be initiated by the adult and directed to the child but they can also be initiated by the adult and directed to the adult herself.
- Who actually performs the subtask (adult or child or not performed)?
- Is the nonperforming partner involved in (or focused on) this subtask (nonperforming means for the particular subtask at hand), is she involved in a parallel activity or is she involved in a completely different task?

Through the combination of these characteristics, this analysis can be used to distinguish between different kind of pedagogical strategies such as adult-initiated and adult-controlled strategies versus those in which the child has more control over her own activities; between strategies in which the child is the main performer and those in which the adult plays a performer's role too; between more sequential patterns in which both participants focus their attention exclusively on the same set of behaviours versus more parallel patterns in which both partners perform more independently from each other. By looking at the relative frequencies of the occurrence of the combination of these four characteristics, one can make inferences about the role division and organisation of the activity as a whole. For instance, if a pair has many patterns in which the adult takes the initiative and performs it while the child is watching, then modelling is an important pedagogical principle. Or if there are many patterns in which the child is asked to perform by the adult while the adult is watching the child, then the so-called 'child as a performer' principle is being applied, and so forth.

All the videotapes were scored with help of the previously described instrument by the researcher and a second observer who also participated in an interrater reliability test (Cohen's Kappa yielded. 85 for the math task and. 90 for the construction task). To investigate group and task effects simultaneously as well as a number of child characteristics, logistic regression analysis (method: stepwise forward, model: partially saturated) was applied for the most frequent sequences (see Appendix for an overview). Thus, through this analysis the differences between the teacher-pupil and the parent-child pairs, between the math and the construction task could be tested in the same analysis. Also, the possible effects of the child's age, the child's sex and grade were tested in this same analysis. The different patterns were defined as the dependent (categorial) variables. For each of the dependent variables the following independent variables were defined and entered in the analysis: group type (categorial, teachers or parents), task type (categorial, math or construction) and child age, child sex and grade (continuous).

Results: How do Mazahua Parent-Child Pairs Organise Learning and What Communicative Patterns Do They Use in Comparison with Teacher-Pupil Pairs?

Qualitative Descriptions

First, how the activity was organised and structured (and thus put into a certain interpretative frame) is discussed, with particular attention to how the activity was introduced and evaluated. Second, aspects related to responsibilities and role divisions are described.

Activity organisation and structure. In Mazahua parent-child pairs, parents would initiate the activity by undertaking actions themselves while at the same time activating the child, mostly by giving the child an assignment. The exact purpose of the activity became gradually clear to the child. For instance, a parent would start the math task by putting a crate into place and say *'vamos a agarrar esto'* [we'll take this up]. Or in another case, a parent would introduce the construction task to the child with *'agarra el nailon'* [take the nylon [sheet]]. Parents did not define the activity in a specific sense (e.g., introduce the activity as a learning activity) nor did they explicitly define the child's role. However, children did not seem to need such an introduction to be able to participate or become motivated to participate. Basically, they were treated as if they were already part of the experience from the start. They were expected to go along with the actions of the parent and were encouraged to do this through concrete orders (rather than instructions) to undertake action. It was not assumed that children needed to be informed about or lured into the activity. The child's presence almost seemed to be taken for granted as if the pair were building upon other previous actions in which their roles and the nature of the activity had already been spelled out. The same applies to how the activity was completed. The whole event was considered completed when the last subtask was finished. There were no specific moments in which the task was evaluated and usually one of the participants (child or adult) would make clear that they considered the task finished with a simple *'ya'* [done]. However, there were moments during task completion in which the meaning of the activity was made clear to the child, particularly in those cases where the child did not fulfil her role as a good 'learner'. For instance, the parent would encourage the child to watch carefully so that the child would be able to fulfil the task independently later. Generally, parents would be concerned with the continuity of the task and the fluidity of the ongoing action and tried to interweave their orientations in meaningful actions that contributed to the completion of the task. Although they would not deviate from the normal problem solving structure, they would, nevertheless, slow down the rhythm and speed of the activity, for instance, to check the child's understanding.

For the teacher-pupil pairs, the activity was organised such that separate phases were distinguished. Before the pair would start a new phase, the teacher would orient the child about the nature of this part of the activity and what the child was supposed to do. This was particularly manifest in how the task was started. Teachers would, before anything else, try to form the child's attitude to the activity. They would make clear that the child was sup-posed to be attentive to the teacher and the teacher would not say or do any-thing before the child would acknowledge this, for instance, by facing the teacher or by showing she is not involved in anything else. Thus, before the teacher would actually start the activity, she would create another plane of activity in which she defined the kind of role division that was supposed to become effective, making clear that, in order for learning to take place, the child was going to be told what to do and the teacher was responsible for tell-ing the child. At the same time, the teachers would use these introductions to point out what the final product of their activity was going to be (e.g., a roof against the rain or sun or a bigger market stall) or explain aspects of the procedure to be followed. In other words, the teachers would explicitly define the task situation beforehand in various ways (role divisions, task goal, task procedure) before they actually would start the activity. As the activity proceeded the teachers would continue to divide the activity into subtasks, often starting a subtask with a specific orientation (e.g., *'ahora vas a amarrar estos palos con los lazos'* [now you will fasten the sticks to the strings]), and ending them with an evaluation of the subtask, indicating how well the child had done. Also, teachers would repeat subtasks as often as nec-essary for the child to perform them independently. This often resulted in an activity structure in which the 'normal' completion of the task was 'given up' and replaced by a structure in which the order and speed of the activity depended on how well the child could perform the assignments given to her by the teacher. For instance, teachers did not mind long pauses after they had asked a question of which the child did not know the answer.

Role divisions and responsibilities. In the Mazahua parent-child pairs, the parent did not need to 'give up' the performer's role to be able to stimu-late the child to perform. Both adult and child were conceived and acted as performers although the child, as a less experienced member of the team, clearly had a different status. Several different participation structures were created for the child, all having in common that the child was considered a genuinely responsible performer who is contributing to the final result of the activity. For instance, children could be given more marginal roles such as bringing in and holding materials that were supposed to support the adult's activities. However, these tasks were considered as serious contributions and had to be fulfilled according to certain standards, otherwise the child would be corrected. At the same time, the child was expected to increase her knowledge of the activity through careful observation of the adult's activity. If children did not fulfil this observer role, parents would react irritated and remind the child of her responsibility to watch the activity. Observational and performance tasks were considered as closely related and equally valuable for the child's learning as was apparent from the smooth shifts that were made between observing and performing. Children were expected to gradually take on more responsible performer roles and many times they started to take more initiatives as the activity developed. However, they were never forced to take on such roles. On the contrary, children sometimes had to struggle in order to take on more responsibility. Once the parent accepted that the child would take on more responsibility, the parent would not incorporate this initiative in the overall task strategy, but create room for the child to enable her to continue with her activities in a relatively independent manner. In some cases children were able to create a 'role breakthrough', that is, they would, at a certain point in the interaction, assume considerably more responsibility than was given to them originally by the parent. In some cases, the parent would temporarily withdraw, or let the child define the overall task strategy. This shows that the role division pattern is a flexible one in which responsibilities are not fixed but can be defined according to the circumstances and needs of the learning child. This kind of role division, that is, a role division in which both the child and adult have similar roles, seems to facilitate identification and modelling compared to a situation in which the adult and child have qualitatively different responsibilities.

For the teacher-pupil pairs, role divisions were set up in a completely different way. Mostly, teachers would reserve the performer's role for the child and dedicate complete attention to guiding and structuring the child's performance. The teacher would prestructure the child's performance through, for instance, presenting her with a number of options or defining a certain procedure the child had to follow. For instance, she would say: Which board would suit us? The big one or the little one? It was clear that the teacher had the overall responsibility for the child's actions and she would only temporarily 'lend' her responsibility to the child to fulfil certain tasks. Those tasks seemed to be a careful selection of aspects that were considered as crucial for the child's learning, such as choosing the right size of string or defining the right board to be placed. Teachers would make sure that pupils would participate in some way in all aspects of the task. It was clear, however, that the tasks set for the child were not considered relevant for the task completion itself but served a different purpose. For instance, suggestions made by the child were not evaluated as a function of what needed to be done, but rather were viewed as a test of her knowledge of the procedure. It did not matter if these suggestions were not 'real' contributions to the task completion. The consequence of this strategy is that the dependency on the teacher's strategy was almost complete and that initiatives of the child were not valued or recognised. If they were recognised, these initiatives were almost immediately incorporated and restructured into the task strategy of the teacher. The role division that was set up remained intact during the whole interaction, except for two pairs where the same kind of role change occurred as was described in the parent-child pairs. However, in these two cases the teachers had almost no teaching experience. Furthermore, the role change had dramatic consequences for the teacher's authority over the child (whereas in the parent-child pairs in such cases the authority relation remained intact).

Pattern Analysis of Participation Structures and Control Strategies

Important differences were observed between the Mazahua parent-child pairs and the teacher-pupil pairs in the patterns that were coded in the analysis (see Appendix for the results of a logistic regression analysis). In particular, the following patterns occurred more frequently for the parent-child pairs than for the teacher-child pairs:[6]

–   The adult takes the initiative and performs while the child is observing. [aaaf]
–   The child takes the initiative and performs while the adult is observing. [cccf]
–   The child takes the initiative and performs while the adult is involved in a parallel activity. [cccp]
–   The adult takes the initiative and performs while the child is involved in another activity. [aaah]
–   The child takes the initiative and performs while the adult is involved in another activity. [ccch]

---

6.   The differences between the groups were statistically significant ($p < .01$) as shown in the regression analysis.

These patterns occurred more frequently for the teacher-pupil pairs:

- The adult takes the initiative and wants the child to perform it, the child performs and the adult is observing. [accf]
- The adult invites the child to take the initiative and wants the child to perform it, the child performs and the adult is observing. [a->cccf]

I interpret these results as follows. The typical patterns for parent-child pairs were characterised by self-initiated and self-performed actions (for both partners). In other words, both the child and the adult were able to take initiatives for tasks and perform them. This means that both adults and children were able to perform relatively independently from each other compared to the teacher-pupil pairs. Although both parents and children would also watch each other's activities with undivided attention, they typically would coordinate their behaviours while being engaged in other activities.

The typical patterns for teacher-pupil pairs were initiated by the adult, directed to the child as well as performed by the child and watched by the adult. In other words, those patterns in which the adult is organising the child's actions and is watching them. Thus, the results provide evidence that parent-child pairs are characterised by parallel (and thus simultaneous) action patterns in which both partners fulfil similar (performers) roles and that teacher-pupil pairs are characterised by a more sequential organisation of activities with more hierarchical roles.

Apart from these group differences, independent task effects were also found (see Appendix). Children had more control over their own actions in the construction task (e.g., they were able to take more initiatives [cccp, ccch]) and their behaviour was regulated more by adults in the math task (adults asked children to perform tasks and were observing the child's activity [accf]). Although these effects clearly indicate that pedagogical models depend on task settings, they also indicate that these effects cannot explain the differences found between the groups. Thus, although the pairs are influenced by the task setting, they do not lose their prototypical behaviour with respect to each other. Furthermore, child characteristics also have a statistically independent effect. Older children fulfilled more challenging roles (they were give more often assignments [accf, accp] and took more initiatives [cccf]) than younger children (who were more often involved in parallel activities in which less independent action is expected [aaap]) and boys show more independent behaviour (they took more initiatives [cccf]) whereas girls take on less challenging roles (they were more involved in parallel activities [aaap]).

Discussion

Different Pedagogical Models Leaning on Different Concepts of Intersubjectivity

If we take the results from both analyses together it is clear that the parent-child pairs start from a completely different organisation of this teaching-learning situation than the teacher-pupil pairs. (The posttask interviews provided evidence that both parents and teachers interpreted the situation as a teaching-learning situation.) The different organisations seem to reflect different assumptions about how a child is supposed to learn, and the contrasts between parents and teachers seem to be grounded in different ideas about setting the stage, collaboration, control and perspective building. In other words, the different pedagogical models used by the teachers and the Mazahua parents seem to be based on different concepts of intersubjectivity. Using the results presented here, I will describe these different models in terms of the underlying assumptions about how intersubjectivity is to be established.

Context creation. For the Mazahua parent-child pairs, no clear boundaries seem to exist between the task-setting activity and the activity both participants were in before starting the task. That is, although it was clear that at a certain moment they started to be involved in the task, the kind of activity did not seem to be of a different kind (i.e., a different way of speaking or acting implied by a different 'contract'). There was no specific 'stage' in their interactions in which the specific nature of the activity, or specific role divisions were pointed out. Parents did not introduce the activity to the child or explain about the role they were supposed to fulfil as if the child did not know anything about this. Nor did they explicitly and regularly check the child's understanding of the task (e.g., after a subtask was completed) but rather assumed such understanding until proven different. Rather they seemed to view the activity as belonging to the same sphere or domain they were both already in together. Both were already considered insiders and knowers who could build upon former experiences and knowledge of social practices, role divisions and specific problem-solving strategies. Differences in interpretation of the situation were solved along the way, while the action was already going on. In terms of the context creation this means that they do not stress the differences between individual worlds and the need to over-come those differences through communicative acts but rather emphasise communality resulting from, for instance, a common history and the link between the here and now with broader dimensions of time and space with which they are connected.

In the teacher-pupil pairs, on the contrary, the teacher made an effort to create a stage for the task activity to separate it from the action that was already going on. The teacher creates a distance between the child and her-self with respect to the assumed knowledge. In particular, the teacher makes clear to the child that she should take on the role of an outsider who needs to be introduced in the activity by the teacher, who was considered as the insider who possessed the relevant knowledge needed to perform the task. In terms of context creation, this means that differences in perspectives and individual interpretations are stressed rather than their communality. It is through the explicit and systemic communicative moves that take place dur-ing the interaction that the child becomes an insider and understands the situation as the adult does.

Identity of the interlocutors. In the Mazahua parent-child pairs, both the child and the adult had 'authentic' performer roles although these roles dif-fered in status. In the role division that was set up, the child was able to take on more responsibility for the organisation of the activity as a whole. That is, role changes were possible between the adult and child and roles were char-acterised as flexible rather than static. This was confirmed in the pattern anal-ysis which made clear that both the parent and the child were able to take initiatives for subtasks and perform them relatively independently. Both could develop initiatives and participate in the overall task strategy in such a way that both their efforts contributed to the task completion. In terms of communicative identities this means that both the adult and the child were considered responsible for establishing intersubjectivity both through the coordination of their actions as well as through their verbal accounts (see also the next section).

The teacher-pupil pairs followed a strict, static role division in which the child was given a performer role whereas the teacher would assume the overall task responsibility. The child's contribution was not 'authentic' with respect to the task completion but was to be interpreted more as a response to the pedagogic design set up by the teacher. This was confirmed in the pattern analysis which showed that the teacher characteristically took initiatives in the teacher-pupil interactions that were directed towards the child. Thus, instead of the relative self-controlled actions in the Mazahua model, here the child's actions are other-controlled. In terms of communicative identities this means that the teacher assumes the overall responsibility for reaching a common perspective through a pedagogical design that in a certain sense is already preestablished. (Of course, the child's responses would influence the course of actions and the strategy that is followed by the teacher.) But it is clear that their communicative roles are of a different hierarchical order and of a different nature, which means that both partners cannot take responsibility for establishing a common perspective to the same degree or in the same way.

Semiotic devices used to reach intersubjectivity. From the qualitative descriptions, it became clear that the Mazahua parent-child pairs were concerned about the fluidity and continuity of the task activity and that the parents would not divide the task into clearly segmented units in order to orient the child. Rather they would orient the child in the ongoing activity through verbal and nonverbal means without breaking up the process of task completion. The pattern analysis was also consistent with this idea. Typical participation patterns for the parent-child pairs were those in which parallel action took place and in which both partners coordinated their actions while being engaged in some other activity. Thus, the semiotic devices used for coordination or perspective building were applied in parallel rather than sequentially, and continuously rather than through segmentation of the activity. Perspective building took place through continuous coordination of action without structuring the activity into turn-taking segments and without the necessity of exclusive common focusing.

In the teacher-pupil pairs an entirely different structure was applied in which the teachers would explicitly divide the activity into segments that were functional for the child's orientation to the activity. They would even forcefully maintain the turn-taking order by obliging the child to come up with an answer. The pattern analysis showed that in teacher-pupil pairs typically both partners would be involved in the same activity, a consequence of the kind of control that the teacher exerts over the pupil. In terms of how semiotic means were used, this implies that a linear, single-focus process was set up to build a common perspective. The process of perspective building was characterised by discontinuity of action and segmentation through turn-taking procedures.

Of course these three aspects just discussed are not independent from each other. For example, role divisions are not independent from the semiotic means used nor from the kind of context creation that takes place. It is clear that the asymmetric role division in the teacher-pupil pairs and the control strategies that result from this role division are closely related to the kind of semiotic means used to establish intersubjectivity. Only through this verbal, turn-by-turn strategy, in which the teacher keeps focused on the child's action, is the teacher able to maintain her role as supervisor. In a more parallel organisation, control strategies are necessarily different because the other partner is involved in another (though similar) activity. Similarly, the kind of context creation that takes place in the Mazahua parent-child pairs is not independent of their identities as interlocutors. The continuity between the task activity and other social spheres seems relevant for how they perceived the child's role (i.e., similar to the kind of roles children normally would have when involved in activities with their parent and taking into account the skills and knowledge that result from those other activities). Still, as I hope to have shown, the three aspects represent distinct perspectives on how presumptions about communication processes are related to pedagogical models.

Implications for Concepts of Learning and Instruction

There are clear resemblances between the assumptions about intersubjectivity as described in the teacher-pupil model in the previous section and the models inferred from sociocultural studies discussed in the introduction. And clear differences emerge between the assumptions about intersubjectivity as interpreted in Mazahua parent-child pairs and the models used in sociocultural studies on learning. These results point to the fact that the concepts of intersubjectivity used in sociocultural studies on learning and instruction are, to say the least, one-sided and seem to be based on particular cultural, school-based practices.

A similar point is also made by Stone (1993) who points out that scaffolding cannot be adequately described by 'asymmetrical structuring of the passive child through a process of breaking down the task' (p. 180). Rather, he claims, scaffolding is a subtle, fluid interpersonal process 'in which the participants' communicative exchanges serve to build a continually evolving mutual perspective on how to conceive the situation at hand' (p. 180). Moreover, he points to the fact that in scaffolding the emphasis one-sidedly has been on verbal means of context creation whereas modelling could be an equally effective means to create contextual meanings (p. 177). Furthermore, he indicates that the emphasis in Rommetveit's concept of intersubjectivity on the 'here and now' is one-sided and that in the concept of intersubjectivity both the current and the enduring aspects of a relationship should be conceptualised (p. 178). Thus, he criticises pedagogical models (in this case one specific model: the scaffolding metaphor) through pointing out the nature of the communicative activity as such. The argument he makes is therefore similar to arguments used by the authors mentioned in the introduction to this chapter when they reflect critically on the concept of learning and teaching from a communicative perspective. However, my point is not just that we should be aware of the communicative underpinnings of pedagogical models but that we should be aware that communicative and semiotic processes are culture specific (as was also pointed out by Rogoff, Paradise, and Matusov). This means that we cannot directly build upon the concept of intersubjectivity 'as such' when elaborating pedagogical models.

Here, I hope to have made clear through a detailed and specified analysis of two pedagogical models that (a) intersubjectivity concepts are not culturally neutral but depend on certain specific cultural practices, and (b) differences in how intersubjectivity is viewed are closely related to differences in how pedagogical models are given form.

This means that if the concept of intersubjectivity is used to theoretically underpin pedagogical models, then it should be formulated in a way that does not draw one-sidedly on specific communicative formats or conceptualisations of those formats. Matusov's (1996) reformulation of the concept of intersubjectivity as a process of coordination of participants' contributions in joint activity (p. 1) seems to be able to encompass both concepts of intersubjectivity described here and therefore seems a better starting point for theorising about the communicative processes involved in learning and instruction. I would argue that further anthropological research is needed in which different practices of learning and instruction as well as the nature of communication practices are studied in order to gain more insight in the relation between learning, culture and communication. And, more important, this research should be taken into account in theorising about learning and instruction so that we do not base our concepts one-sidedly on a specific notion of communication or on specific social practices. This could lead to a more reflective attitude towards our own assumptions on what learning and communication is about, and stimulate us to describe learning and communication more against the backgrounds of the particular sociocultural practices that inform them.

Appendix

Logistic Regressions for Sequences of Participation and Control: Differences between Parent-Child Pairs and Teacher-Child Pairs (N = 2741)

Sequences[a]		Child characteristics			Teacher[c] vs. Parent	Construction Task vs. Math Task	Teacher vs. Parent x Task	Teacher vs. Parent x Sex	Task x Sex	Constant
		Age	Sex[b]	Years of schooling						
aaaf	B			-.28***	-.19***	-.49***		-.17***		-0.95***
	SE			.09	.06	.06		.06		.24
accf	B	.10*			.50***	-.97***				-1.45***
	SE	.05			.05	.05				.40
acaf	B					-1.08***				-4.29***
	SE					.19				.19
cccf	B		.51***		-.51***					-3.85***
	SE		.13		.15					.16
aaap	B	-.49***	-.47***		-.66***	1.49***		-.15*		1.48***
	SE	.05	.07		.07	.13		.07		.47
accp	B	.40***				1.23***	.56***	.16***		-6.78***
	SE	.06				.16	.07	.07		.60
cccp	B	.61***			-.38**	.59***		.31*	.52***	-9.71***
	SE	.10			.15	.19		.15	.15	.99
aaah	B			.39***	-.55***	1.22****	.36***			-4.11***
	SE			.09	.19	.19	.19			.33
acch	B					.46***		-.74***	-.29***	-3.47***
	SE					.13		.10	.10	.14
ccch	B				-1.41***	1.10***				-5.42***
	SE				.36	.30				.45
acnn	B									
	SE									
a -> cccf	B				2.41***					
	SE				.51					

Note. Only significant results are shown in the table. When *B* is positive, the '+' category of the independent variable influences the chance that the (1) value of the dependent variable occurs positively. For example, the second sequence ('accf') is interpreted as: If the adult is a teacher it is more likely that 'accf' takes place. When B is negative, as for the construction task, then it is less likely that the 'accf' sequence takes place.

[a]Sequences that occurred at least 1% of the time:

aaaf   The adult is performing while the child is watching or listening.

accf   Adult gives the child an assignment, child performs it and the adult watches the child or listens to her.

acaf   The adult gives the child an assignment but performs it herself while the child is watching or listening.

cccf   The child takes the initiative to do a task and performs it while the adult is watching or listening.

aaap   The adult on her own initiative performs a task while the child is involved in a parallel activity.

accp   The adult gives the child an assignment which the child performs while the adult is busy with a parallel activity.

cccp   The child takes the initiative to do a task and performs it while the adult is involved in a parallel activity.

aaah   The adult on her own initiative performs a task while the child is involved in another activity.

acch   The adult gives the child an assignment which the child performs while the adult herself is busy with another activity.

ccch   The child takes the initiative to do a task and performs it while the adult is involved in some other activity.

acnn   The adult gives the child an assignment which was not performed.

a->cccf The adult gives the child the opportunity to take initiative, the child performs while the adult watches or listens.

Sequence construction:

1 = who takes initiative (a = adult, c = child, a->c = adult gives child initiative)
2 = at whom directed (a = adult, c = child)
3 = who performs (a = adult, c = child, n = not performed)
4 = involvement of other partner (h = involved in other act, f = involved in same activity, p = parallel activity)

[b]'male' is the '+' category. [c]'+' category.
*$p <. 05$ **$p <. 01$ ***$p <. 001$

References

Brown, A.L., & Palincsar, A.S. (1982). Inducing strategic learning from texts by means of informed self-control training. *Topics in Learning and Learning Disabilities*, 2(1), 1-17.

Bruner, J. (1996). *The culture of education.* Cambridge, Mass.: Harvard University Press.

Haan, M. de (1999). *Learning as cultural practice: How children learn in a Mexican Mazahua community. A study on culture and learning.* Amsterdam: Thela Thesis.

Hoogsteder, M. (1995). *Learning through participation: The communication between young children and their caregivers in informal learning and tutoring situations.* Utrecht, The Netherlands: ISOR.

Hwang, C.P., Lamb, M.E., & Sigel, I.E. (eds.) (1996). *Images of childhood.* Mahwah, N.J.: Erlbaum.

Matusov, E. (1996). Intersubjectivity without agreement. *Mind, Culture, and Activity*, 3, 25-45.

Ochs, E. (1988). *Culture and language development: Language acquisition and language socialization in a Samoan village.* Cambridge: Cambridge University Press.

Ochs, E., & Schieffelin, B. (1984). Language acquisition and socialization: Three developmental stories. In R. Schweder & R. LeVine (eds.), *Culture theory: Essays in mind, self and emotion.* Cambridge: Cambridge University Press, 276-320.

Paradise, R. (1987). Learning through social interaction: The experience and development of the Mazahua self in the context of the market. Unpublished doctoral dissertation, University of Pennsylvania.

Paradise, R. (1996). Passivity or tacit collaboration: Mazahua interaction in cultural context. *Learning & Instruction*, 6, 379-89.

Paradise, R. (1998). What's different about learning in schools as compared to family and community settings? *Human Development*, 41, 270-78.

Philips, S.U. (1983). *The invisible culture: Communication in classroom and community on the Warm Springs Indian Reservation.* New York: Longman.

Rogoff, B. (1990). *Apprenticeship in thinking: Cognitive development in social context.* New York: Oxford University Press.

Rogoff, B., Mistry, J., Göncü, A., & Mosier, C. (1993). Guided participation in cultural activity by toddlers and caregivers. *Monographs of the Society for Research in Child Development*, 58(8, Serial No. 236).

Rommetveit, R. (1974). *On message structure: A framework for the study of language and communication.* New York: Wiley.

Rommetveit, R. (1985). Language acquisition as increasing linguistic structuring of experience and symbolic behaviour control. In J.V. Wertsch (ed.), *Culture, communication and cognition: Vygotskian perspectives.* Cambridge: Cambridge University Press, 183-204.

Scaife, M., & Bruner, J.S. (1975, January 24). The capacity for joint visual attention in the infant. *Nature*, 253, 265-66.

Scollon, R., & Scollon, S.B.K. (1981). *Narrative, literacy and face in interethnic communication*. Norwood, N.J.: Ablex.

Stairs, A. (1991). Learning processes and teaching roles in Native Education: Cultural base and cultural brokerage. *The Canadian Modern Language Review*, 47, 280-94.

Stone, C.A. (1993). What is missing in the metaphor of scaffolding? In E.A. Forman, N. Minick, & C.A. Stone (eds.), *Contexts for learning: Sociocultural dynamics in children's development*. New York: Oxford University Press, 169-83.

Tharp, R.G., & Gallimore, R. (1988). *Rousing minds to life: Teaching, learning, and schooling in social context*. Cambridge: Cambridge University Press.

Trevarthen, C. (1986). Form, significance and psychological potential of hand gestures of infants. In J.L. Nespoulous, P. Perron, & A.R. Lecours (eds.), *The biological foundation of gestures: Motor and semiotic aspects*. Hillsdale, N.J.: Erlbaum, 149-202.

Wertsch, J.V. (1978). Adult-child interaction and the roots of metacognition. *Quarterly Newsletter of the Institute for Comparative Human Development*, 2, 15-18.

Wertsch, J.V. (1985). *Vygotsky and the social formation of the mind*. Cambridge, Mass.: Harvard University Press.

Wertsch, J.V. (1998). *Mind as action*. New York: Oxford University Press.

Wertsch, J.V., McNamee, G.D., McLane, J.B., & Budwig, N.A. (1980). The adult-child dyad as a problem solving system. *Child Development*, 51, 1215-21.

Wertsch, J.V., Minick, N., & Arns, F.J. (1984). The creation of context in problem solving. In B. Rogoff & J. Lave (eds.), *Everyday cognition: Its development in social contexts*. Cambridge, Mass.: Harvard University Press, 151-71.

Wood, D., Bruner, J.S., & Ross, G. (1976). The role of tutoring in problem solving. *Journal of Child Psychology and Psychiatry*, 17, 89-100.

Wood, D., & Middleton, D. (1975). A study of assisted problem solving. *British Journal of Psychology*, 66, 181-91.

11 Lost — or Merely Domesticated? The Boom in Socio-Historicocultural Theory Emphasises Some Concepts, Overlooks Others

Mohamed Elhammoumi

Introduction

The inherent complexity of human thought processes, consciousness and activity requires theories, methodologies, explanations and field experiments that address this complexity. The cognitive revolution and, most recently, cultural psychology, promised to deliver these conceptual tools but have brought only limited success. The cognitive revolution has been concerned with the intrapsychological processes functioning within the individual. Cultural psychology has been concerned with semiotic processes that mediate human higher mental functioning. In both approaches, thought processes, consciousness and activity are analysed as entities independent from the concrete social structures and institutions that form the bases of their structures and meanings.

The evident limitations of these approaches have led contemporary psychologists to turn their attention to the heritage of Soviet psychology of the 1920s and 1930s. In fact, socio-historicocultural psychology[1] in general is viewed as an alternative to the existing studies in psychological science.

*   A debt of gratitude is owed to Seth Chaiklin who has taken the time to read and comment on this chapter. I am deeply grateful to his illuminating comments, invaluable help and editorial advice. I would like to thank Dr. Helena H. Worthen for her careful reading and helpful comments of an earlier draft of this chapter. Cheryl Vinyard Elhammoumi provided assistance in proofreading the manuscript.

1. It is well-known that the concept 'cultural-historical' remains largely undefined in the active research activities inspired by the Soviet school of cultural-historical psychology. The concept of cultural-historical has been translated and interpreted differently by the Vygotskian psychologists. For example, Michael Cole used it as sociocultural approach (Cole 1979, 1990; Wertsch 1995), cultural-historical approach (Cole 1994, van der Veer 1985), sociocultural historical psychology (Cole 1995a), cultural-historical

However, dependence on approaches borrowed from the cognitive revolution and cultural psychology has resulted in oversimplification and misunderstanding of socio-historicocultural psychology, both theoretically and methodologically. Thus contemporary socio-historicocultural psychology is cut off from its explanatory and experimental potential.

In an attempt to reconstruct the links between socio-historicocultural theory as it is practiced today and the materialist conception of history from which it evolved, this chapter brings into focus that the Marxist methodological aspects are missing or inadequately represented within the different trends of the Soviet school of socio-historicocultural psychology. In my view there is a dialectical materialist tradition that was an important source of ideas for Vygotsky, and these aspects have not been incorporated sufficiently into the current psychological works within the tradition.[2]

psychology (Cole 1995b), cultural-historical perspective (Valsiner 1993), sociohistorical psychology (Ratner 1991, 1998), sociohistorical perspective (Wertsch 1987), sociohistorical approach (Wertsch 1991), cultural-historical theory (Engeström 1989), socio-cultural approach (Wertsch 1990). It is important to note that this is not the way in which the concept was used by Vygotsky and his followers in the study of human mental phenomena, consciousness and activity. I have coined the term 'socio-historico-cultural' as a general category that integrates and unites Vygotsky's cultural-historical with Marx's materialist conception of history. Contemporary psychologists working within the theoretical framework of the Soviet school of cultural-historical psychology use the concept 'cultural-historical' in a specific, technical way. The socio-historicocultural approach to human mental phenomena maintains that the social, historical, and cultural basis of the human mind constantly changes in a dialectical process. The socio-historicocultural approach claims that all human mental phenomena are internalised social relations which include social relations of production, psychological means of production, psychological forces of production, psychological relations of production, and psychological mode of production from which human higher mental functions emerge. The production of higher mental functions, the production of consciousness and the production of behaviour were grounded in socially concrete life.

2. Here Vygotsky draws a distinction between Marxist tradition as represented in Marx's writings and Marxism as represented in the different trends of philosophy and political ideology, and Soviet Marxism as traditionally formulated in official doctrine and preached by many psychologists in the Soviet Union. In other words, Vygotsky understood that the connection between Marx and the different trends of Marxism is not tight. He felt that Soviet psychologists inspired by Marxism tended to transform Marx's concepts and discoveries into a simplistic and dogmatic philosophical system. Marx also drew the distinction when he said to Paul Lafargue, 'I am not a Marxist'. This remark can be interpreted as a protest against those enthusiastic followers who transformed his concepts into a simplistic version of Marxism. In this respect, Vygotsky (1927/1997b) said, 'The only rightful application of Marxism to psychology would be to create a general psychology — its concepts are being formulated in direct dependence upon general dialectics, for it is the dialectics of psychology. Any applica-

This chapter argues that socio-historicocultural theory is, after all, an extension of the materialist conception of history. A 'domesticated' version of socio-historicocultural theory is weakened by the absence of links to a materialist analysis. For example, analytic constructs that arise from a materialist conception of history are principles of ownership, production and distribution of wealth and resources. Socio-historicocultural theory needs to draw on these constructs in order to realise its potential to extend beyond the analysis of small scale and individual activity.

However, contemporary theorists of this school typically construe 'socially organised practical life' as taking place on the small, interpersonal 'domestic' scale of the classroom, family or work group. Thus they emphasise intention, shared meaning, individual or distributed cognition, memory, the development of speech, and so forth. This construction overlooks the equally, if not more important, larger scale such as forms of social control and power, distribution of wealth, divisions of labor and social class.

Jean Jaurès stated that when we study history we must take from the past not ashes but fire. This, it would appear, also pertains to the history of socio-historicocultural psychology. Recent investigations of socio-historicocultural psychology are full of the ashes of the classical psychology of the first half of this century.

What follows is an attempt to reopen an old question, that of the nature, foundation, and roots of human higher mental functions, in the light of a return to the fire, the classic texts of dialectical psychology (Vygotsky 1934/1987; Leontiev 1959/1981, 1975/1978). These texts come from the Soviet traditions of socio-historicocultural psychology and the philosophy of the materialist conception of history. These traditions flourished in the 1920s, both inside and out of Russia, and are exemplified by the work of Lev Vygotsky and his colleagues in the Soviet Union, Georg Lukács's reification theory in Hungary, Piaget's psychosocial theory of knowledge in Switzerland, Georges Politzer's (e.g., 1928/1994, 1929/1969a, 1929/1969b, 1929/1969c) concrete psychology and Henri Wallon's (e.g., 1946, 1951/1963) dialectical psychology in France.

tion of Marxism to psychology via other paths or in other points outside this area, will inevitably lead to scholastic, verbal constructions, to the dissolution of dialectics into surveys and tests, to judgment about things according to their external, accidental, secondary features, to the complete loss of any objective criterion and the attempt to deny all historical tendencies of the development of psychology, to a terminological revolution, in sum to a gross distortion of both Marxism and psychology' (p. 330).

Socio-historicocultural psychology is à la mode in Western theoretical and empirical psychological science in general and in theoretical developmental psychology in particular. Over the past two decades, the range of approaches to the analysis of human higher mental functions from a socio-historicocultural perspective have multiplied (Elhammoumi 1997), fuelled partly by increases in interest in the influence of culture on human thought. Today every psychologist claims to be a cultural-historical psychologist, at least in the area of theoretical developmental psychology.

Yet the popularity of socio-historicoculturalism does not mean to say that it is well understood. Andrei Brushlinsky[3] (1997) pointed out that he 'does not hesitate to show his pique over what he sees as a wave of faddish, unscientific enthusiasm in America for the theories of Lev Vygotsky' (p. 9). I think this enthusiasm extends to include Luria, Leontiev and their followers. It is combined with an inadequate regard for the traditions within which their thought developed: the theories of the materialist conception of history and dialectical materialism. Leontiev's, Luria's, and Vygotsky's admirers have focused their attention on the role of sign and word, speech and language, in the development of higher mental functions, consciousness and human action. Thus the main concepts of the socio-historicocultural research program have been lost in the explosive production of studies about Leontiev's, Luria's, and Vygotsky's thought. The most important concepts were excluded.

What are these important concepts? According to the classic texts of socio-historicocultural theory, the whole of human psychological phenomena including human consciousness is derived from socially organised practical activity. Socio-historicocultural theory views *semiotic mediation, symbolic processes, and cognitive processes* as secondary because they derive from the interactions that individuals make in a socially-organised, concrete, practical activity.

Concepts that are primary, that are not derivative but are aspects of socially organised practical activity, include: social systems, ideologies, institutionalised ways of working, institutionalised ways of educating, dialectical

3. Brushlinsky is currently the director of the Institute of Psychology in the Russian Academy of Sciences. He is certainly among the most eminent of students and followers of Sergei Rubinshtein (1889-1960). According to Brushlinsky, Vygotsky's theory relies on an approach based on signs rather than activity. He argues that human higher mental functions are first of all developed and revealed in practical activity. He believes that Vygotsky, after his death, was the victim of Stalin's decrees and now under the free society he is the victim of charismatisation. To learn more about his ideas, see Brushlinsky (1979, 1987, 1990).

materialism, alienation, social relations of production, psychological means of production, psychological mode of production of social concepts and psychological relations of production.[4]

Thus, when psychologists, inspired by Soviet psychology, study shared meanings and understandings instead of socially organised practical activity, they are paying more attention to the ashes than the fire. The consequence of this mistake is that social interaction may be named as a prerequisite to cognitive development but there is no follow-up analysis of the concrete relations of the social interaction. Just as the followers of Piaget ignored the realities of social communication in their account of cognition,[5] so do social constructionists ignore the realities of economic structure (e.g., Gergen 1985; Harré 1986a, 1986b; Shotter 1993), and socio-cognitive conflict theorists ignore the realities of social interaction and economic structure (e.g., Doise & Mugny 1981; Perret-Clermont 1998), rendering their descriptions less promising for practical application. Cognitive processes are reduced to the study of internal laws of a particular development, ignoring that their content is essentially prefigured and governed by the preexisting external concrete social forces. The zone of proximal development has been domesticated in the field of standardised instruments and tests of evaluation which often fail to meet the challenges of complex cognition. The concept of development has been reduced to tracing continuous personal histories. Even the idea that human thought processes are mediated by semiotic signs and technological tools is still underdeveloped theoretically, methodologically and epistemologically. In their analyses of human cognition, socio-historicocultural psy-

4. In the process of production, human individuals enter into social relations which are regulated by the economic conditions of production. These relations of production give rise to the legal and political superstructure, a particular form of social consciousness and an ideological form. In Vygotsky's (1926/1997a) view, the concept of ideology has a place in psychological science: 'The nature of man's education, therefore, is wholly determined by the social environment in which he grows and develops. But this environment does not always affect man directly and straightforwardly, but also indirectly, through his ideology. By ideology, we will understand all the social stimuli that have been established in the course of historical development and have become hardened in the form of legal statutes, moral precepts, artistic tastes, and so on. These standards are permeated through and through with the class structure of society that generated them and serve as the class organisation of production. They are responsible for all human behavior, and in this sense we are justified in speaking of man's class behavior' (p. 211).
5. Piaget (e.g., 1950/1965) paid more attention to the social part of the cognition than his followers.

chologists (Bruner, Cole, Engeström, Rogoff, Valsiner, van der Veer, Wertsch among others) kept out of their theoretical picture any reference to larger forms of human activity and larger processes in social life, such as the realities of economic structure, class struggle, realities of labour activities, and the realities of social interaction.

The temptation to substitute ashes for fire is not new. In his critical review of the Darwinian school, Engels (1886/1940) criticised contemporary views of the materialist naturalists of the Darwinian school as trying to explain human actions as arising 'from their thoughts instead of from their needs' (p. 289). He argued the reverse that the development of labour [human action]

helped to bring the members of society closer together by multiplying cases of mutual supports, joint activity, and by making the advantage of this joint activity to each individual ... they had something to say to one another. (p. 283)

Then, in the process of cooperative activity, communication became both necessary and possible. Thus human individuals created language as a tool but only when the concrete practical conditions and needs for that tool developed. Again, semiotic mediation and symbolic processes are secondary to concrete practical activity.

Engels' chapter 'The Part Played by Labor in the Transition from Ape to Man' played a crucial role in clarifying Vygotsky's ideas. Engels concluded that in the process of anthropogenesis a form of *activity* was born and shaped the course of the human species. This *activity* is called *labour*. In the final analysis, labour marks the distinction between human individuals and animals, and marks the starting point of the historical development of human individuals. In this sense, Vygotsky (1925/1993) pointed out that: 'Labor is that fundamental pivot around which the life of society is structured and erected. Man's social life and his study of nature are linked to activity of labor' (p. 119), and he (1930/1994) added that

The development of material production simultaneously brought with it the progressive division of labor and the constantly growing distorted development of the human potential. (p. 178)

Psychological phenomena have to be explained in terms of actual concrete life, the present social relations of productive activity and current activities. This implies that serious attention must be paid to the concrete social structures in which persons form meanings. The concrete social structures include also the socially organised practical activity such as work, principles of division of labour which govern human action in specific social institutions, the ways of working, ways of schooling and education, distributions of wealth and resources, and division of social classes. They also include practical acts of material production: the forces of production and the social relations of production. They also include the institutions of power which enforce laws. Finally, psychological phenomena must also be explained in terms of the coercive power of social institutions, the collective struggles to transform them, and the collective action to change them.

Socio-Historicocultural Roots of Human Psychological Phenomena

Any modern approach to socio-historicocultural psychology of human thought processes, consciousness and activity must begin by considering the relationship between the forces of production and the relations of production. The contradiction between these two forces is the engine of social development, historical progress and psychological development. In this respect, as in others, Marxism is the conceptual core of socio-historico-cultural psychology. The contradiction between forces of production (including science, education as productive force) and the social relations of production underlies the dynamic of any contemporary mode of thought production (the predominant way of thinking which serves as the basis of the social order of its social organisation). Whatever changes may have occurred in the development of Vygotsky's thought during the decade (1924-1934) of his intellectual achievement, he consistently held to this thesis: that social relations of production form the real foundation for the structure of human mental phenomena. The mode of production in material life regulates the intellectual processes of life. In this sense, Vygotsky (1927/1997b) said that 'each person is to some degree a measure of the society, or rather class, to which he belongs, for the whole totality of social relationships is reflected in him' (p. 317).

It is not the dialectic of human consciousness that explains concrete material life and human history of the members of the society, but it is the concrete material life of individuals that explains human consciousness and history. Human consciousness and human history are only the product of the concrete material life and the properties of objective social life. Similarly, human higher mental functions, consciousness and activity are grounded in historically organised human activity. Human forms of thought and consciousness are framed and shaped by the social relations of production.[6] Vygotsky, repeatedly and with increasing insistence, emphasised that 'social relations of production' constitute the real foundation for the make up of human thought, activity and consciousness.

This does not exclude other influences. Economic conditions may be the single most fruitful point of departure for the analysis of human activity, but Vygotsky explicitly recognised that while understanding material conditions is necessary, it is not sufficient for understanding the emergence or spread of ideas.

Socio-historicocultural theory derives its assumptions from Marx's materialist conception of history applied to the historical development of human beings, which means every human mental phenomenon bears the marks of their history. Cultural development means every human psychological phenomenon bears the identifying marks of their culture. Social development means every psychological phenomenon bears the identifying characteristics of its space-time context. The starting point of socio-historico-cultural psychology is *production*, which is just as creative as is higher mental functions. Human higher mental functions are neither innate nor predetermined, but are created by the historically-developed social relations of production. In this sense, the human individual is the subject of his/her activity. This activity is characterised by its social, historical, and cultural features.

Theses on Socio-Historicocultural Psychology

Following Vygotsky's examination of the nature and the foundation of human higher mental functions, consciousness and activity, we can come up with six theses that have direct practical meaning:

---

6. Vygotsky argues that if human individuals transform the social relations in which they find themselves, a new picture of mental structures and consciousness can emerge. Human consciousness must be explained from the contradiction of material life, from the existing conflict between the social productive forces and the relations of production. In this sense, human suffering has its cause, not in intellectual confusions about the nature of human being, but in the alienated character of the existing social relations of production and practical social life. To understand what is going on in any society as a whole, it is important to start by looking at the economic relations of production in that society and try to fit everything else into that.

First thesis: Human higher mental functions, consciousness and activity in the individual are the *product of social relations of production*.

Second thesis: Human higher mental functions, consciousness and activity are mediated by *signs and tools* which give rise to *labour activity*.

Third thesis: Human higher mental functions, consciousness and activity can be examined only through *developmental* or *genetic analysis*. In this sense, developmental analysis must return to the source and reconstruct all the points and phases in the development of a given structure, '*to study something historically* [developmentally] *means to study it in the process of change*' (Vygotsky 1978, 64-65). In other words, to discover its nature and essence, 'that is the *dialectical method's* basic demand' (p. 65).

Fourth thesis: Human higher mental functions, consciousness and activity are *rooted in historically organised human activity*.

Fifth thesis: In the final analysis, human individuals do not make history, but they make *the instruments and tools of production which give rise to labour activity that regulates social relations of production*. History in our analysis is seen as the final product of the whole of human activity. As usual, *The German Ideology* contains vivid summaries of crucial arguments, Marx and Engels (1846/1970) argue that:

History is nothing but the succession of the separate generations, each of which exploits the materials, the capital funds, the productive forces handed down to it by all preceding generations, and thus, on the one hand, continues the traditional activity in completely changed circumstances and, on the other, modifies the old circumstances with a completely changed activity. (p. 57)

Sixth thesis: Human higher mental functions, consciousness and activity are *framed and shaped by culturally organised human activity*.

In short, human thought and consciousness are rooted in the material conditions of life, which are summarised by materialist philosophy under the name *materialist conception of history*. According to Vygotsky, the anatomy of human consciousness, thought and personality is to be sought in its historical context, social milieu, social position and cultural environment.

The Foundation of Human Psychological Phenomena

The production of material needs or — in other words — the economy is the principal axis of society and its socially organised institutions. Every economic production creates its own social environment and its system of production. In the process of creating a socioeconomic system of production we create social relations between individuals. The nature of these social relations, based on economic production, shapes and makes up social institutions that regulate the division of labour activities, ways of working, ways of schooling and educating individuals, and distribution of resources and wealth. Economic production is thus more important than law, politics, religion, and so forth, in understanding the nature of human psychological and social processes. Similarly, changes in the social relations of production — changes in the economy — precede changes in law, politics, religion, and so forth and must necessarily be understood to lead changes in human psychological processes.[7]

Human higher mental functions differ from each other by the place the individuals occupy in a socio-historicoculturally established system of social production. Their relations (in most cases confined and formulated in law) to the means of production,[8] their roles in the social organisation of labour, and consequently, the dimensions and method of acquiring the share of social wealth, of which they dispose, were the principal components to regu-

7. For a comprehensive treatment of Vygotsky's concept of social relations of production, supported by fuller quotation and documentation, see Elhammoumi (in press). The following quotation provides an interesting point into Vygotsky's analysis of the concept of social relations of production, 'The use of notched sticks and knots, the beginnings of writing and simple memory aids all demonstrate that even at early stages of historical development humans went beyond the limits of psychological functions given to them by nature and proceeded to a new culturally-elaborated organization of their behavior. Comparative analysis shows that such activity is absent in even the highest species of animals; we believe that these sign operations are the product of specific conditions of *social* development' (Vygotsky 1978, 39).
8. By 'means of production' Vygotsky (1926/1997a) means 'From the standpoint of historical materialism, the fundamental causes of all social changes and all political upheavals must be sought not in peoples' minds, Engels said, and not in their views of eternal truths and justice, but in changes in the means of production and distribution. They must be sought not in philosophy, but in the economics of each epoch. Thus, in mankind the production process assumes the broadest possible social character, which at the present time encompasses the entire world. Accordingly, there arise the most complex forms of organisation of human social behavior with which the child encounters before he directly confronts nature' (p. 211).

late their social and mental life. In such a society, the relations of production characterised by exchange value govern, frame, shape, and mediate both the intra- and interindividual relations, so most interindividual relations are reduced to the commodities they produce.

Seen from this perspective, the creative struggle to confront and change the social relations of production ceases to be peripheral or accidental to the study of human psychological processes, but moves to centre stage and becomes essential. A psychology which misses the centrality of the larger forms of human activity and larger processes in social life is less efficient to the task which lies in front of it.

Human individuals live their lives in the process of labour. Engels (1886/1940) pointed out that 'Labor [*activity*] is the source of all wealth ... basic condition for all human existence and ... created man himself' (p. 279). Or in other words, human activity is the rich process of the whole human life. Labour requires tools, instruments and equipment. But just as tools are the equipment of material production, signs (i.e., language) are instruments of mental production. Human cognition requires cognitive tools. Cognitive tools are words, signs and symbols. Words, signs and symbols are means of psychological production of human cognition. Linguistic skills are psychological tools and fundamental means of thought production, and means of relating humans to humans, just as technological tools relate humans to nature.

Psychological Relations of Production

In social production human individuals enter into specific relations with one another. In this process human thought develops and matures. Marx distinguishes between three levels of social phenomena: first, the material productive forces, then, the relations of production, and finally, the level of philosophical and ideological ideas. These ideas fill the consciousness of human individuals at any stage of historical development and change what they are experiencing.

In the past two decades many social scientists in the West, former Soviet countries, and developing societies have expressed renewed interest in examining how culture, history and concrete social conditions affect human higher mental functioning. What motivated researchers in social sciences to revive the archives of the writings of the socio-historicocultural psychology? In my view, this new trend is multiply determined, but one of the major factors in its success has been the failure of the cognitive revolution which integrated most of the key theoretical concepts[9] of behaviourism into its research program. Unfortunately, now we are witnessing the same process of assimilation of the socio-historicocultural theory into cognitive science by American psychology and West European psychology. Most of the leading scholars working within the socio-historicocultural framework have participated in this. Thus socio-historicocultural theory's concepts have been formulated in ways that do not draw faithfully from their original conceptual and philosophical background (Bruner 1996; Holland & Valsiner 1988; Rogoff 1990; Shweder 1990). Socio-historicocultural theory becomes a study of individual mental processes rather than socially organised practical human activity (Ratner 1996, 1997a, 1997b; Sève 1969, 1978, 1999).

Human Activity in Action

Socio-historicocultural approaches, if we do not strip them of their essential concepts, can help us understand the mechanisms underlying the structures of human society, consciousness, cognition and personality.

In this chapter I placed greater emphasis on the role of concrete social conditions, current social relations of production, and organized practical activities in human development, higher mental functions, consciousness and activity. But a focus on the concrete life is an aspect of socio-historicocultural theory. The fact is that one can only appropriate the world by changing it in reality, not simply by interpreting it differently, or changing it in thought. Vygotsky argues that if we transform the *social relations* in which we find ourselves, new visions of thinking, personality, and self can emerge. To test this assumption, Vygotsky and Luria designed a series of experiments known as the 'psychological expedition to Uzbekistan'. The theoretical conceptions underlying the Uzkek experiments were not new. An earlier, detailed theoretical description of the change in social relations of production and the development of the forces of production was provided in 1845-46 by Marx and Engels in *The German Ideology*. Marx and Engels compared earlier modes of production with the capitalist mode of production, paying more attention

---

9. Vygotsky has been misunderstood in the West because psychologists inspired by the socio-historicocultural approach to human psychological phenomena too often project their own common and mainstream concepts of the nature of human being. These approaches (e.g., cognitivism, cognitive neuroscience, and cultural psychology) reduce human activity to individual activity. It is clear that, the attempt to domesticate socio-historicocultural concepts has been a failure, if not a contradiction

to the differences in the individual's relations to others, society, world, and nature. Vygotsky and Luria were interested in what happens to the individual's cognitive development when traditional society begins to modernise. The central idea of their studies was to compare the cognitive processes of active collective farmers (*Kolkhoz*) and peasants living in remote villages not affected by the process of modernisation. The rapid transition from a feudal mode of production to a presocialist social organisation provided the opportunity for examining the concurrent evolution of mental processes. Data analysis of the experiments indicate that not only quantitative changes in the content of mental processes, but also qualitative transformation in their structures was noted in a variety of 'psychological processes, and most of all, higher, specifically human forms of psychological activity, such as voluntary attention, active memory and abstract thought' (Luria 1971, 272). Luria (1979) reported:

In all cases we found that changes in the practical forms of activity, and especially the reorganization of activity based on the formal schooling, produced qualitative changes in the thought processes of the individuals studied. Moreover, we were able to establish that basic changes in the organization of thinking can occur in a relatively short time when there are sufficiently sharp changes in social-historical circumstances, such as those that occurred following the 1917 Revolution. (p. 80)

Tulviste (1999) argues that although 'Luria's research in Central Asia is widely known, it seems that its aim and meaning were not fully understood' (p. 71). Luria's results will be fully understood if we interpret them in the light of the theoretical framework of *The German Ideology*. The Vygotsky-Luria experiments are very important because they demonstrate that changes in the social relations of production give rise to changes in mental processes. Vygotsky-Luria's results provide strong evidence and strengthen our idea that human higher mental functions come into existence through social relations and socially organised practical activity.

Conclusion

Socio-historicocultural conceptions were based on the materialist conception of history. It is important to bear in mind that the core of socio-historicocultural theory is its ability to keep in its picture the Marxist tradition which focuses its primary concern on understanding human mental functions within socially-organised, concrete life.

The reviving of the writings of the Soviet school of cultural-historical psychology has transformed the theoretical field of developmental psychology and cultural psychology. It offers a stimulating set of ideas. The impact is too monumental to embrace at the time when psychological science is struggling for an integrated theoretical framework.

This chapter has integrated the historical and conceptual relations between the Marxist tradition of societal analysis and the mental processes, paying special attention to the social relations of production and the socially organised practical activity. Societal changes not only produce new advances in material progress, they also generate new forms of higher mental functioning in humans. Socio-historicocultural theory as an extension of the materialist conception of history and cultural-historical theory has awakened our understanding that all cultures contain all elements necessary for adequate and sufficient cognitive growth and intellectual development of their members. However, when the transmission of cultural signs and tools from one generation to the next is interrupted by social injustice, social oppression, discrimination, unemployment, poverty, famine, segregation, racism, urban ghetto, war, colonization, etc., then higher mental functioning is inevitably affected.

In my view cultural-historical psychology has had a difficult course since the foundations laid by the Vygotsky-Luria studies in Central Asia. Vygotsky and Luria clearly saw a distinction in Uzbek society, before and after collectivisation. In Luria's (1979) last discussions of the Uzbekistan studies in his intellectual biography, he writes that Uzkek culture

could boast of an ancient high culture which included the outstanding scientific and poetic achievements associated with such figures as Uleg Bek, a mathematician and astronomer who left behind a remarkable observatory near Samarkand, the philosopher Al-Biruni, the physician Ali-Ibn Senna (Avecenna), the poets Saadi and Nezami, and others [such as Abu Nasr Mansur ibn Ali who worked on trigonometry and discovered the sine law]. (p. 60)

Luria explained that the cultural level in Uzbek was

typical of feudal societies, the peasant masses remained illiterate and for the most part separated from high culture. They lived in villages that were completely dependent on wealthy landowners and powerful feudal lords. (p. 60)

This provided fertile ground for further study and application of dialectical materialist psychology. However, because of a changing ideology in the Soviet Union in the 1930s, this work was not developed further or was not fully discussed. In later years, cultural-historical psychologists did not fully incorporate the idea of culture as an explanatory variable in their investigations (see Tulviste 1999). In this way, the domestication of the original concepts began. It remains for us now to reignite Vygotsky's flame and reconceptualise psychology in terms of a materialist conception of history.

References

Bruner, J. (1996). *The culture of education*. Cambridge, Mass.: Harvard University Press.

Brushlinsky, A.V. (1979). The interrelationship of the natural and the social in human mental development. *Soviet Psychology*, 17(4), 36-52.

Brushlinsky, A.V. (1987). Activity, action, and mind as process. *Soviet Psychology*, 25(4), 59-81.

Brushlinsky, A.V. (1990). The activity of the subject and psychic activity. In V.A. Lektorsky (ed.), *Activity: Theories, methodology and problems*. Orlando, Fla.: Paul M. Deutsch Press, 67-73.

Brushlinsky, A.V. (1997, January). Psychology in transitional Russia. *APS Observer*, 10(1), 6-9.

Cole, M. (1979). Introduction: The Kharkov school of developmental psychology. *Soviet Psychology*, 18(2), 3-8.

Cole, M. (1990). Alexandr Romanovich Luria: Cultural psychologist. In E. Goldberg (ed.), *Contemporary neuropsychology and the legacy of Luria*. Hillsdale, N.J.: Erlbaum, 11-28.

Cole, M. (1994). A conception of culture for a communication theory of mind. In D. Vocate (ed.), *Intrapersonal communication: Different voices, different minds*. Hillsdale, N.J.: Erlbaum, 77-98.

Cole, M. (1995a). Socio-cultural historical psychology: Some general remarks and proposal for new kind of cultural-genetic methodology. In J.V. Wertsch, P. Del Rio, & A. Alvarez (eds.), *Sociocultural studies of mind*. Cambridge: Cambridge University Press, 187-214.

Cole, M. (1995b). Cultural-historical psychology: A meso-genetic approach. In L.W.M. Martin, K. Nelson, & E. Tobach (eds.), *Sociocultural psychology: Theory and practice of doing and knowing*. Cambridge: Cambridge University Press, 168-204.

Doise, W., & Mugny, G. (1981). *Le développement social de l'intelligence.* Paris: Inter Editions.

Elhammoumi, M. (1997). *Socio-historicocultural psychology: Lev Semenovich Vygotsky (1896-1934).* Lanham, Md.: University Press of America.

Elhammoumi, M. (in press). *Free conversations with Lev Semenovich Vygotsky.* Lanham, Md.: University Press of America.

Engels. F. (1940). The part played by labor in the transition from ape to man. In *The dialectic of nature.* New York: International Publishers, 279-96. (Original work written 1886)

Engeström, Y. (1989). The cultural-historical theory of activity and the study of political repression. *International Journal of Mental Health,* 17(4), 29-41.

Gergen, K. (1985). The social constructionist movement in modern psychology. *American Psychologist,* 40, 266-75.

Harré, R. (1986a). The steps to social constructionism. In M. Richards & P. Light (eds.), *Children of social worlds: Development in a social context.* Cambridge: Polity Press, 287-96.

Harré, R. (1986b). An outline of the social constructionist viewpoint. In R. Harré (ed.), *The social construction of emotions.* Oxford: Blackwell, 2-14.

Holland, D., & Valsiner, J. (1988). Cognition, symbols and Vygotsky's developmental psychology. *Ethos,* 16, 247-72.

Leontiev, A.N. (1963). L'homme et la culture. *Recherches Internationales à la Lumière du Marxisme,* 46, 47-67.

Leontiev, A.N. (1978). *Activity, consciousness, and personality* (M.J. Hall, trans). Englewood Cliffs, N.J.: Prentice-Hall. (Original work published 1975)

Leontiev (Leontyev), A.N. (1981). *Problems of the development of the mind* (N. Kopylova, trans.). Moscow: Progress. (Original work published 1959)

Luria, A.R. (1971). Towards the problem of the historical nature of psychological processes. *International Journal of Psychology,* 6, 259-72.

Luria, A.R. (1979). *The making of mind: A personal account of Soviet psychology* (M. Cole & S. Cole, eds.). Cambridge, Mass.: Harvard University Press.

Marx, K., & Engels, F. (1970). *The German ideology* (C.J. Arthur, ed.; W. Lough, C. Dutt, and C.P. Magill, trans.). New York: International Publishers. (Original work written 1846)

Perret-Clermont, A.-N. (1998). *La construction de l'intelligence dans l'interaction sociale.* Bern, Switzerland: Peter Lang.

Piaget, J. (1965). L'explication en sociologie. In *Etudes sociologiques.* Genève: Librairie Droz, 15-99. (Reprinted from *Introduction à l'epistémologie génétique: Vol. 3. La pensée biologique, la pensée psychologique et la pensée sociologique,* 1950, Paris: Presses Universitaires de France)

Politzer, G. (1969a). Note sur la psychologie individuelle. In *Écrits 2: Les fondements de la psychologie*. Paris: Editions Sociales, 235-43. (Original work published 1929)

Politzer, G. (1969b). Psychologie mythologique et psychologie scientifique. In *Écrits 2: Les fondements de la psychologie*. Paris: Editions Sociales, 57-131. (Original work published 1929)

Politzer, G. (1969c). Où va la psychologie concrète? In *Écrits 2: Les fondements de la psychologie*. Paris: Editions Sociales, 136-88. (Original work published 1929)

Politzer, G. (1994). *Critique of the foundations of psychology* (M. Apprey, trans.). Pittsburgh, Pa.: Duquesne University Press. (Original work published 1928)

Ratner, C. (1991). *Vygotsky's sociohistorical psychology and its contemporary applications*. New York: Plenum Press.

Ratner, C. (1996). Activity as a key concept for cultural psychology. *Culture & Psychology*, 2, 407-34.

Ratner, C. (1997a). In defense of activity theory. *Culture & Psychology*, 3, 211-23.

Ratner, C. (1997b). *Cultural psychology and qualitative methodology: Theoretical and empirical considerations*. New York: Plenum.

Ratner, C. (1998). The historical and contemporary significance of Vygotsky's sociohistorical psychology. In R. Rieber & K. Salzinger (eds.), *Psychology: Theoretical-historical perspectives*. Washington, D.C.: American Psychological Association, 455-73.

Rogoff, B. (1990). *Apprenticeship in thinking: Cognitive development in the social context*. New York: Oxford University Press.

Sève. L. (1969). *Marxisme et théorie de la personnalité*. Paris: Editions Sociales.

Sève. L. (1978). *Man in Marxist theory and the psychology of personality*. Hassocks, England: Harvester Press.

Sève, L. (1999). Quelles contradictions? A propos de Piaget, Vygotski et Marx. In Y. Clot (ed.), *Avec Vygotski*. Paris: La Dispute, 221-40.

Shotter, J. (1993). Harré, Vygotsky, Bakhtin, Vico, Wittgenstein: Academic discourses and conventional realities. *Journal for the Theory of Social Behavior*, 23, 459-82.

Shweder, R. (1990). Cultural psychology, what is it? In J.W. Stigler, R.A. Shweder, & G. Herdt (eds.), *Cultural psychology: Essays on comparative human development*. Cambridge: Cambridge University Press, 1-43.

Tulviste, P. (1999). Activity as explanatory principle in cultural psychology. In S. Chaiklin, M. Hedegaard, & U.J. Jensen (eds.), *Activity theory and social practice*. Aarhus, Denmark: Aarhus University Press, 66-78.

Valsiner, J. (1993). Comparative-cultural research in Soviet psychology. *Journal of Russian & East European Psychology*, 31(1), 5-10.

van der Veer, R. (1985). The cultural-historical approach in psychology: A research program? *Quarterly Newsletter of the Laboratory of Comparative Human Cognition,* 7, 108-13.

Vygotsky, L.S. (1978). *Mind in society: The development of higher psychological process-es* (M. Cole, V. John-Steiner, S. Scribner, & E. Souberman, eds.; M. Cole and M. Lopez-Morillas, trans.). Cambridge, Mass.: Harvard University Press.

Vygotsky, L.S. (1987). Thinking and speech. (N. Minick, trans.). In R.W. Rieber & J. Wollock (eds.), *The collected works of L.S. Vygotsky: Vol. 1. Problems of general psychology.* New York: Plenum Press, 39-285. (Original work published 1934)

Vygotsky, L.S. (1993). Principles of social education for the deaf-mute child (J.E. Knox and C.B. Stevens, trans.). In R.W. Rieber & J. Wollock (eds.), *The collected works of L.S. Vygotsky: Vol. 2. The fundamentals of defectology (Abnormal psychology and learning disabilities).* New York: Plenum Press, 110-21. (Original work written 1925)

Vygotsky, L.S. (1994). The socialist alteration of man (T. Prout, trans.). In R. van der Veer & J. Valsiner (eds.), *The Vygotsky reader.* Oxford: Blackwell, 175-84. (Original work published 1930)

Vygotsky, L.S. (1997a). *Educational psychology* (R. Silverman, trans.). Boca Raton, Fla.: Saint Lucie Press. (Original work published 1926)

Vygotsky, L.S. (1997b). The historical meaning of the crisis in psychology: A methodological investigation (R. van der Veer, trans.). In R.W. Rieber & J. Wollock (eds.), *The collected works of L.S. Vygotsky: Vol. 3. Problems of the theory and history of psychology.* New York: Plenum Press, 233-343. (Original work written 1927)

Wallon, H. (1946). Matérialisme dialectique et psychologie. In *Cours de l'Université Nouvelle.* Paris: Editions Sociales Internationales, 15-23.

Wallon, H. (1963). Psychologie et matérialisme dialectique. *Enfance,* 1963, 1-2, 31-34. (Reprinted from *Società,* 1951, 7, 241-46)

Wertsch, J. (1987). Collective memory: Issues of sociohistorical perspective. *Quarterly Newsletter of the Laboratory of Comparative Human Cognition,* 9, 19-22.

Wertsch, J. (1990). Dialogue and dialogism in a socio-cultural approach to mind. In I. Markova & R. Foppa (eds.), *The dynamic of dialogue.* London: Harvester Wheatsheaf, 62-82.

Wertsch, J.V. (1991). *Voices of the mind: A sociohistorical approach to mediated action.* Cambridge, Mass.: Harvard University Press.

Wertsch, J. (1995). Discourse and learning in the classroom: A sociocultural approach. In L.P. Steffe & J.E. Gale (eds.), *Constructionism in education.* Mahwah, N.J.: Erlbaum, 159-74.

12 Activity Settings, Ways of Thinking and Discourse Modes: An Empirical Investigation of the Heterogeneity of Verbal Thinking

Mercedes Cubero and Manuel L. de la Mata

The basic aim of this chapter is to present an empirical study to further develop the notion of the heterogeneity of verbal thinking, as proposed by Peeter Tulviste. This notion is based on the ideas of Lévy-Bruhl (1910/1926, 1927/1974, 1975), who stressed the qualitative nature of change which human psyche undergoes as a result of historical change in society, as well as the idea of the heterogeneity of verbal thinking both in individuals and culture. However, Lévy-Bruhl left two questions unanswered: (a) what is it that actually changes in thinking, and (b) what are the reasons for these changes? Tulviste answered these two questions by using Vygotsky's idea of instrumental thinking and Leontiev's theory of activity.

Vygotsky (1934/1986) claimed that different ways of thinking are the consequence of the use of different tools or psychological instruments. Moreover, tools serve a dual purpose: they *mediate* and *transform* psychological processes. The most important mediational means of human activity, among the various symbolic and physical systems, is language. For Tulviste, the mediated nature of cognition can be used to answer our question about what actually changes in thinking during its historical development. Not only the operations of thinking change, but also its basic units, namely, concepts. In this respect, Tulviste follows Vygotsky's (1934/1986) ideas about the development of concepts. Vygotsky's analysis is based on two ideas: (a) the meaning of words — as units of verbal thinking — change, and (b) development consists of a transition to qualitatively new forms of using words for thinking: from a first form of using words as a proper name to a second form in which the word is a symbol of a complex and to a third form, in which the word is an instrument or means for developing a concept.

Tulviste adopted Leontiev's theory of activity, (1975/1978, 1981, 1959/ 1983, 1989), as well as the modifications proposed by Wertsch (1981, 1985), as a theoretical framework for explaining why thinking changes. According to this theory, differences in ways of thinking depend on the activity context within which individual development takes place. Therefore, activity context becomes the key to understanding why verbal thinking changes. As such, the historical heterogeneity of verbal thinking should be seen as a consequence of heterogeneity in activity settings.

Starting from these theoretical assumptions Tulviste (1979, 1982, 1989, 1988/1991, 1992) formulated his ideas about the historical heterogeneity of verbal thinking by postulating the existence of a functional relationship between ways of thinking and activity settings. The demands of each activity setting generate particular ways of thinking that are useful to deal with every-day problems, and are specific to those settings. For Tulviste, the various ways of thinking differ qualitatively in terms of the tools used and the form in which these tools are acquired, but not in terms of the efficiency or superiority of one way over another. Therefore, he maintains that new ways of thinking are added to previous ways of thinking, without replacing them, because each way of thinking is related functionally to different sociocultural activities.

This functional relationship has both a cultural and an individual dimension. For the same individual there exists diverse ways of thinking — just as in a culture — corresponding to the various sociocultural activity settings in which the individual engages. This 'individual heterogeneity' is of particular importance for researchers interested in analysing the influence of macro- as well as microsocial factors in human psychological development. As individuals, throughout their ontogenetic development, participate in the cultural activities of their society, they are required to adopt ways of thinking that are adapted to changes in life circumstances. Thus, an individual will not use a single, homogeneous way of thinking, but different, heterogeneous ways of thinking, depending on context demands.

This functional relationship explains both the universal aspects in psychological processes in different cultures as well as ways in which cultures differ. The universal aspects are explained by the existence of common cultural activities or practices, while the differential ones relate to the specific features of particular practices within a given culture, such as schooling in Western culture.

With regard to the relationship between cognitive processes and language, Tulviste (1988/1991) follows Vygotsky in viewing various forms of verbal thinking as (mediated by) different ways of using words. But Tulviste does not address adequately what actually changes when different ways of thinking are involved. However, extensions to Vygotsky's semiotics are useful for developing that kind of analysis (Bruner 1964, 1986, 1990; Scribner 1977, 1992a, 1992b; Wertsch 1985, 1990, 1991). Concepts such as *discourse genres, types of argumentation* and *privileging of mediational means* provide useful tools for investigating the relationships between thought and language.

Bruner (1986, 1990) argues for a semiotic conception of thinking, in which each mode of thought is associated to a discourse genre. For him there are two ways of thinking, or two ways of knowing: logical-scientific thinking and narrative. Neither way of thinking can preclude the other because they are mutually complementary.

Logical-scientific thinking is based on the use of logical operations of class inclusion and categorisation. It is concerned with general causes and relations, theory generation and hypothesis verification. In logical-scientific thinking, objects are put together on the basis of common characteristics, which make them interchangeable. A major feature of this way of thinking is the search for higher levels of abstraction by transcending the particular attributes of objects. Argument is the typical form in this way of thinking.

Narrative thinking, in contrast, is based on the establishment of particular links between elements. Objects and events are put together on the basis of internal (particular and idiosyncratic) relationships between elements, rather than their belonging to a general class or connected by causal relations. The story (narrative) is the typical form in this way of thinking. As Bruner says, a narrative and an argument are different classes of entities and they differ in their processes of verification. Arguments convince because of their truth, narratives because of their resemblance to life.

Argument and narrative, as different approaches to justifying a text, share certain similarities with the various methods of explanation that Scribner (1977; Scribner & Cole 1981) outlined: theoretical and empirical (or functional) explanation. Argumentation, in Bruner's terms, and theoretical explanation, for Scribner, are ways in which an individual justifies action based on generalisable or decontextualised rules rather than on personal experience; that is, through accepted truths. Both, moreover, would appear to have arisen in the Western tradition of schooling. Narrative and empirical explanation, on the other hand, are based on the personal experience of the individual; they rely on a person's knowledge or beliefs about the world.

Another important issue related to Lévy-Bruhl's unanswered questions concerns the mechanism for generating heterogeneity in thinking, or, what amounts to the same thing, how individuals acquire the various modes of thinking that exist in their culture. To investigate this mechanism, Tulviste studied how problem-solving strategies are learned by children in the course of interaction with adults. However, he has little to say about how individuals learn these skills and make them their own. Rogoff's (1990) reformulation of the Vygotskian concept of internalisation — which she calls *appropriation* — allows us to go a little further into the means by which ways of thinking are transferred to the individual.

In this process of appropriation, we see how the circumstances and requirements of the particular setting in which people participate determine the discourse genre that is privileged within that context. The form of the discourse genre, and the characteristics and functions that this genre takes, depend on the motives, aims, and objectives inherent in the specific cultural activity in which the genre is used. The participants, through social interaction with more expert members of their culture, appropriate not only the different discourse genres specific to each cultural activity, but also acquire control over when and where they should be used.

Moreover, through this appropriation of mediational means and their patterns of privileging, the verbal thinking of the participants changes, by which we mean different uses of words, a change in discourse genres, social speech, and other kinds of mediational means. These changes should be seen as the acquisition of new ways of thinking which are added to those that already exist, and which derive their meaning and priorities for use from different activity contexts. Therefore, historical heterogeneity in verbal thinking must be viewed as a consequence of heterogeneity in activity settings and in the semiotic tools that are available for mediating thought.

Given the perspective just sketched, we believe that it is possible to address the key questions of why cognitive diversity is found both in culture and in the individual, what the diversity consists of, and how it came about? Taking the 'why' question first, we assume that the variety of activities in which individuals participate in a given culture can account for the multiplicity of forms that thinking can adopt. 'What' undergoes qualitative change in thinking is the patterns of privileging, ways of speaking and discourse modes that mediate psychological activity through reference to various semiotic tools. Finally, the question of 'how' mediational means change led us to a particular, developmental view within which the process of appropriation of these tools provides the key to our answer.

This way of analysing the heterogeneity of thinking seems persuasive to us and useful for explaining a broad range of situations involving the uniformity and diversity in ways of thinking. Moreover, it allows us to address the intimate relationship between thinking and language. Lastly, it seems to provide a good account of how social interaction — both at a macrolevel and at a micro-, face-to-face level — decisively influences psychological functions.

We wanted to conduct an empirical study to address specifically the 'what' and 'why' questions (Cubero 1997) — that is, to examine the semiotic mechanisms and their changes over the course of a task. The unit of analysis was *semiotically-mediated action*. This notion of action derives from the work of sociocultural theorists like Zinchenko (1985) and Wertsch (1985, 1998). They have pointed out that although Vygotsky addressed specifically the problem of the unit of analysis of mental functioning, the unit he selected, word meaning, did not accomplish all the requirements that he had previously established. For this reason, Zinchenko (1985) and Wertsch (1985, 1998) proposed the concept of tool-mediated action as a unit of analysis for human mental functioning. This notion of action led to the assumption that the starting point of the analysis should be human beings acting in sociocultural settings, not cognitive processes of isolated individuals. At the same time, the term *mediated* stressed the fact that human action is realised through the use of mediational means such as language and tools. These mediational means, whose nature is semiotic in most cases, shape action in important ways (Wertsch 1991) and give human mind a social character.

In our case, we were interested in analysing how the acquisition of new mediational means (discourse modes) that school promotes was related to new ways of mediating actions in two tasks (ways of verbal thinking). The study was conducted in an adult education school and two tasks were designed to relate to different activity settings. In the first task, the *menu* task, participants (all women) were presented with a set of photographs of food items (e.g., meat, vegetables, fruit, bread) and asked to form a menu for a family's daily meals (breakfast, lunch and dinner). This task was repeated three times, with different requirements for the menus. It was designed to show that uniformity of thinking could be observed in an activity setting, even though the persons who were doing the thinking had different amounts of school experience.

The second task required the participants to classify the photographs in a different way, avoiding the construction of more menus. This *classification* task was considered a school task. Because the participants differed in their previous school experience, we expected to observe differences both in the way in which the participants carried out the task and in the mediational means (discourse modes) employed to mediate task completion. More specifically, we formulated the following hypotheses:

1. Participants should perform the menu task in a similar way, regardless of their literacy level, because task completion was expected to require ways of thinking associated with practical activities. Because participants participated in these kinds of activities in a similar way, regardless of their literacy level, they were assumed to possess similar levels of competence.

2. Participants should perform the classification task in a different way depending on the extent of their schooling experience. In this case, task completion was expected to require ways of thinking that are normally associated with formal educational activities.

3. Finally, as an implication of the previous two hypotheses, participants with a minimal literacy background were expected to perform both tasks in the same way. In contrast, participants with more schooling experience should demonstrate a qualitatively different approach to the two tasks.

Method

Participants

30 women, who were students from different adult education schools in Seville (southern Spain), participated in the study. 15 were in the basic literacy level and 15 came from an advanced literacy level. Participants in the basic level were learning to read and write. The students in the advanced level, in turn, attended courses oriented to getting a primary school certificate. The age of the participants ranged from 50 to 65 years.

Design

Two independent (explanatory) variables were used: (a) *literacy level* (basic and advanced literacy levels), and (b) *experimental task* (menu task and classification task). The dependent or outcome variables were the behaviour of participants as analysed according to the category system shown in Figure 12.1. These categories reflected the unit of analysis — mediated action.

Construction Subtask

Action Plane

Type of action (i.e., what the subjects actually do)
- Orientation
- Location
- Evaluation

Regulation (i.e., who took responsibility for the task)
- Other regulation
- Self regulation

Utterance Plane

Referential perspective (i.e., how were topics brought up in discourse)
- Reference to a single object
- Reference to an object that belongs to a class
- Reference to an everyday category
- Reference to a conceptual category

Justification Subtask

Clustering Analysis

Adjustment to task requirements (i.e., extent to which instructions were followed)
- Nonadjusted
- Adjusted

Clustering forms (i.e., criteria used to cluster)

Menu task
- Simple
- Sophisticated
- Categorised

Classification task
- Menu
- By negation
- Pseudoconcept
- Concept

Discourse Analysis

Discourse mode
- Descriptive
- Narrative
- Argumentative

Figure 12.1. Category system used to describe performance.

Materials

30 cards, 9 × 8 cm, were used, each bearing a coloured photograph that depicted a food item. The depicted items were used commonly in the cuisine of the Andalusian region, in which the participants lived. The items included meat (chicken, pork and beef), fish, vegetables, legumes, dairy products, and fruits.

Procedure

Participants had to complete two tasks: construction of a menu and a classification task.

In the menu task, participants were presented with the 30 cards and asked to construct a menu for a whole day (breakfast, lunch and dinner). After they completed this construction, they were asked to construct a new menu, but avoid repeating the first one (they were told that one should not eat the same menu everyday). Finally, participants were asked to construct a third menu that could be used for a special day (e.g., Easter, Christmas).

In the classification task, participants were asked to cluster the cards using a different criterion than the one used in the menu task. That is, they were asked explicitly to avoid forming menus again. We expected that participants would cluster cards by classes of food.

Both tasks consisted of two subtasks: the *construction* subtask, in which the participants clustered the cards, forming menus or classes of food, and the *justification* subtask, in which the participants explained and justified their clusterings.

Data Collection and Analysis

Audio and video recordings were made while the participants performed the tasks. The video recordings were coded according to the categories shown in Figure 12.1. (The audio recordings were transcribed and used when the video recording was inaudible.) The construction subtask was analysed from two perspectives (*action plane* and *utterance plane*). For the action plane, the type of action and who regulates it is recorded. For the utterance plane, the referential perspective is coded. For the justification subtask, both a clustering analysis and a discourse analysis were used. The clustering analysis made global judgements about the participant's ability to follow the task instructions, and the principle used to form the clustering; the discourse analysis made a global judgement about the discourse mode used to discuss the clustering process.

The clustering principles were different for the menu task and the classification task. For the menu task, the menus were classified as to whether they were simple, sophisticated or categorised. For the classification task, the participants's clustering was categorised as menu (if the items were grouped by breakfast, lunch or dinner), by negation (for items that were grouped because they could not be cooked together), pseudoconcept (for food items that were bought in the same shop or kept in the same place), or concept (for food items put together on the basis of taxonomic criteria). Cubero (1997) provides a more detailed explanation of the category system.

The categorisation process was exhaustive. That is, a participant's performance was always categorised according to each of the categories in Figure 12.1, and always given one of the values for each category. Given the qualitative nature of these data, we analysed them using hierarchical log-linear models (Kennedy 1983), which are particularly suitable for showing relationships between factors in multiple-entry (contingencies) tables. They are similar to χ^2 tests, but can be used with a greater number of variables. For more details about the statistical procedures used in the analysis, see Cubero (1997).

Results and Discussion

This section presents and discusses the results that are relevant to the hypotheses presented in the introduction. We shall follow the same order. After discussing each hypothesis, we shall conclude with a general discussion of the results and consider their implications for the notion of heterogeneity of verbal thinking. In order to simplify the presentation, we only report the statistically significant χ^2 values that were found, and do not present lambda parameters.

Menu-Constructing Performance: A Test for Uniformity of Thinking

We found, as hypothesised, no significant differences between the two literacy levels in their performance of the menu task. More specifically, the results were as follows:

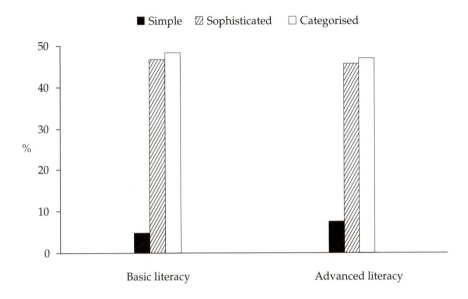

Figure 12.2. Clustering forms used in the menu task by literacy level.

– Participants from both literacy levels performed the task at a very simi-
    lar level (89% and 91% of adjustment to instructions in basic literacy and
    in advanced literacy level, respectively).
– Participants from both literacy levels formed the same kind of clusters in
    the construction subtask of the menu task. Figure 12.2 shows the almost
    identical distribution for the two groups in the percentage of occurrence
    for the three kinds of clustering forms.
– Participants from both literacy levels provided predominantly narrative
    accounts of what they had done (justification subtask). As shown in Fig-
    ure 12.3, the percentage of occurrence for the three kinds of discourse
    modes (descriptive, narrative and argumentative) were very similar for
    the two literacy levels. Participants from both literacy levels provided
    narrative justifications of menu constructions, in which both characters
    and events showed a close resemblance to everyday events in the
    participants's lives.

As the menu task was understood as an everyday problem, it was not surprising to observe that the participants's way of dealing with it also re-

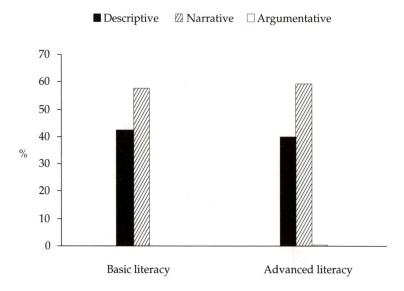

Figure 12.3. Discourse modes used in the menu task by literacy level.

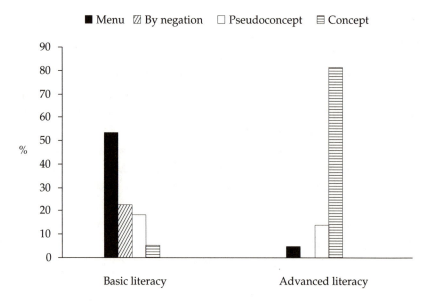

Figure 12.4. Clustering forms used in the classification task by literacy level.

flected real-life strategies. If we consider that the participants from both literacy levels are equally equipped to deal with the circumstances of the problem, then why should we expect to find any difference in the solutions they propose?

Classification Performance: A Test for Cultural Heterogeneity of Thinking

Two findings support our second hypothesis about differences between literacy levels in the ways they performed the classification task.

–   Participants from the basic literacy level showed a significantly lower adjustment to the task requirements in the classification task than participants from the advanced level (42% vs. 76%; $\chi^2(1, N = 30) = 31.90, p <.0001$).
–   The clustering forms at each literacy level were different ($\chi^2(3, N = 30) = 137.85; p <. 0001$). Figure 12.4 shows a clear difference in the distribution of clustering forms used by the participants from the two literacy levels. Participants from the basic literacy level used mostly contextualised clustering forms: 76% of the cases, if we combine menu (53%) and by negation (23%). Participants from the advanced level, in contrast, used predominantly conceptual forms of classification (81% of the clusterings). These participants who, in the menu task, showed no differences in either the manner in which they performed the task or in the items chosen, addressed the classification task in a qualitatively different way (Ramírez 1995; Ramírez & Cubero 1995).

Literacy Level and Task Performance: A Test for Individual Heterogeneity of Thinking

The pattern of interaction between literacy level, task, and referential perspective ($\chi^2(6, N = 30) = 60.47, p <. 0001$) was similar to the pattern for literacy level, task, and discourse modes ($\chi^2(4, N = 30) = 44.87, p <. 0001$). In both cases, we observed no differences between literacy levels in the menu task, but a remarkable difference in the classification task. Participants from the advanced level solved the two tasks in a different way.

–   Focussing first on referential perspective, we found a close resemblance in the distribution of categories of referential perspective used by both

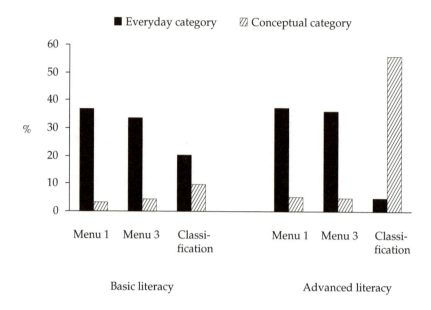

Figure 12.5. Referential perspective used for the two tasks for each literacy level.

the basic and advanced literacy levels in the menu task for the first trial and the third trial (in which they had to prepare a special menu). For both literacy levels, the percentage of explanations in the everyday category was higher than for conceptual categories (see Figure 12.5).

– We also found significant differences between literacy levels in the classification task (see Figure 12.5). While the basic literacy group used everyday criteria to explain 20% of their clusterings, the advanced literacy group did so in only 5% of the cases. Furthermore, the basic literacy group used conceptual criteria to explain only 10% of their clusterings, compared to 56% for the advanced literacy group.

– The same pattern was observed for the relationships between discourse mode, task and literacy level (see Figure 12.6). A similar distribution of discourse modes was observed for both literacy levels in the first and third trials of the menu task

– However, for the classification task, we see a striking difference in the distribution of categories for the two literacy levels. The basic literacy level

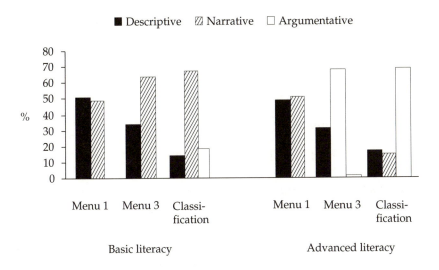

Figure 12.6. Discourse modes used for the two tasks by each literacy level.

justified 67% of their clusterings with reference to a narrative, everyday report, and 18% with more school-like argumentative explanations. For the advanced literacy level, the pattern was reversed: 15% of the clusterings were justified in a narrative way, while 69% of the clusterings were justified with a genuine argument.

It is interesting to note that although the basic literacy level used increasingly more elaborate tools in the classification task compared to the menu task, they did not change the general pattern of performance for the two tasks. That is, their graphs in Figures 12.5 and 12.6 show the same basic pattern for the menu and classification task. The classification task seemed to be understood by this group as, simply, another version of the menu task.

The advanced participants understood things differently. They carried out the menu task in a similar way to the basic literacy participants, but when they had to complete the classification task they performed in a qualitatively different way, both with respect to the basic literacy participants, and to their own performance in the menu task. These qualitative changes, both in the criteria of classification and in the predominant discourse mode used by the advanced literacy participants, could represent a shift in the mediational means privileged by these participants in each task (Wertsch 1991) — that is, a shift in attitude about which tools are considered more appropriate for dealing with the task. It seems to us that the advanced literacy participants conceived the classification task, in contrast to the menu task, as a school-like activity, which demanded the application of tools that are normally associated with school-like activities, namely, the use of decontextualised forms.

Sources of Heterogeneity

Given our theoretical framework, we assumed that heterogeneity in ways of dealing with the tasks would be related to the use of different mediational means (discourse modes). To support this idea, we had to find evidence for the existence of a relationship between ways of thinking and discourse modes. We believe the present study provides evidence for such a relationship. We mentioned some of this evidence when we compared the clustering forms of the two groups of participants (see Figure 12.4). Specifically, the basic literacy group used lists or menus in contrast to the use of genuine concepts by the advanced literacy group. The relationship between ways of thinking and discourse modes adds emphasis to our findings about the relationship between the clustering forms used and the discourse genres employed to justify them. As shown in Figure 12.7, when using a menu or list as the basis for clusterings during the classification task, the participants (combined across the two groups) employed narrative explanations in almost all cases (96%). Conversely, when they classified by using conceptual criteria, classification was almost exclusively justified through reference to arguments (93%).

These results shed light on the ideas of Bruner (1986, 1990) and Scribner (1977; Scribner & Cole 1981) cited previously. When comparing the accounts given by the participants in the basic and advanced literacy groups as they justified their clusterings in the classification task, we found evidence for two ways of thinking. The basic literacy level, who mostly constructed menus, used a narrative or empirical (in Scribner's terms) way of thinking, while the advanced literacy level, for whom the use of concepts was more usual, exhibited a way of thinking that could be described as argumentative or theoretical (see Figure 12.6).

We interpret this result as showing that access to particular ways of thinking that aim to organise experience in a conceptual way — which is typical in formal education — can only be gained by using tools, which are a prod-

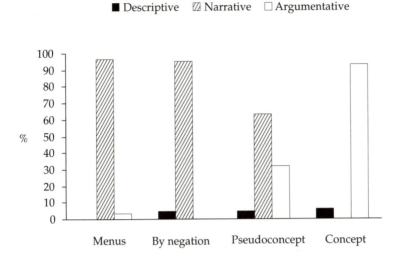

Figure 12.7. Discourse modes used for different clustering forms in the classification task, for the combined literacy levels.

uct of those educational institutions. However, for those with little or no formal education, the use of menus as a way of categorising the items represented an alternative way to solve the problem. This way of categorisation was justified by means of a story, that is, narrative or empirical arguments that draw upon the participant's own personal experience or observed relationship between the task and everyday activities.

Implications

In sum our study shows differences across individuals and tasks (heterogeneity, in Tulviste's terms). These differences can be related to participation in activity settings as 'housewiving' and formal education. Because the former activity setting was shared by the two groups of participants, it does not seem surprising to observe that they had a similar way of completing the menu task. As Tulviste (1989, 1988/1991) would argue, familiar problems will go on being dealt with in a familiar way — if this was successful — as long as the requirements of the activity setting continue to be the same as before. In such a setting the need for change does not arise.

In the classification task, which is related to school experience, we found the predicted differences between groups. When participating in an activity setting, such as schooling, an individual is required to respond to the new circumstances in which she/he finds herself/himself. In other words, she/he has to adapt (psychologically) to the novel situation by learning how to deal with the new problems, specific to this activity setting, in a competent manner.

As Lévy-Bruhl (1927/1974) would argue, we found heterogeneity in thinking both in culture (across activity settings) and in the individual (across tasks in the advanced level). From our perspective, it seems that these forms of heterogeneity are related to the acquisition of new mediational means. But the capacity for reasoning in a formal, decontextualised way does not displace ways of thinking that are characteristic of earlier periods of individual development. Ways of thinking are closely related to the activities in which the individual participates — as Tulviste (1988/1991) argues. Complex cultures, in which various kinds of activity are pursued (which to some degree is true for all cultures), promote various ways of thinking. These ways of thinking must be considered as ways of dealing with different challenges, each of these being adapted to the requirements of specific activities. Similarly, as an individual participates in various activity settings, he/she will have, at his/her disposal, the ways of thinking associated with these activities.

Conclusion

In this chapter we presented an empirical study to address Lévy-Bruhl's unanswered questions about the heterogeneity of thinking, specifically the 'why' and 'what' questions. Our results showed differences in ways of thinking, depending on the cultural experience of the participants and on the nature of the task. As we predicted, women who participated in activity settings such as cooking and housewiving, did not, in general, show performance differences in a task that was related to these activity settings, namely, composing a menu. At the same time, when participants with different literacy backgrounds are presented with a task that was related to school activities (classification of food items), they solve this task in a different way, corresponding to their experience in school activities. The observed differences in the actions performed by participants (i.e., their ways of solving the tasks) can be used to answer the 'why' question. Similarities and differences in the activity settings in which participants are involved account for the similarities and differences in participants's ways of thinking.

What actually changes in thinking? We found a relationship between the literacy background of the participants and the mediational means that were used predominantly to mediate each task. According to our theoretical perspective, the analysis of mediational means focused on discourse modes and on the nature of concepts employed by individuals to justify their clusterings. We observed that clustering forms, discourse modes and referential perspective were quite similar for both literacy levels for the menu task. Here, similarities in the participation of cooking and housewiving are related to similarities in the discourse modes and verbal concepts employed to mediate a task that resembled these activities. In contrast, the different literacy background of the participants was related to differences in the semiotic tools they employed. The co-occurrence between homogeneity and heterogeneity in ways of thinking with specific mediational means supports the idea that these similarities and differences in thinking can be explained by the use of similar or different semiotic tools to mediate participants's actions. The findings about the relationship between discourse modes and clustering forms in the classification task (presented in Figure 12.7) are consistent with this interpretation.

In conclusion, this study dealt with the issue of heterogeneity of verbal thinking, and, in particular, related differences in ways of thinking with the mediational means used by individuals to mediate their actions in solving the tasks. It showed the relationship between, on the one hand, activity settings and, on the other, discourse modes and ways of verbal thinking. At the same time, it has shown formal education to be a source of heterogeneity in thinking and problem-solving.

References

Bruner, J. (1964). The course of cognitive growth. *American Psychologist*, 19, 1-15.

Bruner, J. (1986). *Actual minds, possible worlds.* Cambridge, Mass.: Harvard University Press.

Bruner, J. (1990). *Acts of meaning.* Cambridge, Mass.: Harvard University Press.

Cubero, M. (1997). Escenarios de actividad y modos de pensamiento: Un estudio sobre la heterogeneidad del pensamiento verbal. Unpublished doctoral thesis, Universidad de Sevilla, Spain.

Kennedy, J.J. (1983). *Analyzing qualitative data: Introductory log-linear analysis for behavioral research.* New York: Praeger.

Leontiev, A.N. (1978). *Activity, consciousness, and personality* (M.J. Hall, trans.). Englewood Cliffs, N.J.: Prentice-Hall. (Original work published 1975)

Leontiev, A.N. (1981). The problem of activity in psychology. J.V. Wertsch (ed. and trans.), *The concept of activity in Soviet psychology.* Armonk, N.Y.: Sharpe, 37-71.

Leontiev, A.N. (1983). *El desarrollo del psiquismo* (E. Calatayud, trans.). Madrid: Akal. (Original work published 1959)

Leontiev, A.N. (1989). The problem of activity in the history of Soviet psychology. *Soviet Psychology,* 27(1), 22-39.

Lévy-Bruhl, L. (1926). *How natives think* (L.A. Clare, trans.). London: Allen & Unwin. (Original work published 1910)

Lévy-Bruhl, L. (1974). *El alma primitiva* (E. Trías, trans.). Barcelona: Península. (Original work published 1927)

Lévy-Bruhl, L. (1975). *The notebooks on primitive mentality* (P. Rivière, trans.). New York: Harper & Row.

Ramírez, J.D. (1995). *Usos de la palabra y sus tecnologías: Una aproximación dialógica al estudio de la alfabetización.* Buenos Aires: Miño y Dávila.

Ramírez, J.D., & Cubero, M. (1995). Modes of discourse — ways for thinking: Actual debates in socio-cultural studies. *Philosophica,* 55, 69-87.

Rogoff, B. (1990). *Apprenticeship in thinking. Cognitive development in social context.* New York: Oxford University Press.

Scribner, S. (1977). Modes of thinking and ways of speaking. In P.N. Johnson-Laird & P.C. Wason (eds.), *Thinking: Readings in cognitive science.* Cambridge: Cambridge University Press, 483-500.

Scribner, S. (1992a). Mind in action: A functional approach to thinking. *Quarterly Newsletter of the Laboratory of Comparative Human Cognition,* 14, 103-10.

Scribner, S. (1992b). The cognitive consequences of literacy. *Quarterly Newsletter of the Laboratory of Comparative Human Cognition,* 14, 84-102.

Scribner, S., & Cole, M. (1981). *The psychology of literacy.* Cambridge, Mass.: Harvard University Press.

Tulviste P. (1979). On the origins of theoretic syllogistic reasoning in culture and the child. *Quarterly Newsletter of the Laboratory of Comparative Human Cognition,* 1, 73-80.

Tulviste, P. (1982). Is there a form of verbal thought specific to childhood? *Soviet Psychology,* 21(1), 3-17.

Tulviste, P. (1989). Education and the development of concepts: Interpreting results of experiments with adults with and without schooling. *Soviet Psychology,* 27(1), 5-21.

Tulviste, P. (1991). *Cultural-historical development of verbal thinking: A psychological study* (M.J. Hall, trans.). Commack, N.Y.: Nova Science. (Original work published 1988)

Tulviste, P. (1992). On the historical heterogeneity of verbal thought. *Journal of Russian and East European Psychology,* 30(1), 77-88.

Vygotsky, L.S. (1986). *Thought and language* (A. Kozulin, ed. and trans.). Cambridge, Mass.: MIT Press. (Original work published 1934)

Wertsch, J.V. (1981). The concept of activity in Soviet psychology. An introduction. In J.V. Wertsch (ed.), *The concept of activity in Soviet psychology.* Armonk, N.Y.: Sharpe, 3-37.

Wertsch, J.V. (1985). *Vygotsky and the social formation of mind.* Cambridge, Mass.: Harvard University Press.

Wertsch, J.V. (1990). The voice of rationality in sociocultural approach to mind. In L.C. Moll (ed.), *Vygotsky and education: Instructional implications and applications of sociohistorical psychology.* Cambridge: Cambridge University Press, 109-26.

Wertsch, J.V. (1991). *Voices of the mind: A sociohistorical approach to mediated action.* London: Harvester Wheatsheaf.

Wertsch, J.V. (1998). *Mind as action.* New York: Oxford University Press.

Zinchenko, V.P. (1985). Vygotsky's ideas about units for the analysis of mind. In J.V. Wertsch (ed.), *Culture, communication and cognition: Vygotskian perspectives.* Cambridge: Cambridge University Press, 94-118.

13 The Category of 'Personality' in Cultural-Historical Psychology

Seth Chaiklin

Personality is a fundamental concept in cultural-historical psychology. However, it can be difficult, almost impossible, to notice the importance of this concept when reading classical texts within the cultural-historical tradition. Despite the availability of texts that discuss the idea of personality (e.g., Asmolov 1998; González Rey & Mitjans 1989; Leontiev 1975/1978; Petrovsky 1985), it is apparent that this concept has not been received in much of the cultural-historical research conducted in Western Europe, North America, and South America, and it remains relatively unexplored in concrete empirical investigations (though see Bratus 1988/1990; Fariñas León, this volume; Neimark 1976). This is a puzzle for me. How can a concept be so important, yet receive relatively little attention in current research?[1]

As a contribution to rectifying this problem, the first part of this chapter presents a brief survey of some examples of the personality concept as found in classic texts in the cultural-historical tradition, followed by some examples from pedagogical research. This survey is written especially for people who are trying to learn about the cultural-historical research tradition, and is meant to call attention to the significance of the personality concept, even if it is not well-integrated into current research practice. Among other things, it is possible to identify some common aspects in a cultural-historical analysis of personality. However, there are simply too few concrete examples of empirical research that try to work with the personality concept within the cultural-historical tradition, and, correspondingly, there is little advice about

* Thanks to Mariane Hedegaard and Harris Chaiklin for editorial comments.

1. To get a rough impression of the extent to which the personality concept is used in contemporary cultural-historical psychology, I searched electronically through the 413 abstracts that were accepted for the 1998 ISCRAT Congress. Twenty-two abstracts (about 5%) included the word *personality* at least once, though not always as a technical concept, while only 10 papers (2.4%) addressed personality as a major theme. One of these ten papers was my own, while the others, consistent with my claim that personality has been important within the Soviet tradition of cultural-historical psychology, were from Cuba (3) and former Soviet states (6).

how to approach these problems empirically. This, no doubt, contributes to the difficulties in using this concept.

To move toward an empirical approach, the second part of the chapter further elaborates the meaning and significance of the personality concept in a cultural-historical perspective. The concept is, of course, not unique to the cultural-historical tradition, and it was only starting to be formed as a general psychological concept during Vygotsky's lifetime, so the chapter concludes with a brief discussion of the history of the concept, and a final reflection about some problems to be addressed in using the concept of personality within a cultural-historical perspective.

The Importance of Personality in Cultural-Historical Psychology

To understand why the personality concept is fundamental in cultural-historical psychology, I will survey some classic examples. This survey also provides a background for the discussion in the second part of the chapter. The survey begins with a line of thought that started with Vygotsky, and continued with one of his research associates, Bozhovich. This line has focused primarily on the development of psychological functions. Then I discuss Leontiev's approach, and the approach of another of Vygotsky's research associates, Elkonin, which brings more attention to psychological activity and societal practices. The survey concludes with some examples that show the role of the concept in pedagogical research, and a brief comment about the current status of research in this area.

Vygotsky's Concept of Personality

In some of Vygotsky's texts, the term *personality* is used when discussing other research traditions that have used the term in a characterological meaning or in pathological contexts (e.g., Vygotsky 1931/1998, 137-46). For now, attention is restricted to those instances in which Vygotsky is trying to give a positive meaning to the concept within his own theoretical systems.

Without claiming to have made an exhaustive study of Vygotsky's works, I would suggest that Vygotsky uses the personality concept in (at least) two different ways. One use is generic, in which personality is used to refer to those human qualities of behaviour that result from cultural development, as distinct from biological maturation. A second use is a more precise identification of the specific cultural development, which in Vygotsky's analysis was thinking with concepts, and a self-consciousness of this ability. It is difficult to characterise these two ways as phases or periods within Vygotsky's thinking, because these two uses both appear in texts written during the same period (1930-1931).The following quote illustrates the generic use, shows that Vygotsky rejects a characterological meaning, and relates the concept to its use in pathological studies.

Personality as understood here has a narrower sense than in the usual sense of the word. We will not include here all the traits of individuality that distinguish it from a number of other individualities, that make up its uniqueness or relate it to one specific type or another. We are inclined to put an equals sign between the child's personality and his cultural development. Thus, the personality is a social concept; it encompasses what is supernatural and historical in humanity. It is not innate, but arises as a result of cultural development because 'personality' is a historical concept. It encompasses unity of behavior that is marked by the trait of *mastery* (see the chapter on will). In this sense, the correlate of personality will be the relation of primitive and higher reactions, and in this plan, the concept we introduced coincides with the concept that Kretschmer is establishing in the area of psychopathology. (Vygotsky 1931/1997, 242)

The second way in which Vygotsky used the concept of personality is already indicated at the end of the preceding quote, namely the idea of mastery of psychological functions. This idea is elaborated further in the following set of quotes from Vygotsky's (1931/1998) *The Pedology of the Adolescent*. The main idea is that personality is dependent on the achievement of a unity of psychological functions, which are the inward movement (internalisation) of social forms of behaviour. In Vygotsky's view, psychological functions are unified by the mastery of one's own behaviour, which involves the use of 'will' and requires thinking with concepts. Therefore, personality only starts with adolescence (around age 11 or 12). Consciousness (reflective awareness) of these unified functions is what forms an 'I', and what constitutes personality.[2]

2. Bozhovich (1977) gives a similar summary of Vygotsky's view about personality: 'Consciousness always operates as a complex hierarchical system, the highest form of which is a hierarchy at the top of which stands conceptual thinking. The outcome of this development is that the child becomes a conscious being, capable of controlling his own behavior. Thus, at this stage in Vygotsky's research, the development of generalized thinking and thinking in concepts was seen as the central process determining the development of the human mind, man's consciousness, and his personality' (p. 15).

The importance of thinking in concepts is shown here:

If we try to trace the steps of development during the transitional age ... we will see that ... on the basis of the transition to thinking in concepts, the bases of personality are established in the child. (p. 148)

Self-mastery and self-consciousness of this ability for thinking are indicated in the following:

As we have said repeatedly, the higher mental functions are based on mastery of one's own behavior. We can speak of the formation of the personality only when there is mastery of the person's own behavior. But as a prerequisite, mastery assumes reflection in consciousness, reflection in words of the structure of one's own mental operations because, as we have indicated, freedom in this case also signifies nothing other than recognized necessity. (p. 171)

One could make a much closer textual analysis of Vygotsky's use of the concept of personality, but its value would probably be mostly of historical interest. As can be seen, personality was viewed primarily in terms of intellectual functions. The problem was to integrate emotional aspects into the analysis. As Bozhovich (1977) suggests, the next — uncompleted — stage of Vygotsky's thinking was to investigate 'the development of human affect and needs in light of his theory of the development of higher mental functions and their systems' (p. 17). Bozhovich (1968) developed this stage in her own extensive research program on development of personality among children by examining the crises of childhood.

Like Vygotsky, Bozhovich (1979) considers the importance of the will, as a functional system, in the development of personality (p. 5), because it is 'the functional system that is responsible for a person's conscious control of his own behavior' (p. 6). Although this was considered 'central for a psychological description of personality', Bozhovich's (1980a, 1980b) empirical work makes clear that emotional aspects are also involved in the new functional systems that emerge in a person's lifetime. These systems have both rational and emotional aspects such that

the formation of the personality is not wholly described by the independent development of any one aspect, i.e., the rational, the voluntary, or the emotional. The personality is a genuinely higher integrative system — an indivisible whole. (Bozhovich 1979, 7)

Leontiev's Concept of Personality

In everyday speech, personality is commonly referred to as a collection of traits or attributes that characterise an individual. This view is also expressed in several psychological traditions that consider personality as an array of traits. In these approaches, one imagines personality as the sum total of these various traits, which in turn can be used to explain actions as a result, or at least an influence, of these traits. A cultural-historical approach, as exemplified by Leontiev, does not lend itself easily to this kind of structural model.

[T]he real basis of human personality lies not in genetic programs deposited in him, nor in the depths of his natural disposition and inclinations, nor even in the habits, knowledge, and wisdom acquired by him, including professional learning, but in that system of activities that is realized through this knowledge and wisdom. (Leontiev 1975/1978, 113)

But Leontiev is not attempting to replace a list of traits with a list of activities. That is, personality is formed through a person's actions in a system of social relationships, and these activities are hierarchically organised. This hierarchy of activities 'form the nucleus of the personality', and the integration of these separate activities are not realised 'by the action of biological or spiritual forces of the subject which lie within him, but by that system of relationships into which the subject enters' (p. 114).

Note that this does not really specify what is meant by personality, but only refers to the conditions under which it is formed. Leontiev's (1975/1978) main discussion of personality, where the preceding quote was taken, is found in a chapter titled 'Activity and Personality'. It is difficult to find a single sentence or paragraph among the 44 pages in this chapter where Leontiev presents a clear definition of personality. One has to read carefully to note that he is often writing about the formation of personality, the basis for the formation of personality, or what characterises personality. There are, of course, some places where something resembling a definition appears. For example,

the real basis of personality is that special structure of the entire activity of the subject that occurs at a given stage of development of his human connections with the world. (p. 127)

But then one has to understand the meaning of 'special structure', and here one can infer that this structure is 'those hierarchical connections of motives that form the "knots" of personality' (p. 126). One might want to equate motive hierarchies with personality, but note that these hierarchies only form 'knots' of personality. And these 'knots' do not refer to personality, but to the objective social relations in a person's activities:

We have seen that multifaceted activities of the subject are intertwined with another and connected in knots by objective relationships, social in their nature, into which he necessarily enters. These knots, their hierarchies, also form that secret "center of personality", which we call the "I"; in other words, this center lies not in the individual, not under the surface of his skin, but in his being. (p. 139)

So it would appear that personality emerges from a person's activities which are organised by a hierarchy of motives. That is, 'personality as a new quality engendered by the movement of the systems of objective social relations in which his activity is drawn' (p. 136). But one has to be careful about reducing personality to a mere identification of the social relationships in which one participates, or a changing motive hierarchy. Two paragraphs prior to this statement about a 'new quality', Leontiev writes:

the structure of personality devolves neither to the riches of connections between man and the world nor to the degree to which they are arranged in hierarchies, that their characterization lies rather in the correlation of the various systems developed by the life relationships that engender conflict among them. (p. 136)

That is, the structure of personality is not only reflected by objective social relations or a hierarchy of motives, but is formed by how a person handles specific conflicts between motives that comprise the hierarchy. For example, many upper-secondary school pupils have a motive to get high grades in order to enter a chosen postsecondary education. Another motive is social relationships with friends. Conflicts arise when friends, for example, insist on the pupil coming to a party when the pupil has to take an important examination the next day. The pupil's personality is reflected in how these (and other) conflicts are handled over time.

The correlation that engendered the conflict, mentioned in the previous quote, is not a process in which objective relations dominate or determine the outcome. Rather it is the person's interpretation of the conflict that embodies the consequences of the conflict. 'The making of this movement [of con-sciousness] expresses in itself the making of a connective system of person-al senses, the making of personality' (p. 129). To continue with the previous example, some pupils will choose to attend the party, valuing their social relationships more than the possible consequences for their further educa-tion; others will choose to remain at home. The structure of personality reflects the pupil's personal sense about these choices. That is, some pupils will attend the party with pleasure, while others will attend with guilt or dis-comfort. For the pupils remaining at home, some will be content, others despondent. These personal senses form the system that is denoted as per-sonality.

In sum, we can see that personality refers to the personal meaning of the motive hierarchy that is formed in resolving conflicts. But what exactly is personality here? Is Leontiev being inconsistent in his definitions? Are his ideas insufficiently worked through? My hypothesis (beyond the fact that Leontiev acknowledges that his ideas are incomplete) is that he is trying to express the idea of personality as a movement in the development of motive hierarchies, and it is difficult to formulate this idea linguistically.[3] As Leon-tiev noted, the concept of personality is introduced into the study of activity 'as of an internal moment of activity' (p. 97). But the 'study of personality as a moment of activity and its product constitutes a special, although not *iso-lated* psychological problem' (p. 97). So, we can see that personality is a way to focus attention on changes in activity, but as noted, it is not simply to look at any changes, but to understand the dynamic interactions among the mul-tiple motives that are present in an activity. This idea is similar to González Rey's (1999) notion of *configuration*.

This brief survey of Leontiev's analysis of personality is not meant to be a comprehensive and critical evaluation. Rather, I wanted to illustrate some of the ideas and considerations that characterise a cultural-historical theory of personality, in order to show that this concept is oriented to understand-ing a person's being, as manifested in the main social relations that arise from participation in societal practices.

The concept of personality, just like the concept of the individual, is expressed by the wholeness of the subject's life … [it] represents a whole formation of a special type. (p. 107)

---

3. One needs to read Leontiev's text carefully, crosschecking different statements, in order to extract an understanding that is compatible with Leontiev's view.

Elkonin continues with Leontiev's activity analysis, integrating a Vygotskian view with more attention to the concrete historical practices. Like Bozhovich, Elkonin (1972) noted that Vygotsky pointed to the necessity of viewing the development of affect and intellect as a dynamic unity (p. 233). But, Elkonin believes that:

our concepts of the mental development of the child have suffered principally from a radical separation of processes of intellectual development from those of personality development. (pp. 232-33)

Also like Bozhovich, Elkonin worked with the idea that 'the personality is the highest psychological example of *organization and control* of one's own behavior' (cited from Elkonin's scientific diaries by Venger, Slobodchikov, & Elkonin 1990, 24-25).

   However, his analysis of the development of personality did not focus on the discrete individual and her characteristics, 'but primarily on the system of relations between adults and children' (Venger et al. 1990, p. 25).[4] More specifically, 'the child's activity within the systems "child — social object" and "child — social adult" represents a unitary process within which his personality is formed' (Elkonin 1972, 239). The way to study this process is to consider the genesis and stages of development of societal practices. Crises in the system of adult-child relations (e.g., when the child develops new intellectual capabilities or social responsibilities) result in the development of new dominant activities, thereby changing the motive hierarchy.

   This short survey of some ideas about personality within the cultural-historical tradition has shown certain common points, especially a focus on intellectual and emotional aspects as unified in personality development, the importance of will, or self-regulation of behaviour as an important part of personality development, conflict as a source of development, the importance of subjective interpretation in resolving conflicts, and to some extent the focus on being (i.e., the whole person). Personality (in this analysis) is formed by acquiring societally elaborated experience through social interac-

---

4. Elkonin (1972) criticised Leontiev and his colleagues for only studying activity and not 'the objective-contextual aspect of activity, treating it as an aspect lying outside of activity' (p. 232). This may, in fact, be a valid description of the concrete research that Leontiev and his colleagues conducted, but I do not see anything in Leontiev's theoretical analysis that would exclude or reject attention to the objective-contextual aspect.

tion, and results in a relationship to view oneself as for oneself. By definition, social interactions in a societal practice are necessary for this development, hence the assertion that one is not born with personality (e.g., Leontiev 1975/1978, 107).

This review starts to show one reason for why personality is fundamental in cultural-historical psychology. If we understand that psychological functions develop in activity, but that the meaning of activity is a personal — not an absolute — determination,[5] then a part of understanding the development of psychological functions will require attention to their relation to personality (see the end of Fariñas León's chapter, this volume, for some examples). There are, however, other reasons why personality is a fundamental concept, and these reasons are connected to an interest in promoting human development in societal practices.

Personality in Educational Studies

The analyses from Leontiev and Elkonin are interesting and important for pedagogical psychology, because they provide ways to understand that instructional interventions should be aimed at the development of personality. More specifically, this means developing capabilities (knowledge and motivation) to participate in social relations, which are organised in societally-meaningful activities. The analysis also implies that beyond or instead of focusing on the development of individual capabilities, researchers and practitioners should also consider the possibilities that existing institutional practices offer for acquiring societally-meaningful activities.

Many contemporary pedagogical researchers in the cultural-historical tradition point to the importance of the personality concept (e.g., Hedegaard 1988; Lompscher 1985; Markova 1982). This is not to say that any great progress has been made in trying to analyse the consequences of specific instructional interventions on personality development, but only to indicate that this is an ideal and a direction that cultural-historical psychologists want to realise.

The interest can be understood, to some extent, to derive from Vygotsky's analysis of the relation between teaching and development, in which he argued that instruction should be used to promote development (e.g., Vy-

5. This is not a solipsistic view, because these personal senses are always formed in relation to objective meanings.

gotsky 1934/1987, 194-214). Vygotsky did not consider personality development explicitly in this argument, but as cultural-historical researchers started
to understand development within an activity-theoretic framework, it
became apparent that one could consider instruction as contributing to the
acquisition of activity, which in turn should be understood as the source of
personality development.

The following quotes from Davydov and Markova (1983) indicate the
importance of the concept of personality for pedagogical research within the
cultural-historical tradition.

It is very important to take into account changes not only in the intellectual sphere
but in the moral and personal development of school children as well. In other
words, not just the pupil's knowledge, ... but also, above all, evaluation of the
changes in the schoolchild as a whole personality. (pp. 52-53)

all Soviet theories have in common study of 'the internal link'[6] of the learning process, not as an aggregate of individual mental functions, but as the schoolchild's
active engagement as a subject and a personality (this pinpoints a fundamental
distinction between the view of Soviet psychologists and that of contemporary
neobehaviorist theories, of cognitive psychology, etc.) (p. 54)

It is necessary to create a research program directed at extensive study of the relationships between the development of educational activity and its new psychological formations and the all-round development of the personality of the schoolchild. (p. 74)

As an illustration of the importance of considering intellect and affect together in learning, Fariñas León (this volume) has pointed to the value of
introducing the personality concept in relation to Galperin's theory of the
formation of mental action, and provided some illustrations of the importance of addressing personality in improving the acquisition of mental
actions.

In sum, personality provides an organising theme in relation to learning,
but as noted it has not been common to integrate the concept in these studies.

---

6. Cf. Leontiev (1975/1978): 'In order to overcome the dyadic scheme that dominated
   psychology, it was necessary first of all to isolate that "middle link" mediating connections of the subject with the real world.' (p. 97)

Current Status of the Cultural-Historical Analysis of Personality

The previous sections introduced the concept of personality as found in cultural-historical psychology, and suggested that personality is an important concept, even if it is not developed widely within the tradition. The survey focused primarily on the ideas developed from Vygotsky and Leontiev. There is also a major tradition in cultural-historical psychology that works with similar concepts, but organised around the ideas of Rubinshtein (see Abulkhanova-Slavskaya & Brushlinsky 1996, 187-93), as well as other cultural-historical researchers (e.g., Asmolov 1998; González Rey 1996; González Rey & Mitjans 1989; Petrovsky 1985, chap. 8) who are developing their own approaches, often building on or in relation to the classical ideas.

Despite the importance of the concept of personality, at least in the conceptual logic of cultural-historical psychology, and some agreement on the basic framework, there is still considerable disagreement about the specific details of how to analyse personality. Reviews by Russian psychologists of research on personality carried out in Russia often comment on the difficulty in working on the problem and the divergences in the definitions by different Russian scientists (e.g., Davydov 1988, 87-89), and I can only concur with these evaluations.[7] We do not have a sufficiently elaborated understanding of the notion of personality in the cultural-historical tradition. The difficulties in specifying personality no doubt contribute to the lack of its use in concrete studies. Conversely, attempts to use the concept concretely are likely to yield more theoretical clarification. It is necessary that we try to elaborate the meaning of this concept, not simply to have a comprehensive theoretical model, but also because of the historical (and conceptual) understanding of the relation between the development of our theoretical concepts and intervention in social practices (see Jensen 1999; Seeger, this volume) — interventions that include such practices as education, physical rehabilitation, and social work.

---

7. The divergences are not necessarily wrong or detrimental, but it should serve to warn that one cannot assume that simply because a researcher is writing within the cultural-historical tradition that there is an agreed-upon understanding of the personality concept.

Methodological and Historical Analyses of Personality

The remainder of this chapter starts to amplify and elaborate the meaning and significance of the personality concept within the cultural-historical tradition. I make a series of methodological analyses that seek to clarify this concept within the psychological tradition and its epistemological commitment to dialectical philosophy. The chapter concludes with a brief examination of the historical development of the personality concept, and a reflection about implications.

Why is it Important to Study Personality in the Cultural-Historical Tradition?

What purpose does the personality concept serve? How does it relate to other concepts in the cultural-historical tradition? First let's consider some of the goals expressed in many of the same texts used to introduce personality in the first part of this chapter. Notice that the goals presented here are primarily normative. Bozhovich (1979) argues that studies about the formation of personality are not only necessary to enrich our scientific knowledge

but also to develop an adequate method of upbringing and to determine criteria that may be used to evaluate how successfully a child has been reared. (p. 22)

Similarly, in Venger et al.'s (1990) review of Elkonin's child psychology they note that

the most important question, underlying all the others: What should be (i.e., not what are, but what should be) the specifics of the relations between adults and children in contemporary society. (p. 28)

And finally from Davydov and Markova (1983):

Educational psychology is a theory that sheds light on the conditions that best ensure all-round development of a harmonious personality and mobilize the reserves of development at different age periods of a person's life. (p. 70)

The common theme among these examples is an interest in conditions for realising human potential. This interest does not arise directly from the conceptual and empirical logic of psychological investigations. Main principles of cultural-historical psychology, such as arguments about the mediated nature of psychological development, or the role of societal practice in individual development do not lead to an idea of personality. Vygotsky's focus on the development of psychological functions does not lead automatically to the idea of personality. The need for a mediating link between activity does not have to be formed as a personality concept. Similarly, the concept of personality is not developed in the philosophical and psychological sources that motivated or inspired cultural-historical psychology (such as in the work of Hegel or Marx). Indeed, at the time that Vygotsky was working, the concept of personality was barely established within experimental psychology.

Nonetheless, it is possible to offer some reasons for why the personality concept is important in the cultural-historical tradition. Cultural-historical psychology was developed initially during a revolutionary period in a society where researchers were genuinely interested in creating better conditions for human development. The assumption is that it is important, maybe even necessary, to start analysis with concepts that are meaningful in relation to human life, rather than assume a decompositional model (e.g., analysing basic processes of cognition, emotion, social relations, with the expectation that a meaningful synthesis will emerge or be achieved, see van der Veer, this volume). The interest in starting with human life grows from a desire to be able to understand, analyse, and intervene into ongoing, meaningful human practices.

Ideally, one would like to make interventions in societal practices (in schooling, in workplaces, in psychotherapy) that consider the whole person (i.e., the hierarchical structure of motives that organise one's life). This is precisely why the concept of personality is important in a cultural-historical theory. Human life is conducted and developed through activities. An analysis of personality focuses on the development of a person's capabilities and orientation within these activities. Attention to the concept of personality is, in effect, an attempt to understand the meaning of specific interventions (in teaching, in organising work, in counselling individuals) in the development of the whole person. This desire is as much an ethical intention as it is a scientific discovery, reflecting philosophical and political goals that preceded the appearance of cultural-historical psychology.

Personality as a Category

The title of this chapter indicates that personality should be considered as a category of cultural-historical psychology. The research problem is to form an understanding of the properties of the personality category.[8] Given the materialist position of cultural-historical psychology, it is important to consider whether *personality* should be understood as one more psychological function (along with memory, perception, and thinking)?

It is difficult to provide paradigm examples of 'personality phenomena' in the same way as for other psychological functions. Personality does not have clear operational definitions like perception or memory in which there is an external input and a subsequent behavioural response that can be used to measure the effect of the input. Even if we cannot give complete, unproblematic definitions for memory or perception, there does not seem to be much dispute that the former includes such phenomena as being able to reproduce one's telephone number, or recognising which photograph one saw yesterday, while the latter includes being able to indicate how many large black squares were flashed on a screen. Similarly, for more complicated cognitive processes, like problem-solving or judging, there is often an objective or standard performance against which observed behaviour can be interpreted. In light of these differences, my hypothesis — perhaps distorted by cultural commonsense — is that personality is not in the same category as psychological functions. If personality is understood as a consequence of the development of psychological functions, then perhaps it reflects a different level of description and analysis than commonly used for psychological functions. The different level is, however, still materialistic, because it is dependent upon the development of particular material functions.

Given cultural-historical psychology's orientation to a dialectical theory of knowledge, it seems appropriate to consider Hegel's approach to concepts, in which content determines the form and validity of the category (Hegel 1812/1929, §36). I think the Hegelian analysis of concepts could be useful in clarifying the category of personality because it provides a way to understand the dynamic that Leontiev was trying to express. To use a Hegelian terminology, the concept of personality is no less than the totality of the person-

8. In fact, it is unclear to me whether personality should be considered a specific psychological category, or whether it is a concrete instance of a category like 'emergent phenomena' that includes other instances such as self, identity, and nationality. This needs further analysis.

ality process, comprehended in the 'principle' by which it progresses. For example, Hegel's analysis of true being as something that exists only in the dialectical process that perpetuates it, and the dynamic of negations as a way to understand the resolution of contradictions. This view about the development of concepts can be generalised as a model for understanding the development of personality.[9]

In particular, a notion of personality can be used to formulate the idea of human potentialities to be realised, in relation to societal conditions. In this connection, it may be useful to maintain a materialist position, understanding personality as an ideal, and understanding the development of this ideal in relation to the development of psychological functions. Personality is an interesting candidate for a germcell, providing a way to describe the relation between individual and personality. The individual is the abstract concrete of the surface appearance. The social relations in which the individual enters is the negation of the individual. The personality, as formulated in the cultural-historical tradition is, in fact, a synthesis in which the individual and the social relations are integrated in the concrete individual. With this model, it becomes apparent that psychological research must seek to understand how societal relationships are integrated into personality. Furthermore, the analysis of personality in terms of personal sense reflected in the motive hierarchy provides a non-mechanistic way to bring agency into the analysis.

Personality in a Broader Philosophical Perspective

Just as the concept of personality serves an integrative function in the psychological theory, so does the philosophical focus on realisation of human potential provide a conceptual framework that gives meaning — through societal relations — to the personality concept. The identification of conditions for the development of freedom and the realisation of full human potential were fundamental motivations for the research work of both Hegel and Marx. This motivation was concretised in their life-long intellectual work. For example, the entire structure of Hegel's phenomenology, with its focus on negating the negation as part of realising the universal, and the reality of the universal (as opposed to immediate appearance) are directly linked

9. Whether this model should be ontologised, such as was done in dialectical materialism, seems like an open question, and in any event, it does not readily account for the subjective aspects of personality formation. For now, I prefer to treat it as an interesting heuristic.

to the idea of criticising existing societal conditions in the realisation of the potentialities in persons. Similarly, Marx's turning of Hegel on his head did not entail giving up the idea of realising potentialities nor the idea of freedom. But rather than using the Hegelian notion of reason as the source of freedom, Marx considered the material conditions (social relations) that create the conditions for the development of consciousness.[10] Questions of human freedom are partly an understanding of the potentials that lie in man.

In my estimation, Marx never returned to write directly about the issues of realising human potential, especially those raised in the *1844 Manuscripts*, and this remains an important problem to investigate within cultural-historical psychology.[11] Historically these ideas have been formulated by philosophers, but I think cultural-historical psychology should continue to develop these issues as part of developing an understanding of personality within a historical materialist epistemology. It strikes me that for cultural-historical researchers such as Vygotsky, Leontiev, and Davydov — whose interest in the work of Marx and Hegel was not simply as an externally-imposed necessity — drew direct inspiration from this tradition in their work.[12] For example, the 'whole person' in Hegel is not the empirical person, but the potential that is the person. This can easily be understood in relation to an idea like zone of proximal development.

I think it would be worthwhile to explore the philosophical tradition further — to clarify the relation to the personality concept, not simply to give a philosophical foundation, but also because these analyses provide an important horizon of societal questions within which the psychological analyses

10. 'Only in the collectivity did Marx see the individual as able to develop fully his gifts; only in the collective is the person free. When Marx talks of "personal freedom" he is consciously departing from the meaning that term has in bourgeois society, where the person is free as a bird — free to die of hunger! Freedom can be formal and negative or concrete and positive: the former asks "free from what", while the latter asks "free for what?" Marx shows that only the collective can guarantee freedom in the second sense since it opens the path to full development of the individual.' (Rubinshtein 1934/1987, 127)

11. Philosophical analysis of freedom and human fulfilment has, of course, not stopped with Marx and Hegel. As one illustration, consider the work of Paolo Freire (1968/ 1970), who was inspired in part by Hegel and Marx, and who also writes about freedom as the 'indispensable condition for the quest for human completion' (p. 31), and 'the ontological and historical vocation of becoming more fully human' (p. 52).

12. See, for example, the end of the last quote given here from Vygotsky, or his working notes from 1929 where he writes, 'personality is a totality of social relations. Higher mental functions are created in the collective' (Vygotsky 1979, 68).

should develop. Obviously a few quotes do not represent a comprehensive analysis of the concepts of freedom, human potential, and human essence as found in the works of Hegel, Feuerbach, Marx, and thereafter, nor a sufficient exposition of how these concepts might be employed in psychological research. But one should not overlook what has already been accomplished by way of analysis, nor be frightened by terminology such as 'universal' and 'essence', given that these concepts can be formulated in materialist and constructivist interpretations that are quite compatible with present-day thinking.

No doubt some researchers will be uncomfortable with trying to link philosophical and sociological concepts to scientific, psychological analysis, while others will object to what seems like giving a kind of religious status to the work of Hegel and Marx. But it is easy enough to treat these ideas as hypotheses, to understand them in a historical perspective as reflecting human concerns and interests, which should also be of concern to scientific psychology, and continue from there. This view is consistent with an understanding of cultural-historical psychology as part of a cultural-historical practice (see Seeger, this volume), in which we seek to make our own cultural history.

Historical Consideration of Personality

To this point I have considered the idea of personality primarily from the methodological perspective of cultural-historical psychology. It is also important to consider the historical development of the personality concept more generally, ideally as a genetic study — especially because the term *personality* has became part of everyday language. We should not mistake our everyday familiarity with the term as a sign for the scientific value or validity of such a concept. This is not to minimise the possible value that everyday meanings have for scientific work, but only to point out the necessity for considering the linguistic and scientific history of the concept.

For example, the Russian word for personality, *lichnost'*, is polysemous. 'The Russian term *lichnost'* may refer to "the individual", "the individual personality", or simply to "personality"' (editor in Platonov 1972, 125). According to René van der Veer (personal communication, 20 May 1998), in normal, colloquial Russian, *lichnost'* 'designates the total individual traits of a person', and 'less frequently it denotes just "person" for which Russian has no separate word'. This linguistic fact suggests when one is working with translations of Russian texts, then one must be careful to consider whether the term *per-sonality* is being used in a technical or 'everyday' meaning. Furthermore, when we consider how researchers have used the concept (even within the same research tradition), then we must not unreflectively assume that there has been a delimited, singular meaning associated with the term.

Personality, as a psychological object, was only formulated historically about one hundred years ago. Danziger (1997, 124) noted that the entry for *personality* in the 1901 *Dictionary of Philosophy and Psychology* edited by James Mark Baldwin was entirely medical, referring to the work of French physicians (e.g., Ribot) who viewed the personality as a natural, embodied entity that was prone to disease. The term *personality* had been used prior to the nineteenth century in theological, legal, and ethical contexts, and did not become an object of investigation, at least in American psychology, until the 1920s.[13] Danziger notes historical events that could have contributed to the interest of personality as a concept, including the practical shortcomings of intelligence testing in selecting candidates in non-academic settings. At the time, the psychological quality that was being measured was described variously as temperament, character, and personality. Danziger suggests that the prior medical use of the term *personality* (making it an object of scientific investigation and an assembly of different elements) was a major factor in the emergence of personality as a preferred psychological concept. He also suggests that personality did not have same moralistic connotations as temperament and character.

As part of the historical analysis of personality, it is important to understand the societal problems that were present during the time that researchers were developing the concepts. In the case of personality, it is probably easier to consider the societal context, precisely because it is a concept that aims to describe persons in their social and societal interactions. It is possible that the concept of personality should be understood as a phenomenon that is connected with the ideology of individualism, where the rise of the nation-state may be a critical determinant in the creation of the idea of the individual.

This raises a chicken-and-egg type of problem. Has personality existed since at least the appearance of *homo sapiens*, waiting to be discovered by psy-

13. It is more difficult, according to Thomae (1990), to identify a distinctive European trend in personality theory and research, and he comments that the process-centred approach from Soviet psychology has not received much attention in the mainstream trait-oriented approach (pp. 86-87).

chologists (i.e., the chicken), or was the idea of personality created by psychologists (possibly as a formalisation of a more diffuse societal practice) and used subsequently both to interpret and to develop/modify our own actions and practices (i.e., an egg)? Hacking (1986) discusses a similar problem in relation to the categories of *homosexual* and *split-personality*. He proposed a pragmatic solution to this kind of problem by accepting both aspects as possible. That is, that personality (or homosexuality) always existed and that it was constructed. On his view, then it is a matter of investigating the history of each specific category (p. 234).

It is important to consider that the very idea of personality could be a subtle, generalised form of what Hacking (1986) called 'making up people'. Hacking suggests that this practice is of relatively modern origin (he focuses on the 19th century, which is also when personality appears as a psychological construct), and that it is intimately linked to the idea of control (p. 226). In other words, by formulating an idea like personality, we can better judge what is preferred and what is deviant, thereby justifying intervention, modification, and repression. One could say that this is the dark side of creating visions of human potentials. In creating persons as personality, new realities effectively come into being.

To make Hacking's argument more concrete, consider the arguments of Meyer (1986) who presents two ideas that he thinks are established as constitutive doctrines in modern societies: that human actors 'can and must be systematically socialized' and that this is 'largely effected by institutionalized mass education' (p. 208). 'Individualism is a highly institutional, historical construction; it is not centrally the product of human persons organizing their experience for themselves, but of various bodies of professional officials' (p. 208). Meyer suggests that 'the continuing discovery of new and more abstract elements of personhood: new dimensions of development, new and subjective motives and perceptions, new rights and qualities, new individual capabilities', are necessary in order to maintain the idea that the individual is not entirely under social control (p. 219). While Meyer does not use the word 'free' or 'freedom', it is a reasonable antonym to 'social control'.

It is interesting to juxtapose Meyer's analysis with Bozhovich's (1979) statement that conscious self-regulation is one 'hallmark of the formation of an integral personality free of contradictions' (p. 7). Is personality development meant to serve human freedom and realise human potential, or is it just one more (unknowing) contribution to reproducing social control, giving the illusion of freedom?

There is an interesting tension here. On the one hand, we seek a comprehensive psychological analysis of personality, but we do not want to lose the uniqueness and creativity of the individual. Has Meyer gone too far in focusing only on the ideological? Would Hacking's two-vector metaphor be useful here, in which a community of experts create labels that some people make their own, while the autonomous behaviour of the labelled person creates 'a reality that every expert must face' (p. 234)? Or perhaps Meyer does not recognise that these formulations of human possibilities can be understood as mediating the development of new capabilities; that is, to understand the relation between psychological practice in relation to a general cultural-historical development, and in turn to understand these models in relation to psychological systems. The materialist and social constructivist principles in the cultural-historical tradition may be adequate for understanding these problems more clearly.

It is problematic to form visions of ideals of personality. We may have to recognise, from a historical perspective, that we are trapped into using an individualist perspective for conducting psychology, and that personality is a way to continue that individualist focus, but that, from a dialectical perspective, personality can also be seen as a tool for (self)development that does not have to continue exclusively with an individualist focus. This is precisely where the need for empirical and interventive research becomes clear and where further investigation should be taken.

References

Abulkhanova-Slavskaya, K.A., & Brushlinsky, A.V. (1996). Theory in Soviet psychology: Major dynamics. In V.A. Koltsova, Y.N. Oleinik, A.R. Gilgen, & C.K. Gilgen (eds.), *Post-soviet perspectives on Russian psychology*. Westport, Conn.: Greenwood Press, 187-212.

Asmolov, A.G. (1998). *Vygotsky today: On the verge of non-classical psychology* (J.V. Wertsch, ed.). New York: Nova Science.

Bozhovich, L.I. (1968). *Lichnost i eye formirovaniye detskom vozraste* [The personality and its formation in childhood]. Moscow: Prosveshcheniye.

Bozhovich, L.I. (1977). The concept of cultural-historical development of the mind and its prospects. *Soviet Psychology*, 16(1), 5-22.

Bozhovich, L.I. (1979). Stages in the formation of the personality in ontogeny. *Soviet Psychology*, 17(3), 3-24.

Bozhovich, L.I. (1980a). Stages in the formation of the personality in ontogeny. *Soviet Psychology*, 18(3), 36-52.

Bozhovich, L.I. (1980b). Stages in the formation of the personality in ontogeny. *Soviet* Psychology, 19(2), 61-79.

Bratus, B.S. (1990). *Anomalies of personality: From the deviant to the norm* (H. Davis, ed.; A. Mikheyev, S. Mikheyev, and Y. Filippov, trans.). Orlando, Fla.: Peter M. Deutsch Press. (Original work published 1988)

Danziger, K. (1997). *Naming the mind: How psychology found its language.* London: Sage.

Davydov, V.V. (1988). Problems of developmental teaching. *Soviet Education*, 30(8), 6-97.

Davydov, V.V., & Markova, A.K. (1983). A concept of educational activity for schoolchildren. *Soviet Psychology,* 21(2), 50-76.

Elkonin (El'konin), D.B. (1972). Toward the problem of stages in the mental development of the child. *Soviet Psychology*, 10, 225-51.

Freire, P. (1970). *Pedagogy of the oppressed* (M.B. Ramos, trans.). New York: Seabury. (Original work published 1968)

González Rey, F.L. (1996). *Personalidad, comunicación y desarrollo.* Havana, Cuba: Editoria Pueblo y Educación.

González Rey, F.L. (1999). Personality, subject and human development: The subjective character of human activity. In S. Chaiklin, M. Hedegaard, & U.J. Jensen (eds.), *Activity theory and social practice: Cultural-historical approaches.* Aarhus, Denmark: Aarhus University Press, 253-75.

González Rey, F.L., & Mitjans, A. (1989). *La personalidad: Su educación y desarrollo.* Havana, Cuba: Editora Pueblo y Educación.

Hacking, I. (1986). Making up people. In T.C. Heller, M. Sosna, & D.E. Wellbery (eds.), *Reconstructing individualism: Autonomy, individuality, and the self in Western thought.* Stanford, Calif.: Stanford University Press, 222-36.

Hedegaard, M. (1988). *Skolebørns personlighedsudvikling set gennem orienteringsfagene* [The development of schoolchildren's personality viewed through the social science subjects]. Aarhus, Denmark: Aarhus University Press.

Hegel, G.W.F. (1929). *Science of logic: Vol. 1. Objective logic* (W.H. Johnston and L.G. Struthers, trans.). London: Allen & Unwin. (Original work published 1812)

Jensen, U.F. (1999). Categories in activity theory: Marx's philosophy just-in-time. In S. Chaiklin, M. Hedegaard, & U.J. Jensen (eds.), *Activity theory and social practice: Cultural-historical approaches.* Aarhus, Denmark: Aarhus University Press, 79-99.

Leontiev, A.N. (1978). *Activity, consciousness, and personality* (M.J. Hall, trans.). Englewood Cliffs, N.J.: Prentice-Hall. (Original work published 1975)

Lompscher, J. (1985). *Persönlichkeitsentwicklung in der Lerntätigkeit.* Berlin: Volk und Wissen.

Markova, A.K. (1982). Ausbildung der Lerntätigkeit und Persönlichkeitsentwicklung. In V.V. Davydov, J. Lompscher, & A.K. Markova (eds.), *Ausbildung der Lerntätigkeit bei Schülern.* Berlin: Volk und Wissen, 28-35.

Meyer, J.W. (1986). Myths of socialization and of personality. In T.C. Heller, M. Sosna, & D.E. Wellbery (eds.), *Reconstructing individualism: Autonomy, individuality, and the self in Western thought.* Stanford, Calif.: Stanford University Press, 208-21.

Neimark, M.S. (1976). *Personality orientation* (J. Ipsa, A. Stone, and A. Nakhimovsky, trans.). Englewood Cliffs, N.J.: Educational Technology Publications.

Petrovsky, A.V. (1985). *Studies in psychology: The collective and the individual* (F. Longman, trans.). Moscow: Progress.

Platonov, K.K. (1972). The problem of personality in social psychology. *Soviet Psychology*, 11(1), 123-38.

Rubinshtein (Rubinstejn), S.L. (1987). Problems of psychology in the works of Karl Marx. *Studies in Soviet Thought,* 33, 111-130. (Original work published 1934)

Thomae, H. (1990). How European is personality psychology in Europe? In P.J.D. Drenth, J.A. Sergeant, & R.J. Takens (eds.), *European perspectives in psychology. Vol. 1: Theoretical, psychometrics, personality, developmental, educational, cognitive, gerontological.* Chichester, England: Wiley, 81-105.

Venger, A.L., Slobodchikov, V.I., & Elkonin, B.D. (1990). Problems of child psychology in the scientific works of D.B. El'konin. *Soviet Psychology*, 28(3), 23-41.

Vygotsky, L.S. (1979). Concrete human psychology. *Soviet Psychology*, 27(2), 53-77.

Vygotsky, L.S. (1987). Thinking and speech (N. Minick, trans.). In R.W. Rieber & A.S. Carton (eds.), *The collected works of L.S. Vygotsky: Vol. 1. Problems of general psychology.* New York: Plenum, 39-285. (Original work published 1934)

Vygotsky, L.S. (1997). Conclusion; Further research; Development of personality and world view in the child (M.J. Hall, trans.). In R.W. Rieber (ed.), *The collected works of L.S. Vygotsky: Vol. 4. The history of the development of higher mental functions.* New York: Plenum, 241-51. (Original work published 1931)

Vygotsky, L.S. (1998). Development of higher mental functions during the transitional age (M.J. Hall, trans.). In R.W. Rieber (ed.), *The collected works of L.S. Vygotsky: Vol. 5. Child psychology.* New York: Plenum, 83-149. (Original work published 1931)

14 Toward a Hermeneutical Reconstruction of Galperin's Theory of Learning

Gloria Fariñas León

> *But it is easier to assimilate a thousand new facts in any field than to assimilate a new point of view of a few already known facts.*
>
> L.S. Vygotsky (1931/1997, 1)

Introduction

A fundamental problem for many fields of study within psychology over the past century has been insufficient theoretical work to integrate the continual flow of diverse data derived from empirical investigations. This problem has been expressed particularly in the field that interests me — the theory of learning and its direction. In addition to the problem of insufficient theoretical integration, there is also a serious problem that arises from an atomistic (as opposed to a holistic, systemic) view of psychological facts and phenomena.

Most theories of learning only emphasise aspects of learning processes, which at the same time are decomposed into elements. This atomistic approach prevents a global vision or understanding of learning processes. One consequence of these two problems is that, practical work, such as subject-matter teaching, is not getting the benefits that one would expect from psychological research and theories on learning.

* All the citations in this chapter from Russian and Spanish sources are presented in my English translation. Thanks to Beatriz Macías Gómez-Estern for help in preparing this chapter. I would also like to thank Seth Chaiklin for his work and attention, kindness and patience in helping me edit this chapter.

One theory — one of the most complete theories on the direction of learning — has the potential, however, to avoid these problems. This is the theory of the stage-by-stage development of mental actions, proposed by P.I. Galperin and his followers, especially N.F. Talyzina (e.g., 1984), among others. This theory has traditionally been interpreted in a way that, from my point of view, needs to be modified, in order to achieve a more holistic view of its object of study.

In this chapter, I focus on insights about learning from Galperin and his followers up until the date of Galperin's death in 1988, critically identifying the theory's heuristic potential both theoretically and practically. Then I present a hermenuetic interpretation or point of view that aims to dialectically incorporate the traditional or original interpretation of this theory. This is the reason why I selected the words from Vygotsky as the epigraph for this chapter. Finally, I present two examples from my current research to illustrate and clarify this hermeneutic interpretation.

A Brief and Selective Review of Galperin's Theory of Learning

The main principle that organises Galperin's theory of learning is that mental processes can come into existence in a planned activity so that they become functional organs of this same activity. The planned activity is a group of tasks that is conceived to achieve this internalisation, and conducted under the guidance of a teacher or researcher. In effect, the planned activity creates opportunities for engaging in (material and verbal) actions that lead to the efficient acquisition of the needed mental actions, for example, in logical thinking, attention, mastery of one's native language and foreign language, and metaphorical thinking.

The conceptual frame of Galperin's theory is an identification and analysis of the system of conditions needed to systematically develop mental actions. The system of conditions contains three dynamically related subsystems: (a) the orienting basis of an action (type I, II, III, etc.), (b) the primary and secondary psychological characteristics, and (c) the six stages in the process by which mental actions are internalised. The system of an action's orienting basis is the most frequently praised aspect of Galperin's theory, while the system of stages has been one of the most frequently criticised.

The teacher chooses the type of orienting basis in accordance with the characteristics of the object of learning. The structure of the mental actions required to solve a task depends on the nature of the objects to be learned; therefore, the mental actions that result from learning will have different degrees of freedom, including, of course, those of the 'algorithmic'[1] type. The teacher also chooses the psychological characteristics, which reflect the quality of the learning process and its results, to be developed in accordance with the objectives of the teaching program.

Although the six stages in the process of internalisation are described as a stepwise process, they should be seen as a complex series of interrelated events that aim to create mental forms of action in relation to a given content. The instructional tasks chosen at each stage or moment of learning emphasise one type of understanding or execution, but each moment is not pure. From an early stage in the internalisation process (e.g., the orienting stage), the learner can be incorporating the contents of the activity to the mental form of action. The learner does not have to wait to receive an order from the teacher at the end of the sequence of planned tasks; this is a simplistic understanding of Galperin's theory. The learning process and which stage to focus on depends more on the possibilities of development already acquired by the person in the learning moment; that is to say on the current development rather than the proximal development. But this does not mean that one only uses the learner's acquired knowledge; one of the theory's contributions is specifying the stage or moment in the internalisation process when it is necessary to begin depending on the experience of the learner.

Talyzina (1985, 198) refers to an example that can help to understand this idea: A little child can break a toy because at that moment he is not yet able to represent for himself, in the mental form of action, how the toy is composed internally. When the mental form is not completely formed, it would be practically impossible to incorporate new knowledge and action to be put into practice immediately in this form of realisation; this child has to proceed from the first stage of forming a motivational basis for acting with the toy. The 'entropy' in the formation of mental actions increases when a person has already created a functioning set of action forms at material, verbal, and men-

---

1. Galperin did not like the use of this term in psychology, hence the scare quotes. Some psychologists misunderstand Galperin's theory as implying a preference for a fixed, mechanical sequence of steps, as characterised by algorithmic learning. While this form of learning can be described within Galperin's theory, it is only one kind of learning. The important idea is that the form of the mental action must be adapted to the requirements of the task, and many times this requires that persons must creatively adapt and apply general actions to concrete situations.

tal levels of execution because these forms interact with each other in very different ways. These learner characteristics make it apparent that a stage refers more to what is emphasised at that moment by the person who directs the teaching process. A stage does not have to have a 'topographic' correspondence with all that is happening mentally for the learner at the moment in the teaching process during which it is in focus.

The model presented by Galperin's learning theory has the character of a paradigm and not of a teaching methodology, a technology, or a simple instructional recipe. For this reason, it should be taken more in its spirit than in its letter. Rather than viewing the theory as though it was mechanically specified like a pocket watch, it is more appropriate to understand its ordered structure as analogous to a cloud, dialectically formed between processes of order and disorder. The global shape and movement of the cloud can be specified (i.e., order), even if each specific moment in the process is not determined (i.e., disorder) (Prigogine 1994). From this dialectical view of Galperin's theory, it seems more appropriate to use the theory as a way to understand and adapt to the heterogeneity of the learners in a school classroom, rather than seeking to force them to follow a homogeneous learning process, with a homogenous outcome. In other words, the theory is not meant to be a hypothesis of the learning process that should be subject to classical hypothesis-testing experiments in which one tries to measure direct relationships between teaching methods and learning outcomes. Psychologists should also recognise that in addition to the nomethetic way of interpreting the theory, it is possible, and necessary in my view, to use the theory in a more clinical or idiographic way to interpret singular cases of learning.

The principle that forms direction (the orienting basis of an action), as proposed by Galperin, has great practical value, as demonstrated by diverse learning programs derived from his theory. Galperin's theory is also valuable for explaining the conditions that affect different kinds of learning, and can be used to understand and explain facts and phenomena of the learning process that have only been identified by other theories. Recall, for example, Gagné's (1966) complex typology of forms of learning: trial-and-error, insight, which describes kinds of learning, but does not explain them. Or a form of learning such as proposed by Bandura (e.g., 1963, 1965), which appears to be very distant from Galperin's theoretical focus, can find some measure of explanation in Galperin's theory. I think the explanatory power of Galperin's theory arises for two reasons. First, because of its focus on the essence of the generative process of learning, rather than a focus on the superficial appearances of learning phenomena, and second, because of the use of psychological characteristics as an important part of describing and explaining the facts and phenomena of learning and development.[2]

Rediscovery of Insights from Galperin's Theory of the Development of Mental Actions

Galperin's theory of the development of mental action is not a closed set of concepts and principles. Rather its foundational assumptions — dialectical categories such as social situation of development, zone of proximal development, active character of the subject, genetic-historical approach — reflect its general relation to the cultural-historical psychology tradition, which opens the possibility for integrating or incorporating insights from other researchers in the cultural-historical tradition. Second, the theory has been developed at different levels of psychic organisation: neuropsychological (e.g., Luria), subject (e.g., Galperin, Leontiev, Talyzina), and personality (e.g., Bozhovich). Third, the dialectical philosophical foundation of Galperin's theory should make it possible to incorporate results and theories that were developed from other theoretical starting points, as well as reformulate its own assumptions. And finally, Galperin tried to study essential conditions and mechanisms of learning. That is, his theory is comprehensive in that he has identified the main aspects of any learning process.

There is no doubt about the great value of the theory, produced by Galperin and his collaborators, for the study of the psychological quality of learning processes and their results. The empirical results and practical achievements inspired by this theory are recorded in an extensive bibliography dating from the 1950s, in which many collaborators have enriched the initial thought (e.g., Kabanova & Galperin 1972; Lopez 1969; Pantina 1957).

For all these reasons, I believe that Galperin's theory of the development of mental actions has many possibilities for further development, refinement, extension, and renewal. It could be useful to widen the theory's spectrum, by adding analyses of the interfunctionality between primary and secondary characteristics and between psychological characteristics studied in Galperin's theory and psychological characteristics not usually studied by

---

2. I believe the best clarifications of the place and value of this mechanism for understanding and explaining a psychological point of view are found in Galperin's (1976/1979) book, *Introduction to Psychology*, and his 'Types of Orienting Basis and Types of Learning' (1973).

Galperin and his followers. For example, it is important to extend the study of learning to a higher level of autoregulation, namely, the personality.

In the 1960s, Galperin and his collaborators studied the problems of internal motivation and the types of orientation in learning. After twelve years of work, these studies had not made much progress, which motivated the need to make a theoretical reconstruction of their approach to the formation of mental action. But the reconstructions that have been made have not considered adequately the relations between learning theory and personality theory (González Rey & Mitjans 1989).

In *Introduction to Psychology*, Galperin (1976/1979) faces, with sharpness, the problem of the object of study of psychology. He refers to the existence of different levels of action: the physical, the physiological, of the subject (psychical), and of the personality. He wrote: 'Finally the level of personality, includes physical, physiological and psychic mechanisms of behaviour' (p. 130). Then, he added:

Each higher form of action can and should be studied starting from the aspects and the elemental mechanisms that take part in it, and at the same time, the study of the elemental mechanisms is not enough to study a higher level ... Insufficient in the sense that formation of higher mechanisms from lower ones, is not carried out in accordance with the schemes that exist for the elemental mechanisms; rather they require a new plan, which emerges as a result of the inclusion of new tasks and new relations. (p. 193)

This is not the analysis of a theorist who is ingeniously devoted to the study of the psychic processes without considering the complexity of the higher mechanisms of regulations. Galperin clearly saw these relations, but he was not a personality researcher. Nonetheless, this recognition made room for developing an analysis from the more complex level of regulation, or on the contrary, the theory of personality made room for the formation of mental actions.

Talyzina (1998), in one of her more recent works, approaches the problem of motivation and personality with greater detail and depth. This attention to the relation between motivation and personality constitutes an advance within the theory of formation of mental actions, but an integrated, systemic vision of these two regulation levels (subject and the personality) has yet to be achieved. The education of the personality appears in one of the last chapters of her book. One cannot simply add the topic of the personality at the end of the analysis, rather one has to depart from the idea of personality, and continue using the idea throughout the entire analysis of the efficiency of learning. In short, Galperin and his followers have started to work on the important insight of the need for a holistic learning theory that integrates subject and personality levels of regulation, but there is still much more work that needs to be done. Such an integration would widen the horizons of application for this learning theory, and better achieve one of its main aims, to use teaching to support the development of the person.

A third insight, which historically was perhaps one of the first, was the distinction between primary and secondary psychological characteristics of actions (one of the pillars of this theoretical building). Unlike the primary characteristics such as generalisation, comprehensiveness, and automation, which could be developed in a direct way by the researcher or the teacher, the secondary characteristics, such as reasonableness of action and the conscious character of actions

are never formed in a direct manner … they are always the result of one or more of the primary ones; the way towards them is always taken by means of the primary characteristics. (Talyzina 1987, 69)

This distinction indicates, in my opinion, that Galperin and his collaborators recognised that not everything can be taught directly; there are limits on what can be communicated by teaching. Moreover, psychic life possesses its own internal dynamics, which does not strictly depend on teaching. Therefore, development does not rely in a direct, linear, mechanistic way on teaching, although teaching, in the last resort, leads to development. This differentiation between primary and secondary characteristics implies a nonmechanistic vision of the processes by which mental actions are assimilated. At the same time, this differentiation leads to reflection about and study of learning phenomenology (i.e., a learner's phenomenal consciousness), because secondary characteristics reflect a subjectivity that cannot be understood from examining teaching alone.

Aidarova (1969, 1979), under the guidance of Davydov and Galperin, carried out experiments about the teaching of the Russian language as a first language. In these experiments, which followed a type III orienting basis,[3]

3. The pupils are instructed in a way so that they form a general principle that can be applied to a class of phenomena. For example, in Aidarova's experiments, she taught children in the first grade a 'form-content' principle as a unit of analysis. This principle

Aidarova reported that as a result of the teaching interventions, the pupils displayed a fine sensibility towards the language — not directly taught — like a kind of educated intuition. That is, the pupils developed a 'consciousness of language' in which they have a new point of view or attitude about the nature and meaning of language. This secondary psychological characteristic emerges from the teaching tasks and reflections that the pupils make while working on the tasks. The development of these secondary characteristics is a different criterion for successful learning, than a more traditional focus on efficiency or number of correct answers and solutions to the learning tasks.

Bozhovich (1966/1976), known for her interesting and far-reaching studies about personality development, stated a similar view:

it is possible to speak about a full acquisition of knowledge, only when this knowledge is transformed into points of view; that is, when the student's conception about reality and his attitude towards it change. (p. 198)

Galperin and his collaborators found or looked for qualitatively higher units of analysis from the subjective point of view and for a greater power of regulation such as sensibility towards the language.

Experiments by Butkin, Ermonskaia and Kisliuk (1977), concerning the acceptance of different kinds of orienting bases that were in accordance with the cognitive styles of the learners, showed another insight. These experiments clearly demonstrated that the type III orienting basis — because of its full, generalised, independent nature — was not well accepted by individuals who preferred a metaphorical thinking style over a logical-verbal thinking style. This result, which in my opinion seemed to refute the supremacy of the type III orienting basis, showed the heterogeneous nature of the internalisation process and therefore, of the six stages in Galperin's theory of internalisation. In other words, a learner's comprehension and acceptance of the orienting basis depended not only on the quality of the orientation (i.e., type I, II, or III), but also on individual, subjective preferences as reflected in a psychological characteristic like thinking style.

indicated that there is a relation between morphological form and expressed meaning. The children subsequently generalised this abstract unit of analysis into a method that they applied to all words (i.e., nouns, verbs, adjectives), finding regularities and exceptions. In Galperin's terminology, the unit of analysis and the method of analysis form a Type III orienting basis.

Finally, to end my account of relevant theoretical insights and trails that were developed during Galperin's lifetime, I will discuss the studies by Graf, Iliasov, and Liaudis (1983) about self-organisation of study activity. Researchers often approach the investigation of study activity as a descriptive plan, as an inventory of techniques for study, without being concerned about the place and the psychological mechanism of these techniques in human activity as a whole. Graf et al. generalised the basic principles of Galperin's theory of learning by taking a more strategic viewpoint in their analysis of the study activity by investigating the process of self-direction of learning.

In their projects, they emphasised some of the most important elements of this activity, among them, organisation of time, comprehension, and written text composition. This focus was motivated by, for example, Liaudis, who places great importance on the role of written composition and temporal organisation in developing the study activity. For example, the actions involved in planning one's study time include: sense of planning, control of the conditions, probable forecast, and final control or balance. The research approach was psychopedagogical. In the typical experiment, one group of students was taught actions to learn specific, concrete techniques for studying (such as reading techniques, making summaries of texts, searching for information), while another group was taught general principles for organising and regulating their study activity (such as organising time in daily life, controlling the process and results of study). In general, they found that students who learned general principles performed better on various measures of study activity than the groups that only learned specific study techniques.

Their studies, in my opinion, pointed at the need for further development of Galperin's theory, and their ideas pointed towards a way to reformulate and enrich the theory in a rather independent way. Galperin's theory had typically been used to structure the student's actions, until the moment or stage in which the student reached his independence; that is, when he widened his zone of proximal development. Graf et al.'s results showed the value of giving learners more control of the process of learning at an earlier point in the process.

With this analysis I have tried to call attention to my rediscovery of the theory of stage-by-stage development of mental actions, and to indicate that it is still a fruitful, valuable theory. I stress the fact that the logic of development of this theory sets the main direction for its further development. One of the strongest points of this theoretical model is to demonstrate how the subject can efficiently and productively take possession of the architecture (i.e., the orienting basis, including models of the object, the actions, and the control of action) and the engineering (i.e., the ways to use the orienting basis in the six steps in the internalisation process) of knowledge. This theoretical foundation makes it possible to facilitate the excellence of teaching and learning at different school levels.

With these ends, the conception outlined by Galperin emphasises a series of important requirements for the construction of a theory of learning:

1. A system for conditions for forming the learner's sense comprehension, which is the source of motivation for the object of learning and for forming a comprehension of the meanings of the object of learning, which provides an orienting basis for action.

2. A system of primary and secondary psychological characteristics that express the quality and results of the learning process.

3. A system of dynamic stages that are mediated by teaching (or self-teaching) in the learning process (comprehension and execution).

4. A principled system that governs and orders the teaching process and learning (e.g., the economy of the knowledge in question, the active character of the subject).

There are several explicit or implicit implications from this theory that broadens its value. One is that it emphasises that many difficulties that occur in learning are a result of inadequate teaching forms and methods, rather than inherent limitations or inadequacies in the learner. This view gives considerable possibilities to the development of the education.

Critique and Development of Galperin's Theory of Learning: A Hermeneutic Approach

Galperin's theory is often presented in a cybernetic version. This version of the theory focuses, as a general rule, on how to have strict control over the learning process (through the teaching process), thereby enabling the theory to predict the steps and results of the learning. This cybernetic version has led some psychologists and educators to think that Galperin's theory has a positivistic direction, even though it is within the cultural-historical approach. This criticism, which I believe is deserved, also reflects a major problem with activity theory (of which Galperin's theory is an example).

The theory has focused primarily on the external setup of the instructional influence (i.e., the specific organisation of the teaching process) and emphasises the efficiency of learning and circuits of feedback. In this sense, research and theorising in Galperin's theory can be understood as having focused mainly on the operational concept of zone of proximal development. But this abstract formulation of the concept of zone of proximal development leads to a misunderstanding regarding the complex, tangled system of influences, in which the student lives, not only in the classroom but also before and after coming to it. The theory of stage-by-stage development of mental actions would gain much, if it were interpreted from a hermeneutic position, rather than framing it as a cybernetic model. When applying this model to education, a hermeneutical interpretation would emphasise intersubjective circuits of dialogue in the teaching-learning process, rather than the feedback circuits that are commonly found in the cybernetic version.

The theory has not given much attention to the subjective aspects of learning (i.e., the learner's styles, preferences and personal experiences). A full and deep understanding of this learning requires a continuous and integrated relation to the category of the social situation of development. This integration would allow us to more clearly and easily analyse learning by considering the three levels of relations in the social situation of development — general, particular and singular — and the possible variants of movement between these levels.

I emphasise subjectivity in order to highlight some aspects that were not sufficiently developed in the theory of activity: individuality in a most existential sense, and personal flexibility for achieving an original view of the world and oneself, underlining one's unique creative potential. This implies, in my view, that psychologists should abandon the zeal for homogeneity, and search for diversity, where the singular is part of that diversity.

The critique of the theory of Galperin's model must be followed by a dialectical integration of both interpretations, because one cannot deny or ignore the results obtained in its first (cybernetic) version. This form of complex thinking would contribute to the further development of Galperin's theory. Two additions to Galperin's theory would, from a hermeneutical point of view, widen its potential, and enable it to better draw on the best from the vast body of empirical and theoretical results in the field of learning and human development. These additions are to investigate the relations between psychic and personality levels in the regulation of the process of learning, and to investigate the phenomenology of learning. But new lines of theoretical and empirical investigation should not only add these new dimensions to Galperin's theory; they should also produce new analysis units that synthesise cognitive and affective aspects, where affect refers not only to motivating aspects, but also to its expression in the regulation of psychical and personality levels.

Relations between Psychic and Personality Levels of Regulation in Learning

The interest here is to look at the interactions between the mechanisms of regulation, including self-regulation, at the psychic and personality levels. For example, the relations between consciousness about task solving (in Galperin's terminology) as an expression of psychic regulation, and consciousness about self-style in task solving, as an expression of personality regulation.

Graf et al.'s turn towards the study of self-organisation of learning, could have made it possible to integrate, to a greater extent, a theory of the level of personality regulation, if they had tried to make self-regulation start, for example, from the concept of the person as such, of self-evaluation and self-esteem. But their analysis remained at the activity level, at the level of psychic regulation involved in study techniques. It is known that the mere fulfilment of an activity does not necessarily enrich or develop personality. Personality is not defined by means of the abstract structure of the activity.

Personality does not limit itself to the carrying out of a task towards its final accomplishment ... but rather makes use of its rights to employ its own way of solving the task and introduce it in its life. (Abulkhanova-Slavskaya 1982, 155)

The point is to raise Galperin's conception from the level of psychic regulation (self-regulation), related mainly to the mobilisation and maintenance of psychic activism, to the level of personality regulation (self-regulation), which comprises singular, characteristic ways of acting, the position of the personality within the activity, and the maintenance of a certain personal line which gives stability to the activity. The activity then would improve from personality as a level of higher psychic organisation.

The relations between the two levels of regulation cannot be understood in a static way. For example, in conducting teaching experiments and programs in which the most efficient orienting bases (types II and III) are used, one gets the impression that the learners feel confident about their possibilities for successfully solving the learning tasks being taught. In other words, rationality, which is a secondary characteristic in Galperin's approach, could lead, in a way, to the development of other personality characteristics such as self-respect and pride.

The development of secondary characteristics has an inner dynamic that is not directly determined by teaching. A large part of personality development seems to occur in the same way (i.e., it is not directly determined from external interventions, such as teaching, but emerges from its own inner dynamic). The complexity of the process by which psychic processes affect the development of personality and the ways in which the personality affects the development of psychic processes makes me recall:

all things are helped and helpers, all things are mediate and immediate, and all of them are linked by means of a loop which connects them, even the most distant ones. (Blaise Pascal, cited in Morin, 1994, 422)

It is difficult to discover connections between psychic and personality processes, especially because some may appear unrelated or the effects are indirect, thereby masking the connections. But psychology as a science and as a professional practice needs to develop these connections, which, in my opinion, will require reflection and collaboration among researchers devoted to the study of learning and development with those who study personality development.

Phenomenology of Learning

The phenomenology of learning is concerned with the learner's experience of learning, with an interest to deepen the understanding of the unified (cognitive and affective) experience (*perezhivanie*)[4] of learning and its integration of the functional aspects of this process. Descriptions of learning phenomenology reflect the singular in the learning process.

Investigations of the phenomenology should focus on the 'inner psychological landscape' of the learner's perceptions and feelings when learning, including what the learner gives 'spontaneously' in his/her learning process, and the learner's personal styles, tastes, and preferences for learning. These

---

4. See van der Veer (this volume) for more discussion about *perezhivanie*.

subjective aspects cannot be determined by external influences. They are related to individual, subjective ways of coping with reality.

I think it is necessary to integrate this phenomenology of learning with a functional view of development (i.e., one that takes the social situation of development into account, focusing on how the single person behaves and develops). This integration, in combination with the traditional focus on the teaching process, will result in a more holistic, complete interpretation of learning that acknowledges the learner's contribution (and not only the external teaching conditions).

A Hermeneutic Reconstruction of Galperin's Theory: Some Examples

In this final section, I want to elaborate my suggestions from the previous section by using some themes — learning written expression and learning to organise time — from my own research.[5] My main purpose here is to illustrate what I mean by relating the psychic and personality levels of regulation. The processes of learning and the processes of development of personality are not contained and distinct, like a *matroska*. Rather one should search for the intrinsic nexus in these processes, which means a study of learning from the point of view of complexity: that of personality.[6]

I take the development of consciousness as pivotal in this analysis of how to change the focus in Galperin's theory. This development is often achieved by engaging with the subject as a personality level. I will present some experimental results that show improvements in performance that can be

5. In my other work, that is more theoretical/methodological, I locate expression (written and oral), and the organisation of time in daily life, among other abilities, as responsible for and principle pivots in the functional development of personality (Fariñas León 1993), and the foundation for strategies of learning to learn. My conception about learning has been the foundation for various experiments in primary, secondary, and higher education in Cuba (Fariñas León 1995, 1999c).

6. In Cuba, the study of personality, has received a lot of attention, with a special characteristic approach, stimulated especially by a group of researchers under the leadership of Fernando González Rey (see, e.g., González Rey 1999). My own work is not directly inspired by this approach, but González Rey's ideas were important for stimulating interest in Cuba for the development of psychological theory toward this objective. The sources of inspiration for my conception are from the cultural-historical tradition (especially Galperin, Talyzina, Liaudis, and Iliasov) and from Carl Rogers and Victor Frankl (see my chapter 'Tendiendo Puentes entre Formas de Pensar' in Fariñas León 1995).

achieved if a personality level of regulation is included with the traditional Galperian approach to instruction.

The cybernetic model emphasises mainly the achievement of efficiency through orientational mechanisms, execution and feedback. That is, the theory is oriented mostly toward the object (S-O). I try to amplify these dimensions by also emphasising the subjective spaces of dialogue (intersubjective and intrasubjective). That is, to use a holistic orientation that includes the S-O relation and the subject-subject relation (S-S) equally.

The change from an object-oriented perspective to a holistic perspective also changes the contents of the psychological characteristics. In particular, the development of consciousness as a psychological characteristic is not constrained to understanding the object, but includes the critical interpretation of dialogue with others and with oneself.[7]

The examples that I will present emphasise the S-S relation (including the subject with himself), which takes place through interaction with others (experimenter, teacher, and peers). The subjective conditions are not added mechanically to the conditions of the object, but dialectically integrated (i.e., how I, the learner, see the conditions of the object of learning, how I see myself in the realisation of the learning tasks). This way of learning is not brought to consciousness in a depersonalised manner. From this main idea, I try to localise the problem of personality as a necessary aspect of Galperin's theory of learning.

My goal is to search for niches in Galperin's theory where an integration between the psychic and personality levels is possible. I consider the verbal stage as one of these fundamental niches for the development of this theory from a hermeneutic perspective. The verbal stage is the crucial point in the passage from external to internal and from internal to the external. In Galperin's theory, there is a focus on internal and external dialogue as part of the process of developing mental action, where language serves as a regulating function. My general hypothesis is that teaching interventions that encourage or support learners to focus on their creativity, originality and singularity will result in a more elaborated, richer verbal process, which in turn will improve learning. This focus on creativity and originality is part of what I call a *personality level of regulation*, and it illustrates how a focus on the per-

---

7. This must not be interpreted to mean that Galperin's theory does not pay attention to dialogue (with others and with oneself). Galperin acknowledges a special place for dialogue in the so-called verbal stage, but it has another content and another orientation that is directed more to action with the object of learning.

sonality level of regulation can be related to the development of psychic processes.

Learning Written Expression

In this example, I discuss two studies that emphasise the development of self-consciousness about originality or personal style, without ignoring self-acquisition of the cultural norm of practice (i.e., the type II and III orienting bases of action).[8] These studies show the value of encouraging a subject's internal dialogue, at the personality level, in relation to the performance task.

Teaching experiments that have used a type III orienting basis (such as the experiments of Aidarova) have shown the presence of creativity in the execution of completed tasks. But in our case, we took creativity, or some of its aspects, for the purpose of pointing to an aspect of Galperin's theory that was considered to be insufficient, and that should be developed further. In particular, the problem of self-consciousness, the consciousness of one's singularity in learning a cultural norm, seemed like one of the best places to analyse the problem of subjectivity, in its living aspect, and in the development of Galperin's theory. The self-consciousness of style, of one's own originality, is perhaps one of the most refined elaborations of the concept of the self and this has played an important role in the constant search for human development.

An experiment on learning written expression was conducted with sixth grade pupils (11-12 years old) in a Cuban school classroom (Fariñas León 1999c). First, the students were given an initial diagnostic writing test. Then they all received instruction aimed at forming a Type II orienting basis and motivation that took place over five sessions, each lasting about two hours. The students were then divided randomly into three groups of 10 students, and asked to write a composition.

The first part of the instructions to all three groups was the same: 'Write a composition. The topic is open. You can choose the situation that you want to write about.' Control group A did not receive any additional instructions

---

8. I selected originality as a psychological dimension because it is one of the clearest expressions of the functional development of personality. However, in this case, I do not want to say that Galperin's theory ignores the problematic of creativity, but he handled it in another way (see Kaloshina 1983, among other researchers who have used Galperin's approach).

designed specifically for this situation, but was told to write the text in the way that they usually do it in the classroom. Control Group B and the experimental group were told additionally: 'You must pay attention to the system of actions that we studied in the previous days in the class' (i.e., trying to get them to use the type II orienting basis of action about composing creative texts). Finally, the experimental group was also told: 'Pay attention to the special manner of such things (words, details, images) that could distinguish your composition from other students. Try to find or elaborate your own style of writing.'

The pupils wrote stories that ranged from approximately 300 to almost 600 words. The compositions were scored according to the following indicators of originality in the composition of written texts: richness of details (quantitative indicator), picturesque character of the images, intensity of emotional expressions in a narration, the selection of topic, interesting characters and scenes.

The texts written by pupils in Control Group A showed approximately the same level of quality in comparison with the initial diagnostic task. For both Control Group B and the experimental group, the quality of their compositions improved compared to their performance on the initial diagnostic task. Furthermore, the compositions of the experimental group were better than Control Group B according to the indicators of originality. This experiment shows that one can achieve better performance in the use of an orienting basis if we also engage the use of a personality level of regulation in realising the orienting basis.

A similar experiment was conducted by Zayas (1998), under my supervision, with children in the fifth grade (10-11 years old). The same three groups and instructions were used, but in this experiment, motivational indicators were emphasised to the experimental group (i.e., motivation of being unique, unrepeatable). In this case, to encourage creative texts, the children were requested to make texts that were different from those that they customarily make in their classes, and to seek their own way to elaborate a text that would be different and creative.

The results were similar to the previous experiment explained here. The texts produced by the experimental group were richer in details, and more imaginative (according to three indicators of creativity in the written expression), than the texts of the children in control group B (only had the type II orienting basis and the motivation for the task) and the texts of control group A (who worked under the conditions of their traditional program).

Zayas's experiment demonstrates how the creative yield increased when the child was given instructions that stimulated motivation from aspects that had more to do with the personal identity than when stimulated only with the motivation for the task. Galperin's theory has resources to assimilate the results of these experiments because it states the need for motivation. But in Zayas's experiment, the experimental group is organised in a way that goes beyond the motivation by the task, toward the motivation of personal confirmation, through which one stimulates the search and expression of one's own style. The motivation for the task has more to do with the level of psychical organisation (of the subject), while the motivation that is likely to be created by the instruction 'to be unique and original' has more to do with the level of organisation of the personality. Davydov and Slobodchikov (1991) noted that 'the authentic personality of the human being is discovered in his creative acts' (p. 136).

I think the results from these two experiments speak for the importance of searching for self-understanding of one's own singularity in the process of learning. Theoretical consideration of these data could raise the theoretical understanding of this learning process from the level of regulation of the subject that is referred to in the traditional form of Galperin's theory, towards, as I propose, a personality level of regulation.

Learning About the Organisation of Time in Academic Study

When I previously called attention to the need for widening the variety of psychological characteristics used in Galperin's theory to express the quality of the learning, I was referring precisely to the type of characteristic that I will discuss in the next example. A hermeneutical approach stimulates the study of intersubjective spaces of dialogue. I believe this intersubjective dialogical space is not the objective of the instructional task, as formulated by Galperin. Rather it is incorporated into the students' learning and also in the experimenter's or teacher's view about a pupil's learning processes, as reflected in the instructions and conditions to achieve efficiency of learning through understanding the object of study. This intersubjective space, through the introduction of specific contents, enables the possibility for the development of self-understanding. Self-understanding mediates all the other learning processes.

The example presented here shows that bringing in content in the intersubjective dialogue that relates directly to personality can have advantages in the acquisition of an orienting basis. In my studies on the organisation of time in daily life (Fariñas León 1999a, 1999b), I start with the 'algorithms' or actions system for study developed by Liaudis. But then I seek to demonstrate the original configurations in the subjects by trying to observe the more complex expression of their action from a personalised, idiographic, subjective point of view.

In this research, I analysed the learning of my own students (18-20 years old) in a training course about study techniques in the Faculty of Psychology at the University of Havana. In addition to organisation of time, this course included other topics such as text comprehension, elaboration of summaries, taking notes, and searching for information.

The course was taught in two different versions, with different groups of students participating in each version. (18 students in the first version and 15 in the second.) The training for both groups was six weekly sessions, each of approximately two hours.

In both versions, the same general structure of activities was maintained. Debates were conducted to realise the development of understanding (sense and meaning) of the theme, practical activities for the design and control of the quality of plans. New debates were held for the reflection and evaluation of distinct situations in daily life relations with respect to the organisation of time. That is, there is an intersubjective dialogue in both versions, but the main difference between the two versions of the course was in the way that subject-subject relations were used in the training.

The first version was characterised by a focus oriented to the object, that is learning a cultural standard of practice (i.e., specific study techniques), using the type III orienting basis proposed by Liaudis in Graf et al. (1983). The process of internalisation, as formulated by Galperin, was followed in the ordered, systematic, typical way.

The second version was characterised by a holistic focus, oriented both to the subject-object relation for the acquisition of the cultural standard that was used in the first version and to the subject-subject relation. The focus on subject-subject relations was attempted by including reflection activities that centred on existential themes such as life project, sense of life, and lifestyle (which are considered as problems of the regulation of personality). Specific examples include a lecture and comments on the life of a specific personality, an analysis of daily incidents in relation to problems of time organisation, and discussion of then-current films that were being shown in the cinema. The activities that were conducted did not necessarily correspond to nor did they try to follow Galperin's sequence for learning. Instead, by improvising to use the opportunities and initiatives of the group, it was possible, by the end of the training, to include activities that corresponded to all the stages in Galperin's theory.

Both groups developed a conscious strategy about the organisation of time, because in both versions they had learned a generalised and comprehensive technique (type III orienting basis). This conclusion was based on individual interviews with the students at the end of the teaching experiment. The students in both groups also had the capacity to generalise the strategy to plan time for different kinds of study situations such as composition of texts, comprehension of texts, and solution of problems between other tasks. But the groups also manifested characteristics that distinguished them from each other. In the first group, their newly-developed consciousness was mainly a technique because it is directed fundamentally to the mastery of the operation of time organisation. In the second group, consciousness of the strategy for organising time moved from an operational and technical focus to an existential, transcendental reflection, and a more theoretical thought about organising time. Unlike the first group, they did not show any resistance to the task of designing and controlling how time is used, or argue against the need for planning. Instead, they saw the necessity for making flexible plans that allowed for improvising new activities.

Concluding Remarks

These experiments — about written expression and organisation of study time — illustrate one of the ways in which I see it is possible to make changes in Galperin's theory of learning, by starting from the conceptual relations in the theory, and elaborating or extending consequences or possible implications of these relations. In particular, by bringing content into the verbal stage that is relevant to a personality level of regulation, it is possible to achieve better results in the learning process. These changes, in my point of view, are complementary to the more traditional conception and way of working with this theory. A hermeneutic focus accepts interpretations that emphasise different aspects of dialogue and the most subjective aspects of learning.

If this hypothesis about the value of focusing on personality in learning is accepted, then it becomes clear that it will be useful to better understand learning phenomenology as part of the theoretical clarification of the role of the personality level in learning, and to better identify niches in Galperin's theory where the regulation of the personality can be integrated.

This chapter has only pointed to what I understand must be one possible perspective for the further development of Galperin's theory of the stage-by-stage development of the mental actions. I believe the hermeneutic approach described here would increase the existing potential for understanding learning and its direction.

References

Abulkhanova-Slavskaya, K.A. (1982). Lichnostnye mekanizmy reguliatzii deiatel'nosti [Personality mechanisms of activity regulation]. In E.V. Shorokhova, O.I. Zotova, & A.V. Ryzhov (eds.), *Problemy psikhologii lichnosti*. Moscow: Nauka, 92-98.

Aidarova, L.I. (1969). Rebionok iazyk i humanitarnoie znanie [Child, language and humanistic knowledge]. *Sovetskaya Pedagogika*, no. 6., 11-23.

Aidarova, L.I. (1979). *Psikhologicheskie problemy obuchenia rodnova iasika u mladchij eskolnikov* [Psychological problems in teaching mother tongue to early school children]. Moscow: Pedagogika.

Bandura, A. (1963). The role of imitation in personality development. *Journal of Nursery Education*, 18, 207-15.

Bandura, A. (1965). Behavior modification through modeling procedures. In L. Krasner & L.P. Ullmann (eds.), *Research in behavior modification*. New York: Holt, Rinehart, & Winston, 310-40.

Bozhovich, L.I. (1976). *La personalidad y su formación en la edad infantil* (C. Toste Muñiz, trans.). Havana, Cuba: Editora Pueblo y Educación. (Original work published 1966)

Butkin, G.A., Ermonskaia, D.L, & Kisliuk, G.A. (1977). K probleme individualno-psikhologicheskii raslichii b teorii poetapnogo formirovanii umstbennij deistbii i poniatii [Toward the problem of individual differences in the theory of stage by stage development of mental actions]. In N.F. Talyzina (ed.), *Problemy upravleniia uchebno-vospitatel'nym protsessom*. Moscow: Izd-vo Moskva Un-ta, 9-29.

Davydov, V.V., & Slobodchikov, V.I. (1991). La enseñanza que desarrolla en la escuela del desarrollo (M. Shuare, trans.). In A.V. Mudrik (ed.), *La educación y la enseñanza: Una mirada al futuro*. Moscow: Progreso, 118-45.

Fariñas León, G. (1993). Un viejo debate y un nuevo punto de vista acerca de las habilidades en el desarrollo de la personalidad. *Revista Cubana de Psicología*, 10(2-3), 137-44.

Fariñas León, G. (1995). *Maestro, una estrategia para enseñanza.* Havana, Cuba: Editores Academia.

Fariñas León, G. (1999a). Acerca del concepto de vivencia en el enfoque histórico-cultural. *Revista Cubana de Psicología,* 16(3), 222-28.

Fariñas León, G. (1999b). Hacia un paradigma de complejidad para la educación. *Abstracts from Pedagogía* 1999, 218.

Fariñas León, G. (1999c). *Maestro, para diseñar un programa de aprendizaje.* Havana, Cuba: Editores Academia.

Gagné, R.M. (1966). *The conditions of learning.* New York: Holt, Rinehart & Winston.

Galperin, P.I. (1973a). *Antología de conferencias* (G. Martínez, trans.). Havana, Cuba: Universidad de la Habana, Facultad de Psicología.

Galperin, P.I. (1973b). *Tipos de bases orientadoras y tipos de aprendizaje* (G. Martínez, trans.). Havana, Cuba: Universidad de la Habana, Facultad de Psicología.

Galperin, P.I. (1979). *Introducción a la psicología* (A. Bustamente, trans.) Madrid: Pablo del Rio Editor. (Original work published 1976)

González Rey, F.L. (1999). Personality, subject and human development: The subjective character of human activity. In S. Chaiklin, M. Hedegaard, & U.J. Jensen (eds.), *Activity theory and social practice: Cultural-historical approaches.* Aarhus, Denmark: Aarhus University Press, 253-75.

González Rey, F.L., & Mitjans, A. (1989). *La personalidad: Su educación y desarrollo.* Havana, Cuba: Editora Pueblo y Educación.

Graf, B., Iliasov, I.I., & Liaudis, V.I. (1983). *Osnovy organizatzii uchebnoi deiatel'nosti i samostoiatelnoi* [The auto-organization of study activity]. Moscow: Moscow University Press.

Kabanova, O.Y., & Galperin, P.I. (1972). Linguisticheskoe sosnanie kak osnova formirovaniia rechia v innostrannovo iaszika [Linguistic consciousness as basis for learning a foreign language]. In P.I. Galperin & N.F. Talyzina (eds.), *Rukovodstvo znatelnoi deiatel'nosti studentov.* Moscow: Moscow State University Press.

Kaloshina, I.P. (1983). *Struktura i mekanizmy tvorcheskoi deiatel'nosti* [Structures and mechanism of creative activity]. Moscow: Moscow State University Press.

Lopez, J. (1969). Zavisimost obucheniia o sostava orientirovki osnovi gieitsbiia [Dependence of teaching on the characteristics of the orienting basis]. Unpublished doctoral thesis. Moscow State University.

Morin, E. (1994). Epistemología de la complejidad. In D.F. Schnitman (ed.), *Nuevos paradigmas, cultura y subjetividad.* Mexico City: Paidós, 421-42.

Pantina, N.S. (1957). Formirovanie motorskie nabyki pismennovo rechia v zavisimosti ot tipa orientirovki v zadache [The formation of the motor habit of writing depending on the type of orientation to the task]. *Voprosy Psikhologii,* no. 4, 117-32.

Prigogine, I. (1994). De los relojes a las nubes. In D.F. Schnitman (ed.), *Nuevos paradigmas, cultura y subjetividad.* Mexico City: Paidós, 395-413.

Talyzina, N.F. (1984). *Psikhologiia obucheniia* [The psychology of learning]. Moscow: Pedagogika.

Talyzina, N.F. (1985). Las etapas del proceso de asimilación. In *Los fundamentos de la enseñanza en la educación superior.* Havana, Cuba: Ministerio de Educación Superior, 192-220.

Talyzina, N.F. (1987). *La formación de la actividad cognoscitiva de los escolares.* Havana, Cuba: Ministerio de Educación Superior.

Talyzina, N.F. (1998). *Pedagogicheskaia psikhologii* [Educational psychology]. Moscow: Akademia.

Vygotsky, L.S. (1997). The problem of the development of higher mental functions (M.J. Hall, trans.). In R.W. Reiber (ed.), *The collected works of L.S. Vygotsky: Vol. 4. The history of the development of higher mental functions.* New York: Plenum Press, 1-26. (Original work written 1931)

Zayas, M. (1998). La expresividad en la expresión escrita. Unpublished diplom thesis, Universidad de Havana, Facultad de Psicología.

15 The Ideal in Cultural-Historical Activity Theory: Issues and Perspectives

Peter E. Jones

Introduction

The concept of the *ideal* (as in the terms *ideal form or ideal image*) is one of the most difficult concepts in Marxist philosophy but also one of the most important for research in the cultural-historical and activity theory traditions (henceforth 'CHAT' for convenience). Evald Ilyenkov, the late Soviet philosopher who made the most important contribution to the elucidation of this concept, stressed that 'the problem of "ideality" in its general form is equally significant for psychology, linguistics, and any socio-historical discipline' (1977b, 95). The crux of the problem has to do with the dialectical process through which human productive activity necessarily generates images of itself which are objectified in *ideal* or symbolic forms and come to have an essential role within that activity. This process of *idealisation* and the function of ideal forms within activity are research problems of enormous interest and importance. In more general terms, the significance to CHAT of the concept of the ideal lies in its offering the possibility of understanding the human mind in its interconnections with *activity*. Specifically, it orients research into language acquisition, concept formation, or educational activity, for example, towards an analysis of the relevant forms of symbolic mediation in terms of the logic and developmental dynamic of those activities in which they are generated and function, obliging us, at the same time, to take into

* Heartfelt thanks to Seth Chaiklin without whose support, suggestions, and advice this chapter would not have been written. I am deeply indebted to David Bakhurst on a number of counts: for discussion of these issues over the years, for his encouragement, for his comments on the earlier version of this chapter, and for the copy of Ilyenkov (1991) which he supplied me with. He is, obviously, in no way responsible for the arguments presented here. Passages from Ilyenkov (1991) were translated with the help of Marianna Ivanova. Thanks to those who attended the ISCRAT session where part of this chapter was presented, and in particular to Charles Tolman and Jan Derry for stimulating discussion of the issues.

account the dialectical interconnections between different social practices within the social process as a whole.[1]

The concept appears to be gaining currency in CHAT circles following the ground-breaking study of Ilyenkov's work by David Bakhurst (1991, 1995, especially) and Ilyenkov's contribution to this theme has had considerable influence on some CHAT researchers, Soviet, 'post-Soviet' and Western, since it contains, as Bakhurst (1995, 156) notes, the 'clearest articulation' of the philosophical perspective in which the CHAT traditions are grounded.[2] For this reason, Ilyenkov's work, comprising some of the most powerful and insightful Marxist writings on mind, culture and activity repays serious study, despite the many problems of interpretation (cf. Bakhurst 1991, 175-76). In that connection, it should be stressed that this chapter is intended only as a contribution to the collective effort to get to grips with the concept of the ideal and its import for CHAT and is not meant to be a definitive account.[3]

Bearing in mind the complexity and 'multi-dimensional' character of the problems addressed by Ilyenkov (Bakhurst 1991, 176), this chapter will single out the following three aspects of the concept for detailed discussion: (a) the materialist philosophical underpinnings of the concept of the ideal, (b) the social origins and function of ideal images, and (c) the ideal as *image* or *representation*.

These three aspects have been selected for their direct relevance to current CHAT research interests because they have to do with the philosophical and theoretical foundations of the conception of activity, and more particularly of the role of symbolic mediation in activity, worked out and developed by the founders of the CHAT tradition.[4]

1. See also Beaken (1996) for a discussion of the implications of the ideal for human origins and language origins.
2. Ilyenkov's is not the only important philosophical contribution to the CHAT tradition. There is the brilliant, and even more overlooked (in the West), work of Felix Mikhailov (e.g., 1976/1980, 1990; cf. Bakhurst 1991) and Merab Mamardashvili (e.g., 1992). Indeed, Mikhailov (1976/1980) contains one of the most serious and profound discussions of Marxist philosophy of language.
3. This paper was substantially completed before I saw Lektorsky (1999) which includes new and important discussions of Ilyenkov's conception of the ideal by such authors as V.V. Davydov, F.T. Mikhailov, and A.A. Novikov.
4. Other issues such as the place of the concept in the history of philosophy, the relationship between Ilyenkov's ideas and those of such non-Marxist philosophers as Wittgenstein or McDowell, or the controversies surrounding Ilyenkov's work in philosophical circles in the former Soviet Union will not be examined here (for discussion of such matters see Bakhurst 1991, 1995, 1997).

Overview and Illustration

This section of the chapter gives an overview of the conceptual terrain relevant to each of the three aspects listed above, accompanied by an illustrative example of the application of the concept. The next major section will give a more detailed, and more technical, exploration of each aspect. The chapter will conclude with an examination of some of the general implications and ramifications of the concept, and of Ilyenkov's work on this subject, for current CHAT research.

The Materialist Philosophical Underpinnings of the Concept of the Ideal

The 'problem of the ideal' (Bakhurst 1991, 175) is primarily a philosophical one and concerns the possibility of a materialist (dialectical and historical) explanation of the nature and origins of spiritual or 'nonmaterial' phenomena (cf. Bakhurst 1991, 175) including thought, artistic expression, ethical norms, political ideals and other forms of social consciousness. Such an explanation rejects equally the pseudomaterialist, biological reductionist line of much of modern cognitive science (including the now fashionable 'evolutionary psychology') which attempts to find the source of the properties and forms of human cognition in the structure of the brain, as well as the more straightforwardly idealist conception of human subjectivity as an independent (and indeed primary) realm of spirit, consciousness (or 'discourse') which creates the world in its own image. The dialectical and historical materialist conception involves understanding thinking and all other manifestations of human mental or spiritual life as *images* or *reflections* of the real world of nature and social life which are themselves produced by people in the course of their practical social life activity, and primarily within that productive practice known as *labour*, considered to be the essential, indeed defining, characteristic of human 'species being'.[5] This view seeks the unity of thinking and being, then, within the dynamic of social productive activity, a view to which Vygotsky (1934/1986) alluded when he described 'verbal thought' as 'subject to all the premises of historical materialism' (p. 95).

---

5. This assertion is still rather too general, cf. Ilyenkov (1960/1982, 115): 'Production of labour implements, production of means of production, is not only a universal (both logically and historically) *prerequisite* of all the other forms of human life activity but also a continually reproduced *result* or *consequence* of the social development as a whole'.

The Social Origins and Function of Ideal Images

It follows from the preceding that we must turn to a concrete examination of the dynamic of the real social life process itself (*social being*) in order to understand human thinking and consciousness in all its manifestations. We must study how and why it is that in the course of the social production of objects to satisfy their needs, people also produce a whole world of special objects, termed *ideal*. These have a unique mediating function within that system of productive activity, consisting in their embodying directly, in their *representing*, the intrinsic course, purpose and logic primarily of productive activity and ultimately of all aspects of social life. Consequently, the ideal 'has a purely social nature and origin' (Ilyenkov 1977b, 87) since it is 'the form of social man's activity' (1974/1977a, 265) grounded essentially in the labour process itself. Ideality thus forms a dialectically differentiated moment within human social productive activity seen as a whole.

The Ideal as Image or Representation

The nature of the *representing* or *symbolic* function of the ideal and the logic of its appearance and development is the third aspect of the concept to be discussed here. Ilyenkov argues that ideal forms, such as words, money, or artistic images function as *reflections*, *images*, or *forms* of some other object, process or thing within social activity.[6] Furthermore, the nature of this 'representation' or 'image' is complex and contradictory since the production of ideal forms is intimately connected with the formation of the conscious capacity to think, plan, and set goals for future action — in short to create what does not already exist. However, ideality cannot be considered a product of consciousness or the expression of pre-existing natural cognitive capacities: 'Quite the reverse, the individual's consciousness and will are functions of the ideality of things, their comprehended, *conscious ideality*' (1977b, 87). Ilyenkov argues, then, that the development in an individual of the capacity to think and act consciously is a result of participating in forms of practical social activity mediated by ideal images.

6. Ideal forms are sometimes referred to as 'quasi-objects' (*kvaziob'yekty*), see for example A.A. Leontiev (1997, 95) who also comments on the infelicity of the term. Mamardashvili (1992), basing himself, like Ilyenkov, on a close reading of Marx, employs the Marxian concept of 'transformed form' (*verwandelte Form, prevrashchennaya forma*) with similar meaning (p. 269).

Illustration: The Architect and the Bee

The ideal is a phenomenon peculiar only to the specifically human form of life activity known as labour. It is perhaps easiest to think of it initially as the idea, the conscious goal or aim that people work towards and realise in the course of labour activity. Indeed, Marx himself uses the term in this sense in his often-quoted description of the human labour process:

But what … distinguishes the most incompetent architect from the best of bees, is that the architect has built a cell in his head before he constructs it in wax. The labour process ends in the creation of something which, when the process began, already existed in the worker's imagination, already existed in an *ideal* form. (*Capital*, in Ilyenkov 1974/1977a, 276-77, my emphasis)

This, at first sight, quite straightforward description proves, however, to be fraught with complexities.[7] Ilyenkov warns, for instance, against a 'naturalistic' reading of Marx's phrase about 'building a cell in his head' in which 'the head' is taken to mean 'a material organ of the separate individual's body'. As Ilyenkov (1974/1977a) explains:

The architect builds a house not simply in his head but by means of his head, on the plane of ideas on Whatman paper, on the plane of the drawing board. He thus alters his internal state, externalising it, and operating with it as with *an object distinct from himself.* In changing it he potentially alters the real house, i.e. changes it ideally, potentially, which means that he alters *one sensuously perceived object instead of another.* (p. 280)

Let us therefore examine this case more carefully for what it may tell us about the role of the ideal in productive activity. If we take the whole process of building, say, a house, it is clear that it unites many different types of activity and object. It begins not with the activity of the labourer digging the foundations with shovel on ground but with the specialised mental labour of the architect working with pencil on paper from which ensues the phase of actually constructing the real house. Seen from within this whole cycle of activ-

7. Marx's formulation is, I believe, calamitously misinterpreted by Newman and Holzman (1993) who argue that it shows a 'functionalist bias' and that it is 'both philosophically (analytically) and empirically (descriptively) inaccurate', allowing 'the old philosophical-theological argument of first cause back into play' (pp. 47-48).

ity culminating in the final product, the creation of the design on paper is the erecting of the ideal or potential house. It is this design — an actual object which is passed from the architect to the builders — which is the ideal form of the house, and as the real house is constructed according to the design (with the design 'in mind') it becomes clear that the design was nothing other than that real house itself in a different — *ideal* — form. But the design object per se is merely a work of ink on paper. Its ideality is a function of its role within the house-building process as a systemic whole uniting the activities of architect and builder, the use of pencil and paper and brick and trowel. Indeed, it is only the actual building of the house, in the course of which the plan is concretised (modified, altered, etc.) as it is realised, which constitutes the real unity of ideal and material within social production.[8] Essentially, then, the ideal is a moment within the dynamic of productive activity seen as a constantly renewed cycle of production, consumption, and again production. Ideal, symbolic objects such as the architect's drawing (or language) are a differentiated product of the logic of the entire cyclical movement of the activity system in which they function as a 'momentary metamorphosis' (Ilyenkov 1991, 258) of the activity, objectifying, for a passing moment, the goal of the activity itself. The meaning of such drawings comes from their being used (cf. Bakhurst 1991, 185) as a means within building activity. And this meaning lies in the process of their conversion (back) into the real thing, a process in which they function to enable the accurate anticipation of the course and end product of activity, abstracting and synthesising the intrinsic, objective possibilities of activity, materials and technology in their socially sanctioned use, as a 'premonition' of the product to come. Therefore, from the point of view of its 'objectively conditioned content' (Ilyenkov 1974/ 1977a, 278), the design is an *image* of the real house, even though the real house comes later. The case of the ideal house therefore appears to fit closely with Ilyenkov's (1991) general characterisation of the ideal:

This is being, which however is equal to not-being [*nebytie*], or the present being of the external thing in the phase of its coming to be in the activity of the subject, in the form of its internal image, need, impetus, and goal … The ideal is consequently the subjective being of the object, or the 'nonbeing' [*inobytie*] of the object — the being of one object in another and through another, as Hegel expressed the situation. (p. 218)[9]

8. Therefore we must not make the mistake of thinking that only the mental labour (or 'ideal activity') of the architect is *creative* (cf. Tolstykh et al. 1981, 12).
9. See Ilyenkov (1974/1977a, 264-65) for a similar, less satisfying translation, of this passage.

Only if we understand this contradictory logic of the process of idealisation (cf. Ilyenkov 1997, 185) can we therefore make sense of Ilyenkov's (1974/1977a) definition of the ideal as 'the subjective image of objective reality, i.e. reflection of the external world in the forms of man's activity, in the forms of his consciousness and will' (p. 252). This definition is fully consistent with Marx's own characterisation: 'the ideal is nothing other than the material when it has been transposed and translated inside the human head' (Marx 1867/1976, cited in Ilyenkov 1974/1977a, 252).

This is how things stand from the point of view of the content of the image. From the point of view of its *form*, however, it has immediate empirical existence as an object — a design, a word, etc. — quite separate from (and preceding) the actual activity of building. As Ilyenkov (1974/1977a) puts it:

the ideal is only there where the form itself of the activity corresponding to the form of the external object is transformed for man into a special object with which he can operate specially without touching and without changing the real object up to a certain point. Man, and only man, ceases to be 'merged' with the form of his life activity; he separates it from himself and, giving it his attention, transforms it into an idea. (p. 278)

Ilyenkov argues that this understanding of both the form and content of the ideal is crucial to the distinction between the activities of the architect and the bee. If the ideal is taken to mean simply the 'program', encoded in the body or brain, guiding or impelling behaviour then 'there is no difference in principle, it transpires, between the architect and the bee' (1974/1977a, 277). He explains:

The wax cell that the bee builds also exists beforehand in the form of the pattern of the insect's activity programmed in its nerve centres. In that sense the product of the bee's activity is also given 'ideally' before its real performance. (p. 277)

The crux of the matter is that because the bee's cell-building is an innate form of behaviour the 'form of activity that we can denote as the ideal existence of the product is never differentiated from the body of the animal in any other way than as some real product' (p. 277). Human 'forms of activity (active faculties)', on the other hand, are not innate but are 'passed on only in the form of objects created by man for man' (p. 277). Thus, in house-building, along with the purposeful activity of building plus the real product (the house) there is also the architect's plan. Human productive activity constitutes a whole social system of socially and historically developed practices of producing a real product and of producing the product 'in the head' (i.e., as an image, a design, an aim or goal expressed in a specially created object). Consequently, Ilyenkov is able to clarify Marx's initial formulation of the problem in the following way:

When Marx defined the ideal as the material 'transposed and translated inside the human head', he did not understand this 'head' naturalistically, in terms of natural science. He had in mind the socially developed head of man, all of whose forms of activity, beginning with the forms of language and its word stock and syntactical system and ending with logical categories, are products and forms of social development. Only when expressed in these forms is the external, the material, transformed into social fact, into the property of social man, i.e. into the ideal. (1974/1977a, 262)

Of course, the architect's activity 'on the plane of representation', like the builder's activity, is 'also sensuous objective activity transforming the sensuously perceived image of the thing to which it is directed' but the difference is that in the former 'the thing altered here is special; it is only the objectified idea or *form of the person's activity taken as a thing*' (Ilyenkov 1974/1977a, 280). Thus, the architect, while dealing directly with the representation on paper, is really dealing with the activity of building, a manifestation of 'man's essential powers' (Marx 1844/1975, 352), in a special form. In this way, through the differentiation of activities and capabilities within the social whole, humanity takes its own actions, takes itself as the object of its attention and action. Herein lies the possibility of a genuine materialist explanation of human consciousness as necessarily grounded in labour activity in which human relations to the world and to one another are made into the very object of purposeful productive activity.

Hopefully this brief overview gives an idea of the significance of the concept of the ideal for an understanding of the nature and dynamic of human activity and of the role of symbolic objects such as language or drawings therein. It should be noted, however, that Ilyenkov develops the concept not from a detailed philosophical exploration of language but from Marx's economic work and specifically Volume 1 of *Capital* where the

dialectic of the transformation of a thing into a symbol, and of a symbol into a token, is ... traced ... on the example of the origin and evolution of the money form
of value. (1974/1977a, 273)

This value form, Ilyenkov (1977b) argues

is a typical and characteristic case of ideality in general, and Marx's conception of
it serves as a concrete illustration of all the advantages of the dialectical materialist view of ideality, of the 'ideal'. (pp. 90-91)

Capital is not a philosophical treatise, of course, but an analysis of political
economy. Ilyenkov (1960/1982) turns to *Capital* then, not because money has
any privileged philosophical or historical status in the overall scheme of
things, but because Marx's theory of money forms part of the most thorough,
profound, and consistently developed application of dialectical and historical materialism in any sphere of empirical scientific investigation:

Marx's *Capital* is indeed the highest type of school for theoretical thinking. A scientist specialising in any field of knowledge can use it as a source of most valuable
ideas with regard to the theoretical method of research. (p. 289)

Thus, from a general philosophical and scientific point of view, the fact that
the concept of the ideal is worked out initially on this particular economic
phenomenon is incidental. Ilyenkov's point, however, is that scientific analysis of one typical instance of ideality will reveal the general laws according
to which all ideal forms arise and function — the way in which *things* are dialectically transformed into *symbols* — whatever the particular domain of
social activity in question.[10] On the other hand, it is not always so easy to distinguish between what belongs to the general law and what to its operation
in a particular instance. Indeed, as I will argue later, the complicated relationship between Ilyenkov's general formulations of the problem of the ideal and
the specifics of Marx's theory of value has given rise to misunderstandings
in recent interpretations of the concept.

10. At stake here is actually a key issue of scientific methodology which forms the subject
    of much of Ilyenkov's writing (e.g., 1960/1982, 1997). It involves the limits of induc-
    tion as a method of empirical investigation noted originally by Engels.

Three Aspects of the Concept of the Ideal

Each of the three aspects of the concept examined briefly above will now be discussed in more depth in order to identify those issues of particular relevance to the traditions of CHAT research.

The Materialist Philosophical Underpinnings of the Concept of the Ideal

One of Ilyenkov's chief concerns is to distinguish the Marxian materialist world view from its outdated (but still very much alive and kicking) mechanistic or metaphysical materialist precursors. The old materialism, like Marxist materialism, took the relation between material and ideal to be one of *reflection* of the former by the latter. However, it understood the 'material' to mean 'everything that exists "outside the consciousness"' and the 'ideal' to mean 'existing in the consciousness' (Ilyenkov 1977b, 71-72), a view presented as Marxist by some authors (for discussion of Ilyenkov's polemical exchange with Dubrovsky on this issue cf. Bakhurst 1991, 198). But Ilyenkov (1977b) begins by demonstrating clearly and simply that Marx did not in fact understand things in this way:

In *Capital* Marx defines the *form of value in general* as 'purely ideal' not on the grounds that it exists only 'in the consciousness', only in the head of the commodity-owner, but on quite opposite grounds. The price or the money form of value … is IDEAL because it is totally distinct from the palpable, corporeal form of commodity in which it is *presented*, we read in the chapter on 'Money'. In other words, the form of value is IDEAL, although it exists outside human consciousness and independently of it. (p. 72)

Here is the first advantage of shifting our attention from the usual philosophical topics (ideas, consciousness, language, etc.) to the apparently unphilosophical realm of commodities and money: the pre-Marxian materialist view of ideality can immediately be seen not to work. The value of a commodity in money terms — its *price* — is obviously not primarily an idea or conscious state of the individual's mind since money is a real, external thing passing from hand to hand within the objective sphere of the market. The value form is ideal but is not a fact of individual consciousness but 'a simple social form' (Marx 1867/1976, 195) consisting in the objective relation in which one perfectly tangible thing (money in the shape of a banknote or other form of collateral)[11] stands for or represents all other things as values, a relation founded not on natural affinities or similarities between the objects concerned but on their being commodities and therefore embodying a purely social substance — human labour. I will not find any trace of beer, chocolate, coffee (etc.) in my £10 banknote but nevertheless I can actually convert it back into any and all of them in the act of purchase. It is indeed this act of conversion of the symbolic thing back into the reality symbolised which proves or defines the special function of ideal (symbolic or representative) forms, just as the conversion of the architect's design into the real house or the carrying out of a plan or programme expressed in words also demonstrate the ideal function of drawings, words etc.:

The ideal is immediately realised in a symbol and through a symbol, i.e. through the external, sensuously perceived, visual or audible body of a word. But this body, while remaining itself, proves at the same time to be the being of another body and as such is its *'ideal being'*, its *meaning*, which is quite distinct from its bodily form immediately perceived by the ears or eyes. As a *sign*, as a *name*, a word has nothing in common with what it is the sign of. What is 'common' is only discovered in the act of transforming the word into a deed, and through the deed into a thing (and then again in the reverse process), in practice and the mastering of its results. (Ilyenkov 1974/1977a, 266)

From this perspective it seems to me that David Bakhurst's (1991, chap. 5) insightful presentation and interpretation of the concept of the ideal, which has quite rightly been very influential in Western circles, to some degree weakens the concept by extending its scope beyond the domain of 'symbolic' objects to embrace all the products and means of social life activity. Bakhurst argues for this interpretation on the basis of a discussion of artifacts in general (1991, 181, also Bakhurst 1995, 160-61). The difference between something being an artifact, for example a table, and being a natural object like a lump of wood has to do with human activity: 'When an artifact is fashioned, human activity is somehow embodied [*voploshchennyĭ*] in the natural object' (1991, 182). He explains:

11. Strictly speaking today's pound sterling or U.S. dollar is not really money and therefore not a symbol, in Marx's terms, but a valueless token that represents not the value of the commodity directly but a certain quantity of that commodity (the 'money commodity', typically gold) which functions within the system as the measure of value.

Ilyenkov does not just mean that, when an artifact is created, some material object is given a new *physical* form. This is true, but something a natural-scientific account could capture. Rather, in being created as an embodiment of purpose and incorporated into our life activity in a certain way — being manufactured for a *reason* and put to a certain *use* — the natural object acquires *significance*. This significance is the 'ideal form' of the object, a form that includes not a single atom of the tangible physical substance that possesses it … It is this significance that must be grasped by anyone seeking to distinguish *tables* from *pieces of wood*. (p. 182, also quoted in Cole 1996, 117-18)

He continues:

Ilyenkov sometimes explains this significance by appeal to the concept *representation*. A purely natural object takes on significance when it comes to represent something with which its corporeal form has 'nothing in common', a form of human activity … Objects owe their ideality to their incorporation into the aim-oriented life activity of a human community, to their *use*. The notion of significance is glossed in terms of the concept of representation: Artifacts represent the activity to which they owe their existence as artifacts. (pp. 182-83)

The proposition that 'objects owe their ideality to their incorporation into the aim-oriented life activity of a human community' is surely a correct interpretation of Ilyenkov's position. However, the explanation of ideality from the nature of artifacts in general also implies the converse proposition, which I believe is invalid, namely that objects incorporated into the aim-oriented life activity of a human community are ipso facto ideal. Let us scrutinise the argument point by point.

First of all, if things are ideal because they are created as the embodiment of particular purposes then anything and everything connected with human activity becomes ideal as long as there is, as it were, an 'idea' behind it. So not only the instrument of labour (e.g., the spade I dig with), but the product of labour, the hole I dig, is ideal, since the hole realises the idea of a hole, or the aim of digging a hole, that I worked towards. Not only the bakery, but the bread made in the bakery and which I eat, is ideal. And people too: the parents' aim of having a child is realised in the child, who thus becomes an 'ideal' (as well as a real) person. If everything connected to or involved in human activity is ideal, then the term loses its specific meaning in which it refers to one dimension or 'plane' of the human life process.

Secondly, if we choose to ground ideality in the *use* or *function* of objects rather than the idea behind them, then we immediately run up against a contradiction. The table, as a humanly-created artifact, certainly functions in a socially determined and accepted way (to eat meals off, to support a fruit bowl, etc.) for which its wooden nature, per se, is not responsible. But this function, pace Bakhurst, actually does include or embrace every single atom of the tangible physical substance 'possessed' by the function. The 'table function' has to be exercised by a physical table made of physical stuff (e.g., wood) constructed in such a way as to be strong enough to permit that function; the use of the table (as a table) — its 'significance' in Bakhurst's sense — is indissolubly connected with and conditioned by its precise physical properties. The function itself, furthermore, is governed by laws of physical nature (e.g., gravity) which are independent of our aims and purposes. There is therefore an immediate unity between the socially conditioned function of the artifact and its natural, physical properties. The point is even clearer if we move from tables to instruments of labour:

An instrument of labour is a thing, or complex of things, which the worker interposes between himself and the object of his labour and which serves as a conductor, directing his activity onto that object. He makes use of the mechanical, physical and chemical properties of some substances in order to set them to work on other substances as instruments of his power, and in accordance with his purposes. (Marx 1867/1976, 285)

Consequently, it is impossible to equate ideality — Bakhurst's 'nonmaterial properties' (1991, 175) — directly with the putting to use of the properties and natural affordances of artifacts, tools, instruments of labour, etc., which consists of setting their 'mechanical, physical and chemical properties' to work, something a natural-scientific account could, indeed, capture. In short, ideality does not mean use or function in general.

Thirdly, there is a problem with Bakhurst's interpretation of Ilyenkov's notion of *representation*, a notion that will be examined more closely later. Artifacts do not as a general rule represent the activity to which they owe their existence and in which they function: the mechanical digger or the power station do not *represent* the digging process or the process of generation of electricity; they do not stand for anything else in that process and are simply used (and, indeed, used up) as instruments without any kind of representative function at all. As their natural properties are consumed in the process so are their functions.

Similar over-extensions of the concept can be found, I believe, in other recent accounts. Michael Cole (1996), drawing on Bakhurst's interpretation, makes the following claim:

By virtue of the changes wrought in the process of their creation and use, artifacts are simultaneously *ideal* (conceptual) and *material*. They are ideal in that their material form has been shaped by their participation in the interactions of which they were previously a part and which they mediate in the present. Defined in this manner, the properties of artifacts apply with equal force whether one is considering language or the more usually noted forms of artifacts such as tables and knives which constitute material culture. What differentiates the word 'table' from an actual table is the relative prominence of their material and ideal aspects and the kinds of coordination they afford. No word exists apart from its material instantiation (as a configuration of sound waves, hand movements, writing, or as neuronal activity), whereas every table embodies an order imposed by thinking human beings. (p. 117)[12]

On this account, anything upon which human activity has had (and continues to have) an impact becomes ideal. This would include not only every aspect of human culture narrowly construed but the whole planet's ecosphere to the extent that it has been altered (e.g., polluted) by human economic, military and scientific activity. That the table 'embodies an order imposed by thinking human beings' is not in doubt, but this assertion does not settle but merely poses the question as to the origins and nature of the power that ideal forms have to serve as conductors of the human 'ordering' of nature.

There is also the issue of the 'relative prominence' of material and ideal aspects in words and artifacts. It is quite true, obviously, that words (and, indeed, all ideal forms) must have a material existence ('presented to the mind in an objective mode', Marx 1857-8/1973, 145).[13] A word is just as material as a table if we are considering its physicality. But then we are considering it independently of the system in which it functions; we are no longer considering it as a word. When we look at it functioning within social activity it is ideal, purely ideal, 100% ideal, as it were. By the same token, the instrument of labour is 100% material. *Material* and *ideal* therefore refer to

12. A slightly different version of Cole's argument is also cited in Wells (1994, 46).
13. Interestingly, Wertsch (1998, e.g., 30-31) tends to go to the other extreme, emphasising the 'materiality' of symbolic mediational means rather than treating them as ideal.

quite distinct, and opposed, categories of phenomena having to do with how things function within the system of human activity.[14] As Ilyenkov (1991) puts it, ideal forms exist

outside the individual head, and are perceived by that head (by hundreds of such heads) as external 'objects', visible and tangible. However, if, on that basis, you put, say, 'Swan Lake' or 'King Lear' in the category of *material* phenomena, you commit a fundamental philosophico-theoretical error. A theatrical representation [*predstavlenie*] is precisely that — a *representation*, in the exact and strict sense of the word, in the sense that something different, something *other* is represented in it. (p. 234)

Now of course instruments of labour are the products of social activity exactly as language and other ideal forms are. But while the making of the tool is a social act, it is also a natural process and it is to nature — whether in the raw or transformed in the production process — that the tool owes those properties for which uses are found in the course of historical development.[15] The natural properties of the useful thing and its purposive use form an immediate unity.[16] With the word, the situation is exactly the opposite: the properties that the word owes to nature (e.g., the audible gestures that compose the spoken word) 'have no relation to its existence as a symbol' (Ilyenkov 1974/1977a, 273) which is due solely and wholly to the forms and patterns of social intercourse that it idealises and expresses in 'transformed form'. Like the value form, the word is a 'simple, social form'.[17]

Engeström (1996) in his interesting discussion of the relationship between Activity Theory and the work of Bruno Latour argues that Ilyenkov 'developed the concept of the ideal to deal with the sociality of things' (p. 263), a view which is quite justifiable if we have in mind such 'simple social forms' (Marx, cited earlier) as the value form. However, Engeström appears

14. This is quite possibly what Cole has in mind with his distinction between 'kinds of co-ordination', although the term is left unexplained.
15. 'When man engages in production, he can only proceed as nature does herself, i.e. he can only change the form of the materials' (Marx, 1867/1976, 133).
16. 'The usefulness of a thing makes it a use-value. But this usefulness does not dangle in mid-air. It is conditioned by the physical properties of the commodity, and has no existence apart from the latter. It is therefore the physical body of the commodity itself, for instance iron, corn, a diamond, which is the use-value of the useful thing' (Marx 1867/1976, 126).
17. Cf. Marx (1867/1976): 'the characteristic which objects of utility have of being values is as much men's social product as is their language' (p. 167).

to take the 'sociality of things' to apply to all things involved in social activity, including instruments of labour. Engeström suggests this with the help of a quoted excerpt from Ilyenkov which in fact appears to directly contradict the interpretation I have been attempting to defend here:

Ideality includes *'all the things* that "mediate" the individuals that are socially producing their life: *words, books, statues, churches, community centres, television towers,* and (above all!) *the instruments of labour,* from the stone axe and the bone needle to the modern automated factory and the computer (Ilyenkov 1977, 98).' (Engeström 1996, 263)

However, if we turn to the whole passage from which this quoted extract is drawn, we may be led to a slightly different picture:

For this reason the 'ideal' exists *only in man.* Outside man and beyond him there can be nothing 'ideal'. Man, however, is to be understood not as one individual with a brain, but as a real aggregate of real people collectively realising their specifically human life activity, as the 'aggregate of all social relations' arising between people around one common task, around the process of the social production of their life. It is 'inside' *man thus understood* that the ideal exists, because 'inside' *man thus understood* are *all the things* that 'mediate' the individuals that are socially producing their life: *words, books, statues, churches, community centres, television towers,* and (above all!) *the instruments of labour,* from the stone axe and the bone needle to the modern automated factory and the computer. It is in these 'things' that the ideal exists as the 'subjective', purposeful form-creating life activity of social man, embodied in the material of nature. (Ilyenkov 1977b, 98)

Note that the list of 'things' in the partial quote in Engeström (1996) is not actually Ilyenkov's list of ideal forms, but a more general list of 'all the things that "mediate" the individuals that are socially producing their life'. It seems to me that the list is clearly subdivided: the first half contains ideal forms ('words, books', etc.) and the second instruments of labour. The latter, he argues, mediate the process 'above all', implying that they have a primacy within the process of social production in relation to the 'things' in the first half of the list. Hence the whole passage, arguably, presents the following ideas: (a) ideality is an aspect of the human activity of social production and arises only within that activity as a form of mediation; (b) social production is nature-directed activity mediated primarily by instruments of labour and secondarily by symbolic objects; (c) ideality is immediately embodied in symbolic objects but only exists within the whole system of human productive activity as a function of the complex interrelations between the diverse objects (tools and symbols) produced and employed in that system.

It is true that instruments of labour are fashioned for a particular purpose and can therefore be regarded ('within a materialist framework', as Ilyenkov insists in clarification) as 'organs of the human brain created by man's hand' (Ilyenkov 1960/1982, 115, quoting Marx's *Grundrisse*). However, this does not make the tool an ideal image or give it a semiotic nature. It is the purpose itself which is ideal and as this purpose is gradually realised through the material activity of tool production, that activity results in a material (and not an ideal) thing.[18] The activity of using a tool according to its purpose in social production (in other words, the labour process itself) comprises a dialectical unity of the material properties and action of the tool with the conscious purpose or goal of activity expressed in ideal forms such as words, a unity consisting in mutual transformations between all sides of the process. The categorisation of instruments of labour as ideal, on the other hand, in effect inverts the relationship of material to ideal as this relationship is conceived within materialist philosophy.

I believe that this overextension results from a slight misunderstanding of Ilyenkov's use of Marx's economic analysis. Marx treats the commodity as a double-sided entity having a *use-value* and an *exchange-value*. Crudely speaking, the former is the use to which it is put and the latter how much it costs. Use-value is a function of the natural properties of the thing which are realised in the thing being used in production or consumption. Exchange-value (or *value* for short), on the other hand, is realised in the *circulation* process in which commodities are bought and sold prior to their use. Exchange-value has nothing to do with the naturally conditioned useful properties of things but concerns only the relative amounts of human labour objectified within them. While nature and labour are the source of use-values, exchange-value is the result of labour, of society, alone. This is why Marx (1867/1976) distinguishes between the 'natural form' of the commodity (as a use-value) and its 'value form' (as an exchange-value) (p. 138). While use-values 'constitute the material content of wealth, whatever the social form may be' (p.

18. Cf. A.N. Leontiev (1977): 'Activity is by no means simply the expresser and vehicle of the mental image objectivised in its product. The product records, perpetuates not the image but the activity, the objective content which it objectively carries within itself' (p. 188).

126), the value form is entirely due to the particular social form — commodity production — within which use-values are produced: 'their objective character as values is therefore purely social' (pp. 138-39) and, as we have seen, it is the form of appearance of value (as exchange-value or price) which is ideal. 'The mystical character of the commodity', as Marx puts it, 'does not therefore arise from its use-value' (p. 164) but from its being a value.[19]

Bakhurst's interpretation of ideality, therefore, does not distinguish between the two logically different and opposed aspects of the artifact: the 'plain, homely natural form' (Marx 1867/1976, 138) of commodities as *use-values* or useful objects and the *form of value* of commodities which is 'distinct from its natural form' (p. 152), and is purely social, purely ideal:

A chair with four legs and a velvet canopy is, under certain circumstances, a *throne*; therefore this chair, a thing that serves as a seat, is not a throne through the nature of its use-value. (Marx and Engels Archives, quoted in Ilyenkov 1960/1982, 119)

The more general issue forming the backdrop to this problem is that in *Capital* Marx is developing a single line of argument that unites two different levels of abstraction.[20] Marx's analysis involves seeing capitalism as a unity of the general or universal features of the human labour process with the peculiar features of capitalism as a sociohistorically specific instance or stage of development of that labour process (i.e., as a specific mode of production). Thus, Marx (1867/1976) begins by considering 'the labour process independently of any specific social formation' (p. 283) and it is to this section that the famous passage involving the architect and the bee belongs. Here Marx describes the labour process 'in its simple and abstract elements' as:

purposeful activity aimed at the production of use-values. It is an appropriation of what exists in nature for the requirements of man. It is the universal condition for the metabolic interaction [*Stoffwechsel*] between man and nature, the everlasting nature-imposed condition of human existence, and it is therefore independent of every form of that existence, or rather it is common to all forms of society in which human beings live. (p. 290)

19. 'Not an atom of matter enters into the objectivity of commodities as values; in this it is the direct opposite of the coarsely sensuous objectivity of commodities as physical objects... their objective character as values is therefore purely social' (Marx 1867/ 1976, 138-39).
20. Here my argument follows closely that in Pilling (1980).

Therefore, when we look at capitalism abstractly as a labour process, we will find that 'the worker uses the means of labour as his tools' in order to transform the object of labour into a product (p. 988). On the other hand, when we look concretely at this specific mode of production (i.e., at the valorisation process), the situation looks quite different. Now 'it is not the worker who makes use of the means of production, but the means of production that make use of the worker' (p. 988). He explains:

Living labour does not realise itself in objective labour which thereby becomes its objective organ, but instead objective labour maintains and fortifies itself by drawing off living labour; it is thus that it becomes *value valorising itself, capital*, and functions as such. The means of production thus become no more than leeches drawing off as large an amount of living labour as they can. (p. 988)

Thus while ideality is in general an irreducible internal dimension of the labour process (cf. the architect vs. the bee) it is not in general a property of artifacts (i.e., of the products of labour, whether tools or objects of direct consumption). The products of labour are produced as commodities and have an ideal value form only within the capitalist labour process (valorization) specifically. Nevertheless, since the value form, although historically specific, is ideal, and is the product of the labour process in this specific form, its analysis helps to uncover the general laws according to which ideality arises and functions within the labour process.

The Social Origins and Function of Ideal Images

Since ideality is a dimension of social practice, its origins, nature and functioning must be understood in relation to the logic and dynamic of the practices responsible for its creation. For Ilyenkov, following Marx, the practice that creates the need for, and then the reality of, the 'ideal plane' of existence is human labour during which 'the object of production' (i.e., the outcome of productive activity) is converted into (or 'ideally posited' as) 'an internal image, as a need, as a drive and as purpose' (Ilyenkov 1974/1977a, 260, quoting from Marx's *Grundrisse*). The crux of the matter is that the labour process itself is not a consciously created phenomenon. It arises 'not deliberately, but spontaneously' (Marx and Engels, in Ilyenkov 1991, 213) as a process 'beginning and continuing completely independently of thought' and it is within that process that 'idealisation of reality, nature and social relations is completed, and the language of symbols is born as the external body of the ideal image of the external world' (1974/1977a, 266-67). For Ilyenkov, then, in order to understand the origins, content and functions as well as the very forms of ideal images one must penetrate analytically the process by which material production generates its own ideal forms of mediation and then work out the dialectical logic of the development of this new system moving now through the interaction of its material and ideal poles. While the ideal appears to exist directly in the objects 'possessed' by this symbolic function, adopting this viewpoint allows one to see that this symbolic 'charge' is a purely social phenomenon, something bestowed on these objects only by virtue of their constant emergence from and re-engagement within the activity to which they owe their origin. In this way the whole system of productive activity develops dynamically through a constant 'pulsation' or alternation between the processes of idealisation and re-materialisation (through practice) of ideal forms as a consequence of which the latter take on ever newer forms, increasingly more distant in appearance from their objective source to which, nonetheless, they are inescapably linked by ever more complex mediations reflecting the social division of labour with (in class society) its accompanying social antagonisms, conflicts and contradictions.

Thus, the ideal or symbolic nature of money for example is due to its emergent role within 'an already formed system of relations between people mediated by things' (Ilyenkov 1974/1977a, 272), namely, the historically specific system of commodity production. Specifically:

It arises as a means of resolving the contradictions maturing in the course of the circulation process, and within it (and not inside the head, though not without the help of the head), as a means of satisfying a need that has become immanent in commodity circulation. (Ilyenkov 1974/1977a, 268)

Briefly, commodity production as a generalised social form of production (not to mention capitalism, its highest form) is impossible as long as exchange-value is manifest only in the localised and accidental acts of reciprocal, direct exchange of commodities (barter) in the market. Progress is possible only if that common social substance inherent in commodities can take a form that is independent of the particularised shapes of the whole mass of commodities and in which it can appear and be measured directly in its pure, stable, socially valid state. But 'exchange value as such', exchange value *per se*, 'can of course only exist symbolically' (Marx 1857-8/1973, 154). Therefore the problem is resolved 'by one commodity "being expelled" from their equal family and being converted into the immediately social standard of the socially necessary expenditure of labour' (Ilyenkov 1974/1977a, 268-69). One commodity — typically gold — becomes the universal symbol or 'ideal image' of the value of all other commodities. The role assigned to it by social activity is that of representing each commodity only as a product of abstract labour resulting from the application of socially necessary labour time. Consequently, as money, it does not embody the 'sensuously perceived image' of the commodity 'but rather *its essence*, i.e. the *law* of its existence within the system that in general creates the situation being analysed' (Ilyenkov 1974/1977a, 272).

But this is still a partial picture of the way in which this particular ideal form arises and functions. Ilyenkov (1974/1977a) emphasises that the actual use of gold as a medium of circulation (i.e., for payment) grows out of an earlier stage in which it 'functioned initially as money purely ideally' (p. 271). At this stage, it was a matter of regulating the direct exchange of commodities by calculating how much gold each commodity in turn would fetch. Here, gold 'does not enter bodily into the exchange' but 'is all the same involved in the act of exchange, since it is also present only *ideally*, i.e. in the idea, in the mind of the commodity-owners, in speech, on paper, and so on' (p. 269). But this is no more a psychological matter than the real exchange since the calculation must be done 'not only in the head of the individual but in the conception held by society (directly, the conception held by the participants in the process of buying and selling)' (Marx, 1857-8/1973, cited in Ilyenkov 1974/1977a, 271-72). From being an ideal measure of value in an ideal act of exchange, gold becomes real money, mediating the real acts of sale and purchase through its uniting in one 'thing' the functions of measure of value and means of circulation.

Of course, the analysis of the value form concerns the idealisation of a relatively narrow and historically restricted dimension of productive activity whereas 'all nature is idealised in man and not just that part which he immediately produces or reproduces or consumes in a practical way' (Ilyenkov 1974/1977a, 276). The human life process, therefore, constantly generates an increasing number of 'ideal forms' or forms of 'ideal image' mediating the myriad forms of developing social practice:

So all the things involved in the social process acquire a new 'form of existence' that is not included in their physical nature and differs from it completely — their ideal form. (Ilyenkov 1977b, 86)

The Ideal as Image or Representation

I have argued that when Ilyenkov (1991) speaks of 'ideal form' he is referring to 'things' like language or the value form which take on a special symbolic or representational function:

By 'ideality' or the 'ideal', materialism has to mean that quite specific — and identifiable by strict criteria [*strogo fiksiruemoe*] — correlation between (at least) two material objects (things, processes, events, states) within which one material object, while remaining itself, takes on the role of *representative of the other object*, or, more exactly, of the universal nature of this other object, the universal form and law of *this other object*. (p. 253)

Ideality is not the whole of culture but 'an aspect of culture, one of its dimensions, determining factors, properties' (Ilyenkov 1977b, 96) although the concept extends to a much broader class of phenomena than language:

the image is objectivised not only in words, and may enter into the system of socially evolved knowledge not only in its verbal expression. The image is objectivised just as well (and even more directly) in sculptural, graphic and plastic forms and in the form of the routine-ritual ways of dealing with things and people, so that it is expressed not only in words, in speech and language, but also in drawings, models and such symbolic objects as coats of arms, banners, dress, utensils, or as *money*, including gold coins and paper money, IOUs, bonds or credit notes. (p. 79)

However, it would be wrong to simply and directly equate ideality as a phenomenon with words or other symbolic objects, since their ideality is due entirely to those forms of practical social activity with which they are indissolubly connected and integrated (albeit in highly mediated fashion).[21] The ideal is not in the word or in connections between words (in 'discourse') for

---

21. See Bakhurst (1991): 'according to Ilyenkov, the ideal cannot be reduced to a "static" property at all, be it either a quasi-natural property, or a property of mental states' (p. 184).

'language of itself is as little ideal as the neuro-physiological structure of the brain. It is only *the form of expression* of the ideal, its material-objective being' (Ilyenkov 1974/1977a, 262-63). A person who 'operates with symbols or with tokens and not with objects, relying on symbols and tokens', he emphasises, 'does not act on the ideal plane but only on the verbal plane' (p. 274). Indeed, 'it very often happens', he argues, that 'instead of discovering the real essence of things by means of terms, the individual sees only the terms themselves with their traditional meanings, sees only the symbol and its sensuously perceived body', in which case 'the linguistic symbol is transformed from an instrument of real activity into a fetish, blocking off with its body the reality that it represents' (p. 274). Ideality, then, is not a thing but an aspect of activity, to be found not in words but in the use of words in the actual doing of something. The material is really 'idealised', as Ilyenkov (1974/1977a) puts it, only under the following conditions:

(1) only when it is expressed in immediately, generally significant forms of language (understood in the broadest sense of the word, including the language of drawings, diagrams, models, etc.), and (2) when it is transformed into an active form of man's activity with a real object (and not simply into a 'term' or 'utterance' as the material body of language). In other words the object proves to be idealised only when the faculty of actively recreating it has been created, relying on the language of words or drawings; when the faculty of converting words into deeds, and through deeds into things, has been created. (p. 263)

To think and act in a human way, Ilyenkov argues, is to enter and participate in this social system of material and ideal production, to

be able to reproduce the forms of activity that endow the world with ideality, to mould one's movements to the dictates of the norms that constitute humanity's spiritual culture. (Bakhurst 1991, 197)

The only way to learn a language is to become an active participant in those forms of activity or patterns of social intercourse mediated by words since the functional use of words is created only within such forms and patterns. This is the foundation of Ilyenkov's radical 'anti-innatism' (Bakhurst 1991, 219). Since human thinking is a capacity which develops from and is exercised through the use of objects (i.e., tools and ideal forms) produced by people, it cannot be the expression or externalisation of some putative biologically fixed structure or behavioural pattern. Human mental capacities in the broadest sense — language, memory, perception, thinking, planning, etc. — are themselves produced and reproduced as necessary aspects of the whole dynamic of productive activity itself and are specifically tied to the production and use, within activity, of a mediating layer of ideal objects. The human senses and intellectual capacities grow through the active 'training and exercising' of our natural bodily capacities and potential 'on objects created by man for man' (Ilyenkov 1974/1977a, 261) within already existing forms of practical activity. In and through these objects in our active engagement with others on joint tasks we learn to find the expression of human subjectivity — that of others and of ourselves — in all its forms.

The example of money shows, further, that the concept of *ideal image* does not imply the mechanical and passive reproduction of already empirically given states of affairs. Money comes into existence, as noted above, because of a need 'which appears in the form of an unresolved contradiction of the commodity form' (Ilyenkov 1974/1977a, 268). Thus, the money form constitutes an entirely new and irreducible quality within the system afflicted by contradiction. Its appearance — at first ideally in the 'conception held by society' and then in actuality as real money — is the very resolution of that contradiction and its effect is to allow the generative forces within the system to break through the partial and confining forms in which they have hitherto grown up. It helps to conduct a transformation, a revolutionising and a universalising of the activities and relations within the system itself as a response to real problems posed by life. Similarly, the architect, constructing the house ideally on paper, is engaged in a genuine thinking process directed at real problems posed by the practical building task. Conflicting conditions or contradictory demands, potentially disastrous consequences for the real house, must be actively addressed and resolved in advance of the actual construction. The very form of the design must capture and distil the general, in the sense of essential, properties and relations that will obtain within the real object. Thus, the ideal form reproduces the things involved in human activity in 'their universal, socially-human significance, their role and function within the social organism' (Ilyenkov 1974/1977a, 273). The ideal is people's capacity for creative and transformative action represented as a separate thing or system of things with their own peculiar structure and relations; it incarnates and expresses in an abstract, condensed, maximally sharp outline the real potential and force, as well as the real contradictions, of their productive power as a collectivity.[22]

It is precisely because the ideal image comes to express the essence or law-governed nature of things that the dynamic of social practice undergoes a peculiar inversion, with activity on the ideal plane shifting to the beginning of the activity cycle where the course of activity can be consciously antici-pated, checked, modified, etc., where contradictions within social practice can be identified, reflected on and resolved 'in the head'. Ilyenkov's (1991) general formulation of the situation is characteristically paradoxical:

In thinking [the ideal] is generated before the contradictions will be resolved in reality (i.e., before its own objective realisation). This original position, when the image is born earlier than the object that it reflects, also creates the whole difficulty of the problem of the ideal, which is unresolvable for metaphysical materialism with its version of the theory of reflection. The object as an immediately visible thing does not yet exist while its image is already there. (p. 210)

There is, then, a dialectic of ideal and material in human social production. The ideal exists within material production as a 'nonmaterial image', dialect-ically reacting back on its material matrix, the whole process realising itself in a cyclic or spiral movement (cf. Ilyenkov 1960/1982) in which the mate-rial is idealised (translated into symbols, images) and the ideal in turn is con-verted back into matter. This movement is one manifestation of the

dialectics of all real development, in which the universal necessary condition of the emergence of an object becomes its own universal and necessary consequence, this dialectical inversion in which the condition becomes the conditioned, the cause becomes the effect, the universal becomes the particular, is a characteristic feature of internal interaction, through which actual development assumes the form of a circle or, to be more precise, of a spiral which extends the scope of its motion all the time, with each new turn. (p. 115)

As a final point, it is easier to see the architect's activity as 'activity on the ideal plane' than, say, the activity of the artist, composer, or conductor, not to mention the priest or shaman. What, after all, does a piece of music repre-sent?[23] Music is obviously not the same thing as draughtsmanship or science. Nevertheless, Ilyenkov's general position on the ideal is not invalidated by

22. See also Mamardashvili (1992): 'The syncretic nature of the transformed form allows the system to work … summarily [*summarno*]', that is 'without taking into account or actually manifesting all its connections' (p. 278).
23. This issue was raised by David Bakhurst (personal communication, August 20, 1998).

this fact. The capacity to create, to appreciate, and to be moved by music is necessarily itself as much a social fact as the capacity to design houses on paper. One should also bear in mind Mikhailov's (1990) point that:

the objective world of spiritual production, the *product* produced by it, is not only music and theory, poetry and arithmetic, sculpture and ideas. Outside the developed capacity to see these objects as such, i.e. as one's own, as inner things merged with oneself, they have in themselves absolutely nothing spiritual about them, they are simply vibrations of the air, coloured marks on paper, blocks of marble, etc. The products of spiritual production are primarily the very people capable of creating music and delighting in it, capable of seeing the world as organized according to the 'laws of beauty' and truth. (p. 116)

The musical or dramatic 'thing', like all ideal images, represents the real world of collective human life activity. In separating and condensing our emotional relations and attitudes to life's problems and possibilities it helps to create and then develop that special human 'space' between thinking and doing, a 'space' of anticipation and reflection albeit according to the logic of feelings rather than of theoretical abstractions.[24] But the links between the musical 'image' (or any other aesthetic artifact) and social life, ultimately social production, are undoubtedly far more complex, far more highly mediated than the links between the architect's design and the productive activity that it serves. And these links and mediations, as well as the specific peculiarities of artistic form, cannot be deduced from the general definition but need their own empirical investigation and theoretical elucidation.[25]

Conclusions and Implications

In conclusion, let us turn to a brief look at some of the issues and implications for research within the CHAT tradition raised by the preceding discussion.

In my interpretation of Ilyenkov's work, I have argued that his concept

---

24. 'The totality as it appears in the head, as a totality of thoughts, is a product of the thinking head, which appropriates the world in the only way it can, a way different from the artistic, religious, practical and mental appropriation of this world' (Marx 1857-8/1973, 101).
25. For Marxist discussion of aesthetics see, for example, Ilyenkov (1984) and Slaughter (1980).

of the ideal affords a materialist understanding of the origin and irreducible role of symbolic objects or objectivised 'images' within social productive activity. However, I have argued against extending the concept to embrace all the objects, processes and products of the labour process. To do so would be to reject, or at least to obscure, the secondary, derived nature of ideal forms as 'images' of material objects and processes, thereby depriving the category of its materialist content and severing its connections with historical materialism as an approach to social processes in general. The logical outcome would be a view not so different from Hegelian objective idealism which sees all of human material and spiritual culture as the objectification of an idea existing in advance.

Arguably, we find this kind of objective idealism in the linguistic work of Michael Halliday, for example, where the whole of human culture is viewed as a system of meaning. Such a position, in which material, linguistic, and educational activities are all regarded as essentially 'semiotic' (or 'discursive') in nature is hardly in keeping with the Vygotskian tradition of language research (pace Wells 1994; cf. Bakhurst 1991, especially chap. 3; Jones 1997) informed by historical materialism. Proceeding from historical materialist premises Ilyenkov (1997) argues that each of the 'superstructural' spheres of activity (e.g., artistic, legal, political, educational)

must be understood and revealed as a system of concretely specific, historically developed forms of reflection of economics, of the sphere of social being of humanity. (p. 182)

These 'superstructural' spheres, consisting of specialised forms of mental or ideal activity, are the result of a dialectically developed differentiation within the concrete social whole. Although they attain a relative independence from the process of material production they ultimately owe their existence, functions and power to their being a (highly mediated) 'image' of the former.

The materialist view, then, insists on the crucial philosophical and theoretical distinction between material and ideal activity and as a result obliges us to push beyond the apparent independence of the different social spheres of activity to look for their essential interconnections within the concrete whole.[26] A.N. Leontiev (1977) himself emphasised this general connectivity of different spheres of activity within the social whole:

26. See Jones (1998) for a critique, from this perspective, of the 'Critical Discourse Analysis' of Norman Fairclough (e.g., Fairclough 1992).

no matter what the conditions and forms in which man's activity proceeds, no matter what structure it acquires, it cannot be regarded as something extracted from social relations, from the life of society. (p. 182)

Indeed, if we lose sight of this system of social activities and relations then we lose the very possibility of explaining the functioning of the symbol which 'does not belong to it as such but only to the system within which it has acquired its properties' (Ilyenkov 1974/1977a, 273), with the result that 'some form or other of fetishisation both of the external world and of symbolics develops' (p. 275).

Of particular significance in this connection is Marx's discovery, noted earlier, that social processes when viewed abstractly may look upside down. To see them the right way up means to discover their place within the concrete dynamic of the entire system. Ilyenkov (1991) observed that Hegel, for example, saw the sphere of education abstractly as 'an autonomous sphere of the development of "spirit"' rather than concretely 'as a sphere which in its own specific form actively reproduces the distinctions caused by the form of social division of labour', a view which 'constitutes the chief advantage of the Marxist conception of abilities over the Hegelian' (p. 380). But it is also important to see such a theoretical inversion as the consequence and expression of a social fact, that is of the division of theoretical (mental) and practical (manual) labour within class society into separate and mutually antagonistic activities, where the development of knowledge in all its forms is the exclusive province of specific social groups and layers.

The resulting separation of symbolic forms from actual practical engagement with real objects is obviously a fact of general social significance and concerns the phenomenon of *alienation*, with all the ideological ramifications of that notion.[27] One of its manifestations is the fetishisation of ideal forms and with it the subordination of the individual mind to the fetishised 'image':

When ... the individual only masters the ideal image formally, as a rigid pattern and sequence of operations, without understanding its origin and links with real (and not idealised) actuality, he proves incapable of taking a critical attitude to this image, i.e. as a special object differentiated from him. Then he merges with it, as it were, and cannot treat it as an object correlated with reality and alter it accordingly. In that case, strictly speaking, it is not the individual who operates with the ideal

27. See Bakhurst (1991, 189-95) for a discussion of the distinction in Ilyenkov between *objectification* and *alienation*.

image but the dogmatised image that acts in and through the individual. Here it is not the ideal image that is a real function of the individual but, on the contrary, the individual who is a function of the image, which dominates his mind and will as an externally given formal scheme, as an estranged image, as a fetish, as a system of unarguable rules coming inevitably from somewhere out of the blue. (Ilyenkov 1974/1977a, 282)

Ilyenkov (1991) applies his understanding of the process of fetishisation of ideal forms, allied to his distinction between *ideal* and *verbal* planes noted earlier, to a common problem besetting the then Soviet education system. The problem is that of 'applying knowledge in life, in practice' (p. 381) connected with the problem of 'verbalism' (i.e., the gap between 'knowledge' expressed in words and the ability to handle and resolve real problems in the real world). Ilyenkov shows that under certain conditions in the classroom, the relationship between real things and the words expressing these things and their relations can be inverted in such a way that 'knowledge' is taken to be little else than the learning and manipulation of ready-made verbal formulas rather than the process of cognising the object. This produces a sterile movement 'from a ready made image to its verbal expression', while

the decisive section of the path of cognition — from the object to the image (and back — from the image to the object) — here remains outside the bounds of the activity of the student himself. (p. 385)

Under these conditions

is formed that definite type of mind for whom the word (language) is not a means for mastering the surrounding world but on the contrary the surrounding world acquires the significance of an external means for mastering and fixing verbal formulas. (p. 384)

and the result of this

is that a person who is educated in such a fashion is made a slave of ready made 'formulae' already in the very act of contemplation in the process of living perception — he is trained to see in the object that and only that which has been given to him in a verbal form, that which exactly corresponds to the words. (p. 386)[28]

28. See in this connnection Engeström's (1990, chap. 1) discussion of 'the manufacture of misconceptions'.

Ilyenkov's response to this problem is to urge a restructuring of educational practice based on a reconceptualisation of the learning process in which words come to function genuinely as ideal images of things, as concepts reflecting the logic and essential interconnections of material processes independently of the mind. What is required, he argues, is 'activity directed straight towards the object. Activity changing the object and not the image of it' since 'only in the course of this activity does the image arise for the first time' (p. 387). Consequently:

Genuine *thinking* is formed in real life precisely and only when the work of language is inseparably united with the work of the hand — the organ of immediately objective activity. Not with the hand drawing letters, words, and 'utterances' on paper, but with the hand *making a thing*, i.e. changing the immediate, intractable and wayward material and only here manifesting its objective nature, character, and 'obstinacy' without depending on words or ready-made 'images'. (p. 387)

Ilyenkov also developed his position in relation to other issues of both theoretical and practical (e.g., educational) significance such as the relationship between language and thinking (e.g., pp. 270-74) and between word meaning and concept (1960/1982, 1997; see also Beaken 1996, and Jones 1999).

Finally, Ilyenkov's conception of the dialectic of 'spiral development' of activity systems has profound implications for any analysis of human activity and its symbolic mediation (see Jones, 2000, for more detailed discussion). His insights are valid not only for the 'impersonal' logic of sociohistorical development on a broad scale, but also for the plane of individual psychological development, as can be seen if we briefly turn to Vygotsky's own exploration of the 'truly dialectical character of the development of functional systems' (1984, 88) in the shape of his analysis of the relationship between language, cognition, and practical activity. Vygotsky's (1930/1984) conception of the 'planning function of speech' (*planirushchaia funktsiia rechi*, p. 35) was developed from analysis of the way in which, in children, 'symbolic activity begins to play a specifically organising role, penetrating the process of tool use and ensuring the appearance of forms of behaviour new in principle' (p. 21). He summed up the situation as follows:

the child's speech, which previously accompanied his activity and reflected its main to-ings and fro-ings in a disconnected and chaotic form, is transferred more and more to the pivotal and initial moments of the process, and begins to antici-pate action, illuminating action that has been conceived but still not realised. (p. 34)

And therefore:

The activity of the child who possesses speech is divided into two successive parts: in the first, the problem is solved on the speech plane, with the help of speech plan-ning, and then, in the second, the problem is solved in the simple motor realiza-tion of the prepared solution. (p. 24)

Here, then, is the path of development of *'conscious ideality'* in Ilyenkov's terms (1977b, 87). Thus, the logic of the individual psychological mastery of the means of symbolic mediation reproduces in essence the social logic of genesis and evolution of ideal forms. This intimate connection between the Vygotskian and Ilyenkovian accounts serves as a powerful reminder that we must not artificially counterpose the *social* and the *psychological*, or the *social* and the *individual*, since the development of the individual as an acting and thinking being is in fact the social process itself.[29] We note also that Vygot-sky's account of the role of language in planning activity penetrates beyond Ilyenkov's 'verbal plane', that is beyond relationships between language units (e.g., utterances) involved in activity, so insightfully analysed in Wertsch's (1991) discussion of the role of dialogicality in internalisation, to the 'ideal plane' of the relationships between language and the practical 'object-oriented' activity it mediates.

References

Bakhurst, D. (1991). *Consciousness and revolution in Soviet philosophy: From the Bol-sheviks to Evald Ilyenkov.* Cambridge: Cambridge University Press.

Bakhurst, D. (1995). Lessons from Ilyenkov. *The Communication Review,* 1, 155-78.

Bakhurst, D. (1997). Meaning, normativity and the life of the mind. *Language & Communication,* 17, 33-55.

Beaken, M. (1996). *The making of language.* Edinburgh: Edinburgh University Press.

29. Here I follow Marx (1844/1975): 'It is above all necessary to avoid once more estab-lishing "society" as an abstraction over against the individual. The individual *is* the *social being'* (p. 350).

Cole, M. (1996). *Cultural psychology: A once and future discipline.* Cambridge, Mass.: Harvard University Press.

Engeström, Y. (1990). *Learning, working and imagining: Twelve studies in Activity Theory.* Helsinki: Orienta-Konsultit Oy.

Engeström, Y. (1996). Interobjectivity, ideality, and dialectics. *Mind, Culture, and Activity,* 3, 259-65.

Fairclough, N. (1992). *Discourse and social change.* Cambridge: Polity Press.

Ilyenkov, E.V. (1977a). *Dialectical logic: Essays on its history and theory* (H.C. Creighton, trans.) Moscow: Progress. (Original work published 1974)

Ilyenkov, E.V. (1977b). The concept of the ideal. In *Philosophy in the USSR: Problems of dialectical materialism.* Moscow: Progress, 71-99.

Ilyenkov, E.V. (1982). *The dialectics of the abstract and the concrete in Marx's* Capital (S. Syrovatkin, trans.). Moscow: Progress. (Original work published 1960)

Ilyenkov, E.V. (1984). *Iskusstvo i kommunisticheskii ideal* [Art and the communist ideal]. Moscow: Iskusstvo.

Ilyenkov, E.V. (1991). *Filosofiia i kul'tura* [Philosophy and culture]. Moscow: Politizdat.

Ilyenkov, E.V. (1997). *Dialektika abstraktnogo i konkretnogo v nauchno-teoreticheskom myshlenii.* [The dialectic of the abstract and the concrete in scientifico-theoretical thinking]. Moscow: Rosspen.

Jones, P.E. (1997). Comments on G. Wells' 'The complementary contributions of Halliday and Vygotsky to a "Language-based theory of learning"'. Unpublished manuscript, Department of Communication Studies, Sheffield Hallam University, United Kingdom.

Jones, P.E. (1998). Critical discourse analysis as social theory. *Proceedings of the Association of Media, Communications, and Cultural Studies (Future perfect?),* 181-99.

Jones, P.E. (1999). The 'embodied mind': Contrasting visions. *Mind, Culture and Activity,* 6, 274-85.

Jones, P.E. (2000). The dialectics of the ideal and symbolic mediation. In V. Oittinen (ed.), *Evald Ilyenkov's philosophy revisited.* Helsinki: Kikimora Publications, 205-27.

Lektorsky, V.A. (ed.) (1999). *E.V. Il'enkov: Lichnost' i tvorchestvo.* [E.V. Ilyenkov: Personality and creativity]. Moscow: 'IAazyki russkoi kul'tury'.

Leontiev, A.A. (1997). *Psikhologiia obshchenie.* [The psychology of social interaction]. Moscow: Smysl.

Leontiev (Leontyev), A.N. (1977). Activity and consciousness (R. Daglish, trans). In *Philosophy in the USSR: Problems of dialectical materialism.* Moscow: Progress, 180-202.

Mamardashvili, M.K. (1992). *Kak ia ponimaiu filosofiiu* [How I understand philosophy] (2nd ed.). Moscow: Progress.

Marx, K. (1973). *Grundrisse* (M. Nicolaus, trans.). Harmondsworth, England: Penguin. (Original work written 1857-58)

Marx, K. (1975). Economic and philosophical manuscripts (R. Livingstone and G. Benton, trans.). In *Early writings*. Harmondsworth, England: Penguin, 279-400. (Original work written 1844)

Marx, K. (1976). *Capital: Vol. 1* (B. Fowkes, trans.). Harmondsworth, England: Penguin. (Original work published 1867)

Mikhailov, F.T. (1980). *The riddle of the self* (R. Daglish, trans.). Moscow: Progress. (Original work published 1976)

Mikhailov, F.T. (1990). *Obshchestvennoe soznanie i samosoznanie individa* [Social consciousness and individual self-consciousness]. Moscow: Nauka.

Newman, F., & Holzman, L. (1993). *Lev Vygotsky: Revolutionary scientist*. London: Routledge.

Pilling, G. (1980). *Marx's* Capital: *Philosophy and political economy*. London: Routledge & Kegan Paul.

Slaughter, C. (1980). *Marxism, ideology and literature*. London: Macmillan.

Tolstykh, V.I., et al. (1981). *Dukhovnoe proizvodstvo: Sotsial'no-filosofskii akspekt problemy dukhovnoi deiatel'nosti* [Spiritual production: The socio-philosophical aspect of the problem of spiritual activity]. Moscow: Nauka.

Vygotsky, L.S. (1984). Orudie i znak v razvitii rebenka [Tool and sign in child development]. In A.V. Zaporozhets (ed.), *Sobranie sochinenii* (vol. 6). Moscow: Pedagogika, 6-89. (Original work written 1930)

Vygotsky, L.S. (1986). *Thought and language* (A. Kozulin, ed. and trans.). Cambridge, Mass.: MIT Press. (Original work published 1934)

Wells, G. (1994). The complementary contributions of Halliday and Vygotsky to a 'language-based theory of learning', *Linguistics and Education*, 6, 41-90.

Wertsch, J.V. (1991). *Voices of the mind: A sociocultural approach to mediated action*. London: Harvester Wheatsheaf.

Wertsch, J.V. (1998). *Mind as action*. New York: Oxford University Press.

Index